YOUR BEST LIFE LATER

YOUR BEST LIFE LATER

What Every Daughter and Son needs to Know

by

Andy McQuitty

Endorsements

Your Best Life Later is a refreshing glimpse into the heart of a father who has God's best in mind for his children. The excerpts of Andy McQuitty's journals gifted to his children are full of intentionality, humility, transparency, and a vulnerable authenticity not often found in a leader. My friend Andy is a man who sought to pastor his children and not just the churches he served. The book is a good model for those who want to be godly mentors.

Mark Bailey
President of Dallas Theological Seminary (Ret)

We all need people in our walk with Christ that are further along to help shepherd us along His path. We also need people that may be a few steps behind us so that we can pass down our own experience and knowledge and put those tools to use for the Kingdom. This book by my friend Andy McQuitty serves as both. It beautifully outlines lessons in life that we may learn for ourselves and pass down to others. The truth and vulnerability displayed in these pages are great reminders of both God's love for us and the love we must share with others.

Justin Leonard
1997 PGA Open Champion

"As a father of three, I was brought to tears reading Your Best Life Later. Through twenty-five years of journal entries, Pastor Andy gives a unique glimpse into the spiritual and life lessons that a Christian father passes along to his five children. I've known Andy and his wonderful wife Alice since my wife and I began attending Irving Bible Church in 2006. We have often asked them for advice and spiritual direction as we navigate the turbulent waters of parenting. Your Best Life Later is a beautiful (true) story of the advice given during peaks and valleys of parenting and childhood, the relationships that are built and evolve in a Christian household. It contains biblical guidance that all parents and children should follow. I'm thankful that Andy had the wisdom to understand that these loving journal entries to his children should be shared with the world. I'm equally thankful that Julie, Elizabeth, Bonnie, Jon, and Jeff raised a great dad!"

Mark Teixeira
Major League Baseball All-Star

Forward

At the young age of 30, Andy McQuitty began journaling words of wisdom for each of his five children—on topics including discipline, marriage, authentic faith, work ethic, politics, and so much more. He gave each child their journal as a surprise when he took them to college—and now the content has made its way into a book to impact others. I've always admired Andy McQuitty, and now my admiration is even greater. His journals were unquestionably an expression of unconditional love—from a father seeking to share what he believed to be wise counsel. This book is a genuine treasure, with insights that are just as relevant today as they were several decades ago. Readers will be blessed by what this father shared with his children, and many parents will be inspired and led by the Lord to follow Andy's example.

JAMES ROBISON
Founder and President, LIFE Outreach International
Fort Worth, Texas

For Worldwide Distribution through Ingram

ISBN: 978-1-951648-07-7

LEADERSHIP
Thoughtful, Relevant Leaders From Around The World
BOOKS

LeadershipBooks.com

Dedication

This book is dedicated to the same precious five to whom I originally wrote personal journals over a quarter-century ago: Julia Kathleen, Elizabeth Grace, Bonnie Caroleen, Jonathan Andrew, and Jeffrey Lee.

Hey gang, you were then, are now, and evermore shall be my life's greatest pride and joy!

All five of the McQuitty kids ...

Acknowledgement

I wish to acknowledge the true hero behind this book who is, ironically, the only member of our family whose name (until now) has not even been mentioned. Alice, my wife of forty-two years, not only gave birth to our small army of five but schooled them at home for eighteen years after which she earned her Th.M., wrote three books and continues to pursue a vibrant Biblical teaching ministry all the while on her knees daily in supplication for our family. If I've been privileged to contribute anything of value to the success of our children, it's only because of her—the very heart and soul of our home, the keeper of our dreams—Alice my hero.

Table of Contents

Preface .... *xii*

Introduction 1

Preamble 6

PART 1: JULIA KATHLEEN'S JOURNAL | 10

8   Self-Esteem; Is best not to be rooted in the opinions of othes (SP)

19   Steady-On; Because success is never final and failure never fatal

32   Nothing Wasted; Everything you endure in life has purpose

PART 2: ELIZABETH GRACE'S JOURNAL | 86

6   Whom to Please; Choose God over man every time

19   Christ's Soldiers; Better to suffer for right than wink at evil

23   Sowing Seeds; Never underestimate the power of planting

47   Poiema; You are God's Poetic Masterpiece

PART 3: BONNIE CAROLEEN'S JOURNAL | 183

12   Presumption; When we bypass the Lord, we also bypass His blessings

20   Success; The greatest asset in any life is the blessing of God

27   Character; The depth of your character determines the
height of your achievement

45   Big Change; Don't cry because it's over. Smile because it happened!

PART 4: JONATHAN ANDREW'S JOURNAL | 271

10 Sabbath; Smell the roses, there's more to life than work, effort and achievement

18 Dreams; Shoot for the moon, even if you miss, you'll land among the stars!

19 Motives; The right motive in following Jesus is not a reward, but to be with Him

27 Self-Denial; He who hates his life in this world shall keep it to eternal life

PART 5: JEFFREY LEE'S JOURNAL | 338

9 Benchmark; Grasping God goes both ways, and He will never let go of you

18 Trials; God's way to bring maturity and blessing, so embrace them, be thankful

19 Independence; Freedom of choice brings responsibility, accountability, consequences

AFTERWORD | 378

– Julie 378

– Elizabeth 381

– Bonnie 383

– Jonathan 386

– Jeffrey 389

Preface

I Can't Believe I
Finished The Whole Thing

For obvious reasons, they (whoever 'they' is!) say never write a book on the family until you're at least 50 years of age. This leads me to confess here at the outset that I started writing the volume you hold in your hand on August 15, 1986, when I was just shy of 31. My sincere excuse for this blatant contravention of wisdom is that I wrote *not one* word of this volume with designs on future publication. And even if I had fancied the prospect of someday publishing the journal, I started for my then five-year-old first-born daughter in the summer of 1986, I'm quite sure the dream would have quickly evaporated if the Lord had given me a heads-up that He would be sending *four more* arrows into our quiver. That meant that I would not jot my last entry in my youngest of five's journal until August 19, 2011—almost 25 years to the day after I began. I still can't believe I finished this thing!

Perhaps the best explanation for me finishing this quarter-century-long project is the heart-shredding love that God gave me for each of my five children. The great Apostle Paul writes of all God's children, 'For we are God's handiwork, created in Christ Jesus to do good works, which God prepared in advance for us to do' (Ephesians 2:10, NIV). The word 'handiwork' is a translation of the Greek *'poema,'* literally, a poem or work of art. I saw my children as divine poetry-in-the-making whose beauty would radiate from accomplishing their God-appointed good works according to Proverbs 21:21: 'Whoever pursues righteousness and love finds life, prosperity and honor.' And my job as their Dad? To simply point my precious ones to the Master Craftsman and to encourage them in the way by biblically describing his artistic brushstrokes on the canvass of their lives.

This all sounded good to me until I realized that, while our children were still small, Alice and I were in a season of parenting best expressed in this poignant tweet from a frustrated mom. 'My daughter just accidentally dropped her snotty tissue into my coffee and if that's not a metaphor for parenting I don't know what is' (@sarabellab123). I remember being frustrated by the fact that parents' basic shepherding of their small children's physical challenges of growing up must often postpone their teaching of deeper life lessons. There were simply so many exhortations I wanted to make to them *now*, so many things I was learning that I wanted to teach them *now*, and so many warnings that I wanted to raise with them *now* but that they wouldn't be able to receive until years later as mature young adults.

In those days I concluded what is written in the updated post-script to the first entry in Julie's journal:

'P.S. (2021): It's better to write heartfelt words before their time than to never write them at all.'

So began my not-for-publication journals project for each of what turned out to be my five children. Except for Julie, whose journal I began when she was five, I started one for each of the other four from their infancy. In each journal I would periodically write over the years as one adult to another, even though in real time the child might not yet have even graduated from diapers! Five times then, I presented my journal to my young adult children when we moved them into their freshman college dorm room. Because I had not breathed a word of this project to any of the children growing up, Julie's journal was a complete and total surprise to her. But word got out about what was afoot and the other four kids were expectant and appreciative (if not surprised) when they received their journals as well. Again, I still can't believe I finished this thing!

Here's one last irony. I presented the last of the five journals to Jeff over nine years ago. He and his older siblings have since graduated and married and built careers and traveled the world. Over that time, I forgot all about those journals! Until, that is, the staff of Irving Bible Church threw me a celebration dinner in January 2019 as I retired after 31 years as their Senior Pastor. Without my knowledge, my long-time assistant Donna O'Reilly arranged to fly all my kids in (except Bonnie who was a missionary in China … but who still attended the dinner by video!). Each one spoke at the dinner *from the journals I had written for them*! (Their comments at that banquet appear in the Afterword to this book). How did Donna even know about these journals? Before I gave each one to the kids in their freshmen dorm room hundreds of miles from home, I asked Donna to make a backup copy. As the Irish are wont to say, 'I may be crazy, but I'm not daft!' Donna remembered those journals and arranged for the five grown McQuitty siblings to read from them at the dinner to several hundred attendees, many of whom badgered me for weeks afterward to put them in print.

This project has been no small undertaking. As I said before, I never wrote these journals for publication. Add to that the fact that the originals are handwritten in spiral notebooks with my dubious penmanship, and you have the obvious need for painstaking digital transcription and some light editing in places for clarity, completeness, and format. That I have done along with putting titles above each entry to help you navigate them and adding the real time year 2021 postscripts below them so that the journals can be used as daily devotionals. All that editing and supplementing notwithstanding, you still have in blessed transcribed form an estimated 98% of the original, unvarnished content of those old spiral notebooks. And now for the third time I have to confess: I still can't believe I finished this thing—again! But by the grace of God, here it is. My sincere prayer is that the words on these pages would be used by the Master Artist to apply brushstrokes of beauty to you and your family forever.

Introduction

The Eternal Benefits Of Paying Attention To God In Time

I originally handwrote these five journals in spiral-bound, school notebooks for my children beginning when each of them was born (except for the oldest, Julie, who had attained the advanced age of five when I finally put pen to paper). What on earth possessed a busy young, nearly 31-year-old pastor to embark on a twenty-five-year (as it turned out) writing project? Simply this: I wanted to help my little ones learn as early as possible the eternal benefits of paying as close attention to God as He pays to us according to Psalm 34:15. "The eyes of the Lord are on the righteous, and his ears are attentive to their cry."

King David goes on to assert in that psalm that when our eyes are on the Lord and our ears attentive to His word, we are invited to "... taste and see that the Lord is good" (verse 8). Notice the invitation is not "come" and see, but "taste" and see. Paying close attention to God does not merely bring us into closer proximity to God. It graces us with the even better real-world experience of His goodness that makes life truly worth living. What I wanted for my children in writing their journals is exactly what I want for you, my dear readers, through this years-later publication of said journals. I long for you to master the art of paying close attention to God in time throughout your life with the result that you experience deeply His goodness and grace.

In publishing these now decades-old writings, I am acutely aware that my original audience for the handwritten journals that started in 1986 is not the same as the audience for this book published thirty-five years later, in 2021! Today's audience is bigger and more diverse, and consists of two basic demographics— serious

Christ-followers (especially but not limited to young adults) and secondarily, parents intent on raising serious Christ-followers. I have labored to present these old writings in a way particularly designed to assist, bless, and inspire those two main groups (of which, dear reader, I hope you are one!) referred below.

A. For serious Christ-followers (especially, but not limited to young adults) ...

All serious Christ-followers have discovered the soul-restoring benefit of spending daily time praying and meditating on scripture. Eight hundred years before Christ's birth, King David famously wrote about "that great Shepherd of the sheep" (Heb 13:20): "He makes me lie down in green pastures, He leads me beside quiet waters, He refreshes my soul." (Ps 23:2-3). The Hebrew text, in verse 2 says, "He settles me down." Sheep settle down when they are fed. Ancient middle-eastern shepherds fed and refreshed their sheep with green grass and still waters.

The Great Shepherd spiritually feeds the souls of His sheep with the Word of God as He invites us daily to refresh our souls for fruitfulness. "I am the Vine; you are the branches. When you're joined with Me and I with you, the relation intimate and organic, the harvest is sure to be abundant ... if My words are at home in you, you can be sure that whatever you ask will be listened to and acted upon. This is how My Father shows who He is—when you produce grapes, when you mature as My disciples." (John 15: 5-8, MSG)

Such spiritual maturity is ultimately what we serious Christ-followers are all about, right? An intimate relationship with Jesus Christ and the fruitfulness of a faithfully lived life are non-optional keys to the joy, purpose, and meaning which God promises to His children who practice one simple discipline. "Blessed are those who listen to me, watching daily at my doors, waiting at my doorway." (Proverbs 8:34)

"Watching daily at my doors" is why I have presented these journal entries to you as devotionals. I want them to be your occasion for listening to God, watching, and waiting daily at His doorway. Converting journal entries into devotionals required digitizing the original handwritten text of the journals and then supplementing each journal entry with titles and postscripts. I added titles over each entry so that you would know the basic theme or topic of the entry. And I summarized the basic message of the entry in a Postscript –"**P.S. (2021)**" (the year of this book's publication) so that you can carry away the basic truth or principle of the entry in the form of a memorable scripture verse, quote, phrase or aphorism.

As you read through the daily devotionals, (I suggest you bite off one per day!), I encourage you to highlight any scripture references in your own Bible while reading the larger context surrounding them. For "extra credit," you could even start your own Bible study journal in which you add your thoughts, interpretation, and application! Oops! … I think I just gave away my main reason for engaging you in a daily devotional. It's not just about sharing important biblical principles for life. It's more importantly about wanting to jumpstart you into the daily discipline of spending time in God's Word which you'll learn over time to unpack for yourself.

A last word to my serious Christ-follower audience, especially you "young adults." I am painfully aware of the growing legions of young adult Christians who are launching out into the wide world without the spiritual encouragement of a believing father behind them. If that's you, I can't fully imagine the sense of loss you must feel when reading the words I wrote to my own kids to speed them on their heavenly way. At the risk then of seeming impertinent, would you grant me the honor of being your 'stand-in spiritual Dad' through the pages of this book? Put your name in place of my kids' names in the daily entries and read every word as written to and for you. I have already implored our loving Heavenly Father to make it so should you desire it.

B. To parents intent on raising serious Christ-followers ...

Earlier in these pages I wrote that I can't believe I finished writing these five journals to my children. But actually, I can believe it when I think back to this verse which motivated the whole project in the first place.

"The fear of the Lord is the beginning of knowledge, but fools despise wisdom and instruction. Listen, my son, to your father's instruction and do not forsake your mother's teaching. They are a garland to grace your head and a chain to adorn your neck."

–Proverbs 1:7-9, (NIV)

I envisioned my young child reading that verse and asking the Lord, "My father's instruction? What instruction? Where is it?"

Uh oh. Dads (and Moms too!) really are on the hook to give spiritual instruction to their kids. But as a Christian parent intent on raising your children to be serious Christ-followers, I know you already know that! The only question is, how will we convey said instruction to our sons and daughters? I'd like to suggest two ways that this book might help you accomplish that responsibility.

- First, give this book to your young adult kids. It contains biblical instruction which will be to them a 'garland of grace.' But before you give it, read it first and validate its truth for yourself so that when you do give it, it's *your* personally endorsed instruction to your children by proxy!
- Secondly, you can give spiritual instruction to your children by writing your own journals using this book as a model and guide. That's what my son Jonathan is doing already. He's using the journal I wrote to him as a model for the journal he has already begun writing to my grandson!
- Should you go this route, I would encourage you to note several elements in these journals that you might want to incorporate in your own writings:
- Consistently highlight key scriptures vital for your children's' life and character ...
- Be (painfully!) authentic: admit your own failures and disclose lessons learned ...

- Regularly visualize achievement for your kids and watch their confidence grow …
- Build your kids' self-esteem by accentuating their positive character qualities …
- Share how scripture relates to your own real experiences and thus teach them to apply scripture to life …
- Build each child an unassailable castle of security by constantly assuring them of your unfailing love …
- Never delay writing, because your writing is imperfect. Better to write imperfectly than to never write at all! Besides, if you stick with it, you'll get better as time goes on and I guarantee you'll never regret your early imperfect attempts!

Shall we then take a walk back in time and begin a daily journey that will last 150 days? Let's do it! And when the 150 days are up, let's continue the trek on our own because you know that blessed are those who listen to God, watching daily at his doors, waiting at his doorway!

Much Love,
Dad (Pastor Andy)

How It All Began

As a pastor recently retired after nearly forty years of ministry, I had occasion on a long road trip last month to ponder how this all began. On our way from Dallas to Orlando, we stopped off in Shreveport to visit my parents' graves.

While I knelt by Dad's headstone which announced his eternal homegoing in 2009, the words of a letter he'd written me forty-four years ago resonated in my heart as God's call to ministry that they turned out to be. He'd plunked out the following sentences on an old manual Royal typewriter and snail-mailed them to me when I was a college sophomore making some monumental life decisions about my future:

As I write these words, I'm nearly twenty years older than my dad was when he typed out this generously white-outed letter to me! Yet, after all these years, I am profoundly moved when I read it. I'm sure that's partly because God used my dad's words to cement the course of my ministry life. But I think it's also because there's just something extraordinarily powerful about a dad writing from his heart to his children about things that matter.

Perhaps this is why I felt compelled to pick up a Bic ballpoint and start writing in a spiral school notebook, words from my heart to my children about things that matter. Dad's 1976 letter to me had had such a profound effect on my life that I decided to start a series of journals to my children with the first one in 1986. My father, Eric McQuitty (he was born in Ireland where they didn't give middle names back in the day!), wrote to Eric Andrew McQuitty (that's me of course—I got the middle name so people could tell us apart!), who wrote a journal to my son Jonathan Andrew McQuitty (and his four siblings!), who has recently started writing a journal to his son (my grandson), Eric Andrew McQuitty II, … and the beat goes on!

So yes, it's indisputable to me: there's just something extraordinarily powerful about a dad writing from his heart to his children about things that matter! A forty-six-year-old Irish Presbyterian wrote a letter to his son in college which launched a life of ministry, five journals written over a span of twenty-five years to five children, new journals being started for future generations, and now yes, this book—that's how it all began!

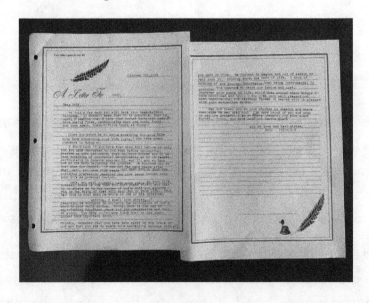

October 7th, 1976

A Letter To Andy

Dear Andy,

In just a few days you will have your twenty-first birthday. It doesn't seem that it is possible, that is until I realize that I have just turned forty-six myself. Time really flies, particularly when one turns forty. But then again, doesn't life begin at forty?

Since you have asked me to write something for your life notebook concerning your life goals, I now take great pleasure in doing so.

I don't know if you've ever been told before or not, but you were dedicated to God even before conception. Because we were believers, that is your mother and I, we knew something of Covenantal Relationship as it is taught particularly in Genesis chapters 15 and 17 and so took God at His word believing the promise. We claimed you at that time for Christ. It was not too many years after that, well, you were five years old when you, in your own childlike profession, received the Lord Jesus Christ into your life as personal Savior.

Andy, you will probably have many goals in your life. However, there is one that you must place first, and that is to always be in the center of God's will and glorify Him in the doing of that will each day of your life. Paul had this in mind when he wrote in one of his Epistles:

"Living, I shall live Christ ... "

Secondly, be diligent in applying the principles of God's Word in your daily living. Truly, this is the way of experiencing happiness, peace, and joy unspeakable and full of glory. How many Christians there must be who overlooked this important truth.

Thirdly, remember that you have been saved by the Grace of God and that you are to share this marvelous message with all you meet in life. Be instant in season and out of season as Paul puts it, "Holding forth the Word of life." I know of nothing of any greater importance than being instrumental in pointing the unsaved to Jesus our Savior and Lord.

Whatever your goals in life, build them around these things I have mentioned and truly I shall be very well pleased, but most importantly, our Heavenly Father in Heaven will be pleased with your dedication to Him.

May God bless you in your studies at Wheaton and wherever else He may lead you. I'm very proud of you and wish to say how grateful I am and very thankful for your sweet spirit. Truly, you have made our hearts glad!

All my love and best wishes,
Eric, -- 2Tim. 1.9

Part 1

A Journal for Julia Kathleen

EAM

August 22, 1999

Dearest Julie,

Over the years, I've been writing to you. Today, I finally get around to delivering the mail! This way, I get to keep talking to you even though I'm not there. Neat!

I Love You.
Dad.

P.S. Gig 'em,
Aggies!

Dr. E. Andrew McQuitty 2435 Kinwest Parkway Irving, Texas 75063

There are 35 entries in Julie's journal, from Aug 15, 1986 August 22, 1999.

... and just so you'll appreciate what was presented to Julie for her reading pleasure as we dropped her off at college, here is a photostat of that backup copy my secretary made, and has since challenged the transcribers, editors, and book designers who turned it into the typed text you get to enjoy today. You're welcome!

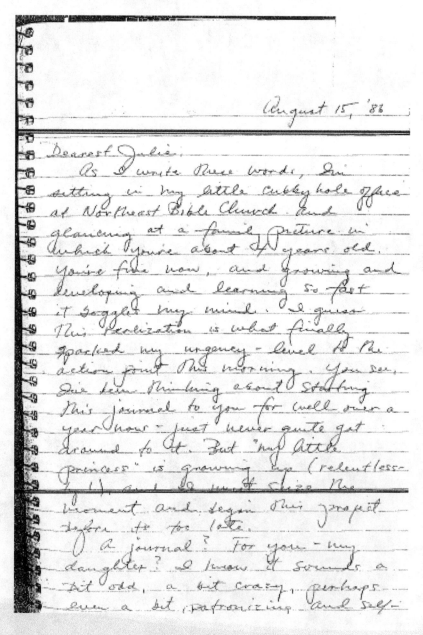

WHY I WRITE

August 15, '86

Dearest Julie,

As I write these words, I'm sitting in my little cubby hole office at Northeast Bible Church and glancing at your little one-year-old face in a family picture. You're five now and growing and developing and learning so fast that it boggles my mind! This realization is what finally sparked my urgency level to the action point early this morning. You see, I've been thinking about starting this journal to you for well over a year now ... just never got around to it! But my little princess is growing (relentlessly!), so I'd best seize the moment and begin this project before it's too late.

A journal? For you, my daughter? I know it sounds a bit odd, a bit crazy, perhaps even a bit patronizing and self-important. I hope you won't think so after you read it, however (I hope you can read it—my penmanship never did even come close to that of your mother's!). I do admit that probably a large motivating factor in my writing is the somewhat selfish desire to give expression to my own thoughts and feelings. You see, as I watch you grow—and as I grow and learn each day—I want so badly to share with you what our Lord is teaching me that sometimes I feel as though I'll pop if I can't express to you a truth or insight that's become real to me, or a warning that's gripped my heart for you. But when I come home to a tender little 5-year-old girl, our conversation is (and appropriately so) centered on your drawings and dolls and swim lessons-i.e., things close to a child's heart.

And so, I have determined by God's grace to carry on a conversation with you which will be (obviously) totally one-sided for a good number of years! I look forward joyfully to the day when I can give you these ramblings of mine and, as a young woman, you can read and understand them and (hopefully!) enjoy them and perhaps even humor your poor old daddy by giving him to understand that they were an encouragement to you. And so, until that wonderful day not too far down life's road when this monologue gives way to genuine dialogue with you, my eldest daughter, I will write occasionally of the things which fill my heart. Thanks for being my daughter, and thus giving me the inestimable privilege of doing so!

Love,
Daddy.

P.S. (2021): It's better to write heartfelt words before their time than to never write them at all...

࿔   ࿔   ࿔

HANDLING CRITICISM

9-12-86

Dear Julie,

I've just discovered this afternoon that there are certain individuals in our church who do not believe that I should be associate pastor or elder. For whatever reasons, they have set themselves up against me. Thus, what I am about to write, I write for me as much as for you.

I think the following statements are generally true: Anyone who leads or takes a stand (or maybe we should just plainly say everyone) will encounter opposition. You will always find people who are against you. Also, more important than the hurtful criticism you occasionally receive is your response to these charges. So how are we to respond when hurtful things are said against us?

1. Don't despair! This too shall pass.
2. Listen to the criticism. Sometimes we can learn our most valuable lessons from those who oppose us if we will be brave and wise enough to listen to what they are saying. Much of it may be chaff but much of it may have truth embedded which we need to hear. Never be too proud to listen, especially when you are the subject!
3. Use this as an occasion for self-examination. Search your heart. Is it true what they're saying? Partly true? Are there things you need to do to bring about reconciliation? Do you need to change, take action, seek forgiveness?
4. Humble yourself before God and men. God gives grace to the humble but resists the proud (James 4:7). I believe that God sends painful experiences like this every so that I'll

come humbly back to him. Nothing so causes us to feel our inadequacy as painful breaches in our relationships with others.

5. Determine if you need to take action, and if so, what action. Then do it.

6. Keep guard on your lips. Where many words are, there also is transgression (Proverbs 18:18). Remember that God is able to make even our enemies to be at peace with us if our ways are pleasing to him. That's why we must be careful never to answer a fool according to his folly, lest we be guilty before God of similar folly. Be circumspect, hold your tongue, humble yourself, trust in the Lord, and wait patiently for Him to work. Perhaps all this can be boiled down to walking humbly with the Lord. Let the hurts that will inevitably come to you drive you closer to Jesus. That's not a bad place to wind up!

Well sweetheart, I must go now to practice what I've just preached. Funny, when you read this, I will have forgotten all about this incident; but right now, I do have a heavy heart. Perhaps there is hope for us in this: What seems so serious and awful today... usually isn't ...!

Love you, Dad.

P.S. (2021): Never fear, deny, or avoid criticism because it affords such wonderful opportunities to correct, improve, and grow.

⦵ ⦵ ⦵

SELF-SUFFICIENCY

Nov. 13, 1986

Dear Julie,

I confess to you that my most paralyzing shortcoming in the ministry and the Christian life as a whole is self-sufficiency. I am prone to the mistaken assumption that I can pull off God's work with my ability. I've always been deft at faking my way through problems and organizing my way out of difficulties. But though I have thereby been able to avoid embarrassing catastrophes in ministry, I seriously doubt that I've ever seen the kind of lasting fruit that God produces by His Spirit only through usable vessels which are humble and weak.

I'm writing you these words because I suspect that you will be susceptible to the same tendency. Why? Because you're an exceptionally bright person—articulate and multi-talented (a strictly objective analysis by your dad!). You too will find achievement easy; you too will find that you can impress others. The question is, will you impress God? He's the only one who counts. Let me share some profound words of Chuck Colson (Loving God p. 24-5) with you:

"My life of success was not what made this morning so glorious—all my achievements meant nothing in God's economy. No; the real legacy of my life was my biggest failure—that I was an ex-convict. My greatest humiliation—being sent to prison—was the beginning of God's greatest use of my life. He chose the one experience in which I could not glory for His glory... only when I lost everything I thought made Chuck Colson a great guy had I found the true self God intended me to be and the true purpose of my life... God doesn't want our success. He wants us.

He doesn't demand our achievements; He demands our allegiance. The Kingdom of God is a kingdom of paradox, where through the ugly defeat of a cross, a holy God is utterly glorified. Victory comes through defeat; healing through brokenness; finding self through losing self."

I hope these words challenge your spirit and humble you as they do me.

Bye for now,
Dad

P.S. (2021): God produces lasting fruit in and through the lives of those who gladly yield their self-sufficiency to Him.

જ૦   જ૦   જ૦

BEING THE FIRSTBORN CHILD

12-23-86

Dear Sweetheart,

Little Bonnie came home from the hospital yesterday after being in the NICU for 2 ½ months. Naturally, all eyes were on her—almost. My eyes were often upon you. I watched you as you held Bonnie for the first time, carefully cradling her head and speaking gently to her. I watched as you alternated between petting and stroking Bonnie like a cuddly kitten and dancing gleefully around her like a maypole! It gave me joy to witness your joy. As I watched you, I was reminded of myself, and I thought how similar you and I are both in personality and role as the oldest of 3 siblings. You'll find that somehow people expect more of you than the younger ones; you're older, and you'll do things earlier than the others. In short, you're something of a surrogate mother as I was to Tim and Phil growing up.

If you're like me, the time will come when you'll resent this. You'll feel singled out and "put upon" and held to a double standard. And you know what? That'll all be true. But it's not all bad. Looking back on my experience from my present age of 31, I realize that God built some strengths and qualities into my life through my "responsibilities" as the oldest that never would have been there otherwise.

But going back even further, God equipped me for the task before birth. It's no accident I was born first. It's the same with you, Julie. God gave you to us first. That means He's equipped you as a leader, a teacher, and a responsible all-round person. You've been given a privilege to set an example for your sisters.

One last thought. Privilege involves sacrifice. Your unique gifts and personality with which God has fitted you will sometimes make you feel a misfit in the crowd. Your interests and priorities will often run counter to the crowd. I often felt this way growing up—different somehow. And I was. And you are. But it's a glorious difference—a difference of privilege; a difference like the "ugly duckling." Someday you will rejoice to be who you are even as did the "duckling" turned swan.

You are my oldest and I know what it will be like for you. You will have some pain, but God will use it to purify and strengthen the mettle of your character. Don't fight your uniqueness. Accept it, affirm it, and nurture it. It is your glory from the Lord.

Love,
Dad

P.S. (2021): God-granted privileges in life are freighted with solemn responsibilities; the full glory of the former is achieved only by the cheerful fulfillment of the latter.

৪০   ৪০   ৪০

SELF-WORTH

1-22-87

Hi Julie,

I've been a bear to live with for the last 24 hours over a foolish thing I'm ashamed to admit. But confession is good for the soul and this writing is therapy for me—so here goes.

Never tie your self-image to your performance in any given area. If you do, you will either be happy or sad based on relative values of little ultimate worth. Yesterday afternoon I got into a racquetball battle with a guy down at the health club. He was a very good player. Problem was, he was a real pain about making bad calls and complaining. I was irritated with him and found myself playing as hard as I could so that I could beat him and "put him in his place." Trouble is, he "waxed" me. Seems silly, I know, but ever since I've felt like such a failure—just because I couldn't win a crazy racquetball game!

Now I know that my view of myself—my sense of self-worth—is not sourced in what I can do, but in who I am as a child of God. That's where your self-worth is to be based too, Julie. The point is that we can relax in the knowledge that, in reality, we need "prove" nothing. I don't need to prove myself worthy, for Jesus has already definitively done so by dying for me!

So, go and enjoy this day with confidence!
Dad

P.S. (2021): Our self-worth as God's Children is never measured by what we can accomplish, but by what Jesus has already accomplished for us.

෮ ෮ ෮

INTEGRITY

2/27/87

Dear Julie,

Sorry it's been so long since last I wrote! Life has been rather hectic lately. I've announced to the elders our intention to seek God's will for us to move to a pastorate. We're a bit anxious as the uncertainty of the future hangs over us. And yet, we're confident in God's leading. Our nation is in the midst of the throes of another political scandal, the "Irangate" scandal (or "Iranamuck" as I've heard it called!). I found a proverb which seems especially apropos in this context, and which I've taken to heart myself:

> He who walks in integrity walks securely but he who perverts his way shall be found out.
> — Proverbs 10:9

Simple, but profound. "The righteous are bold as a lion," (Proverbs 28:1) and this proverb explains why. Do right until the stars fall, Julie, and you'll have nothing to worry about. A clear conscience is the foundation for security.

All my love,
Dad

P.S. (2021): A clear conscience makes a bold heart.

∞   ∞   ∞

SELF-ESTEEM

3/14/87

Dear Julie,

"Self-esteem" is a huge concern for many people, and an increasing issue in our culture. Recently I read where the State of CA is looking into a program to raise the self-esteem of their citizens in an effort to reduce the crime rate (the faulty premise here is obvious)! I know it's important how we feel about ourselves. Your self-image impacts your relationships and your performances.

So how do we develop a good self-image? When you're in a group of people that display great talents and personality, how do you have self-esteem when your own qualities are less visible? How can a quiet, reserved person feel confident though surrounded by more vociferous types? Etc. ...

Here are some thoughts:

1. Self-esteem is exactly that—self-esteem. How well feel about ourselves is not an objective effect wrought by others, but a subjective effect wrought within our own minds.
2. The question of my self-image, now, must be separated from the influence or opinions of others.
3. If self-esteem rises from within a person, then, the real issue is to define what qualities you personally respect and admire and seek to develop them in your life. (N.B., I didn't say talents, which are often God-given; qualities can be developed through diligence.
4. Show me a person who can honestly say that he or she is sincerely pursuing the highest and best in life to the best of their ability, and I'll show you a person who has confidence

and self-esteem. Corollary: perhaps people who have a negative self-image deserve to because they've pursued what is worthless. The good news is that it's never too late to get about doing what is right!)

5. Don't compare yourself to others, then, and never let others determine how you view yourself. Let your confidence lie in the knowledge that you're living for God's best and that He who knows all knows that!

6. Warning: don't let this attitude lead you to a kind of reverse snobbery with which you seek acceptance and worthiness by exalting yourself. Self-confidence born of such pride is destructive and unsatisfying, and only leads to greater insecurity because no one can always be "better" than everyone all the time!

7. Live right, think right, speak right in the sight of God. If you do, you will find that your confidence and self-esteem flourish because both are rooted, not in the opinions of others, but in the inner sincere virtues of the heart.

Love you!
Dad

P.S. (2021): Positive self-esteem flourishes with the growth of esteem-worthy virtues in our life.

According as His divine power hath given unto us all things that pertain unto life and godliness, through the knowledge of Him that hath called us to glory and virtue: Whereby are given unto us exceeding great and precious promises: that by these ye might be partakers of the divine nature, having escaped the corruption that is in the world through lust.

And beside this, giving all diligence, add to your faith virtue; and to virtue knowledge; And to knowledge temperance; and to temperance patience; and to patience godliness; And to godliness

brotherly kindness; and to brotherly kindness charity. For if these things be in you, and abound, they make you that ye shall neither be barren nor unfruitful in the knowledge of our Lord Jesus Christ. But he that lacketh these things is blind, and cannot see afar off, and hath forgotten that he was purged from his old sins.

Wherefore the rather, brethren, give diligence to make your calling and election sure: for if ye do these things, ye shall never fall ....

–2 Peter 1: 3-10

TOUGH LOVE

4-23-87

Hi Julie!

Bob S is a friend of mine. In our discipleship group this morning, he related an incident in which he confronted a neighbor on behalf of that man's son who plays regularly with Bob's son, and is a wild, rebellious sort of little guy. Bob has noticed this, and also the fact that the boy's father is rarely home and spends virtually no time with him. Bob saw that man come home last week and went to talk with him about the son. Bob challenged him to consider where his son would wind up in 10 years if things continue as they are. The man stalked off and slammed the door in Bob's face.

> ... the wicked man flees though no one pursues, but the
> righteous are as bold as a lion.
> —Proverbs 28:1

Julie, we are to be salt and light in this world, and that will involve confrontation from time to time. I myself shrink from such scenes as described above; most people do. But God uses His people mightily when they stand for right and speak truth with conviction. That neighbor may have slammed a door in Bob's face, but Bob's "arrow" of truth had found its mark. That man will have to do some serious thinking now that Bob confronted him with truth. Perhaps he already has. It seems he stayed home all week—more time than Bob's ever seen him around his son in the years they've been neighbors!

Be bold. Speak truth–lovingly. People may curse you then, but chances are they'll thank you later.

Love,
Dad

P.S. (2021): Sometimes only tough love can effect deep change.

   ≃   ≃   ≃

THE TREASURE OF GOD'S WORD

6/14/87

Hi Julie!

Having seen Walt Disney's "Sleeping Beauty" recently, you've taken the alias "Flora" and began flitting about with a stick as a wand pronouncing little fairy poems with a British accent! You'll never need a wand to cast your spell over this guy, though!

I just read Psalm 119 which affirms that God's word "... is eternal; it stands firm in the heavens". (Psalm 119:89) That's why those who meditate upon it are wiser than all their enemies (Psalm 119:98) and have more insight than their teachers; (Psalm 119:99) that's why those who obey it have more understanding than their elders. (Psalm 119:100) It is in submitting to truth that we find true liberty and self-expression: "I run in the path of your commands for you have set my heart free...." (Psalm 119:32) And the result of all this is wonderous peace: "Great peace have they who love your law, and nothing can make them stumble." (Psalm 119:165) For more reasons, we should consider the worth of God's word to be <u>inestimable!</u> "The law from your mouth is more precious to me than thousands of pieces of silver and gold." (Psalm 119:72)

Hope you'll find time today for greatest of treasures!

Love you so,
Dad

P.S. (2021): God's wisdom through His eternal Word is the greatest asset of our earthly lives.

෫෪   ෫෪   ෫෪

GODLY PARENTS

7-16-87

Dearest Julie,

I sat with two good friends talking this morning about our respective upbringing. Tom G and Randy M, two of the most dedicated Christians I know, were relating to me the harshness and heartache of their childhood. Both shared that their main problem was their father. In both cases, their fathers were belligerent, verbally abusive, and violent. The shocking thing to me is that one of these dads was a believer and local church leader. Here were two grown men, close to tears, remembering the hurtfulness of their pasts! They will bear these scars, albeit healed, for the rest of their lives.

I'm sharing this with you because I want you to sense, with me, the inestimable privilege of having parents who love God and love you—and treat you with a kindness commensurate with that love. I am so grateful to God to have been spared such heartache in my own life. It is a heritage, a blessing, and a mercy to grow up in a godly and happy home. I guess I never quite realized how blessed I am until this morning. I just wanted to give you a little jump on the game.

Much love...Through God's grace,
Dad

P.S. (2021): Parents and especially fathers have incredible power to promote good or provoke ill in their children's lives.

🙰   🙰   🙰

THE MILK OF THE WORD

Oct 16, 1987

Dear Julie,

Life holds many changes in store for us, changes which often come so rapidly and radically that they scare us. I'm writing this in my new office at Irving Bible Church. We moved here Oct. 3, and I'm only preaching my second sermon here this week. How we rejoice at God's leading. You've already made some good little neighborhood friends in Ricky, David, and Miriam S!

I just saw again this morning that people are people—no matter how low and outcast or high and mighty they are! Dr. Tim W asked me to lead his men's Bible study at the Cooper Aerobics Center in Dallas. I took Skip B there with me this morning. Twelve of us sat in plush leather chairs around an impressive walnut conference table to study John 15:1–8. These guys represent the power brokers in Dallas—some with great wealth and influence.

I was a bit intimidated as I walked in, but when we prayed and began the study, anxiety disappeared completely. As opened the word, I just realized that these men had needs that only God can meet, and that they are humble before God and accountable to the Word just as I am or anyone else. What a joy to boldly and confidently teach them from the word, knowing that this is life and strength to men who, by virtue of their station in life, have few other needs that I could address in myself.

My point is this—get to know God and his Word. If you do, you'll never be intimidated by the trappings of wealth and power because you'll already possess what all people, great and small, need.

The knowledge of God and his word and the resulting wisdom are the true riches. And they're available for the humblest believer to make their own.

Love always,
Dad

P.S. (2021): God's Word is essential food for the human soul.

Bow down thine ear, and hear the words of the wise, and apply thine heart unto my knowledge. For it is a pleasant thing if thou keep them within thee; they shall withal be fitted in thy lips. That thy trust may be in the Lord, I have made known to thee this day, even to thee. Have not I written to thee excellent things in counsels and knowledge, That I might make thee know the certainty of the words of truth; that thou mightiest answer the words of truth to them that send unto thee?

–Proverbs 22:17–21 (KJV)

ဆ ဆ ဆ

PICTURES

10/30/87

Dear Julie,

Thanks for your hard work and creativity in making my 32nd B – Day so special! Here's the main B-Day card you made for me; thought you'd enjoy having it these years later! I love the way your pictures tell a story.

Love,
Dad

P.S. (2021): That chocolate birthday cake was fabulous! (especially with vanilla Blue Bell ice cream on top!)

SUFFERING AND FORGIVENESS

11/23/87

Dearest Julie,

Compassion, mercy, and forgiveness are Christian qualities which often come through great suffering. Our old church recently split when 19 young families walked out. They were led by about 5 families all characterized by youth and wealth. Observing this fact, one of the older ladies commented: "their problem is that they have never suffered very much in their life; if they had, they'd be far quicker to forgive."

It is true. These people were generally used to having all they wanted when they wanted it. Never having experienced significant setbacks, limitations, and the humiliations of suffering, they were constitutionally incapable of responding graciously when denied their way in the church. Never having learned the priorities of life which suffering so thoroughly teaches, they became unwilling to forgive or show mercy.

I also say this as one who has suffered little. My hope is that one who seeks wisdom might avoid the necessity for much suffering in learning how to live! Anyway, my point is that the values of mercy, compassion, and forgiveness are greater than personal "rights." Please never be one who reverses these values! If you set yourself so, you will perhaps avoid hard lessons God might have had to teach you in the fire of suffering, while sharing the wisdom of those who have suffered and responded well through it.

Be positive, humble, selfless, compassionate, patient, and forgiving. If you are, the happiness you create will ultimately be your own.

Much love,
Dad

P.S. (2021): Compassion is hardest for unbroken hearts.

છ્ક   છ્ક   છ્ક

DOING THE HARD THING

Dec. 10, 1987

Dear Julie,

The weeks are rolling on, and Christmas is about to crawl unsuspectingly into our laps once again! We taped "The Nutcracker" with Baryshnikov, and you've been infatuated with it-dancing around the den to the music as if you were Clara. Perhaps one day you'll dance it for real!

This week I met with our board chairman, Rick K-a man who's been through a lot and is very wise. We were discussing a hard personnel issue at our church, and I commented that I didn't even like to think about it for more than 2 seconds at a time. Rick's response was something like this: "Never hesitate to do the hard things, even if it causes pain or brings trouble, if it is the right thing. In the end, doing the right thing is the only way to lasting peace and progress." He went on to note that that's why I'm at IBC-they had asked for my predecessors' resignation-a hard thing but the right thing.

You know, Rick's right. And now, I've seen why in my own experience at NEBC. We elders, back 8 months ago, avoided the pain of confrontation with J and H. It was too "hard," and we feared losing them from our church. Now, these men have left anyway and split the church in the bargain. By avoiding a little pain early, we're reaping a lot of pain later.

It reminds me of Winston Churchill's famous comment upon Chamberlain's spineless ceding of Czechoslovakia to the Nazi's in a vain attempt at appeasement: "He had a choice between war and shame. He chose shame, and now he shall have war."

Julie, as Bob Jones Sr. used to say, "Do right until stars fall."

Love,
Dad

P.S. (2021): Doing the hard thing in the beginning is actually doing the easy thing in the end.

Forsake the foolish, and live; and go in the way of understanding. He that reproveth a scorner getteth to himself shame: and he that rebuketh a wicked man getteth himself a blot. Reprove not a scorner, lest he hate thee: rebuke a wise man, and he will love thee.

–Proverbs 9:6–8, KJV

        ꙮ   ꙮ   ꙮ

COMPASSION

1-27-88

Dearest Julie,

I want to warn you that, in this life, you will encounter people whose actions and attitudes are absolutely atrocious and debased. It will be a surprise and shock to you to learn how low, how childish, how selfish, and how evil people can be!

I was shocked the other day just playing racquetball at the athletic club. I was with the best player in the joint, a guy who constantly beats all comers. I'd played him before, and noted then that he was a bit reclusive, a bit arrogant, and lacking in goodwill. I was playing him pretty tough when he hindered me from making a shot and I called it.

I could scarcely believe his reaction. He began cursing and screaming at me and ran over to the service line vehemently urging himself on to just wipe me out. It took me so by surprise that I was speechless. (My concentration was also shot so that I quickly lost the game, too!).

Looking back, it's hard to understand why a grown man would behave that way over an unimportant point in an unimportant game of racquetball. I have never before witnessed such a childish, jerky display of temper and vindictiveness from an adult. Surely this indicates severe problems in this man's life, and I have prayed for him and forgive him. And I have also learned to be wary. Don't be surprised at people's behavior; it can be so depraved.

Julie, you have such a tender spirit that such people as this will tend to hurt or intimidate you, and I want to buttress your heart a bit. Forewarned is forearmed; having a healthy respect for depravity may spare you from undue discouragement when you brush up against it!

I Love You,
Dad

P.S. (2021): Hurt people hurt people, but forgiven people forgive hurt people.

Bear with each other and forgive one another if any of you has a grievance against someone. Forgive as the Lord forgave you.

–Colossians 3:13, NIV

ɞ   ɞ   ɞ

SPIRITUAL WEEDS

4-14-88

Dear Julie,

Whatever your schedule may be today, I hope you'll take some minutes to quiet your spirit and open your soul to the Lord for reflection and refreshment. Life is not meant to be a frenzied race, but a measured journey. So slow down; look around, look inside. It'll make your day focus on what's really important and thus prove to be time well spent.

Sometimes you may even sense a need to take extended time from the routine to "get centered" spiritually. I believe that God wants us to do an occasional "overhaul" to tune our internal engines.

I was reading of good King Josiah's reforms in Judah this morning.

> "I got rid of ... household gods and all the other detestable things ... to fulfill the requirements of the laws .... Neither before or after him was there a king like him who turned to the Lord as he did-with all his heart ... soul ... and strength ...."
>
> -2 Kings 23:25

Seasons of reform were necessary for the nation, and they are necessary for individuals. With time, weeds grow up around our souls, and we're only wise to take time to uproot them when necessary. I wonder if "detestable things" or "household gods" have crept in the back door of your life lately? I hope you'll do as Josiah did-get tough with them and "smash them to pieces..." (2 Kings 23:12)

I've allowed the TV—not that old household god—back into the sanctuary of our home. Forgive me. Out it goes when I get home today! Julie, you'll be upset with me for unplugging it, but maybe by the time you read these words, you'll understand.

I Love You,
Dad

P.S. Your first puppy, "Ruffles", came to us from the S family 2 weeks ago. I'm proud of the way you're caring for her!

P.S. (2021): Beauty blooms in the garden of a well-weeded soul.

ॐ   ॐ   ॐ

TROUBLE

6/14/88

Dear Jewels,

I had an adventure last night (this morning actually!) of the sort which I suspect you too will experience at some point! I was driving home on the freeway at 1:30 AM in Dallas when the timing belt on the engine broke. I coasted to a stop and began walking! [N.B. This was obviously long before the luxury of cell phones!]

I also began praying for several reasons.

1. Broken timing belts = big money to fix = DEPRESSION! Also,
2. Walking alone at that hour on the Freeway isn't the safest thing to do!
3. I had just a few dollars cash-no checks, no credit cards (because I lost my wallet last week and stopped our Mobil/ Visa cards; it was a Mobil station I finally reached first for help, and the hotels in the area would have taken VISA!) Great timing! I didn't know if I could get a tow-truck or if it would take me all the way to Irving and if not, where I would stay.

As it turns out, I walked @1.5 miles, found a pay phone, called a 24-hour wrecker service, and did get towed safely back to Irving. Even got to witness to "Walter," the driver. (Perhaps that's why the Lord let all this happen!)

Here's the point, Julie. Things like this will happen. When they do, we have a protector: "Let all who take refuge in you be glad ... spread your protection over them ... for surely, O Lord, you bless the righteous; you surround them with your favor as with a shield." (Ps. 5:11-12)

(By the way, should you ever break down on the road under similar circumstances, stay in your locked car w/ emergency flashers on and open up only when a police officer comes by! Better to sleep in your car than take unnecessary risks!)

Love,
Dad

P.S. (2021): The darker the night, the closer the Lord—and God's children never walk alone.

ʚ   ʚ   ʚ

STEADY ON

12-1-88

Hi Julie!

You've lost your two top front teeth ... as of two days ago and the permanent teeth appear to be coming in crooked. Perhaps as you read these words you'll have braces, though I hope not for your sake (and mine!).

Don't be surprised at the cyclic nature of life, Julie. God has made us to operate in cycles, as all of nature. The sun's daily appearance, the moon's monthly game of hide and seek, and the year's annual schedule of seasons teaches us that though things remain the same, they change.

That'll be the case with you too. Emotionally, you'll have your ups and downs. Mentally, you'll be on and off. Physically, you'll wax and wane. And spiritually you'll soar and struggle. The point is that you shouldn't be discouraged. Life is a process. The important thing is not where you are ... but where you're going.

Winston Churchill said it best. "Success is never final; failure never fatal."

Where are you today? Down? Hang in there; things will look up. Up? Rejoice and pursue, but humbly, for no one can pursue the moon indefinitely.

Love,
Dad

P.S. (2021): The seasons of life are beautiful to those with the faith to acknowledge God made them.

To everything there is a season, and a time to every purpose under the heaven:

A time to be born, and a time to die; a time to plant, and a time to pluck up that which is planted.

A time to kill, and a time to heal; a time to break down, and a time to build up.

A time to weep, and a time to laugh; a time to mourn, and a time to dance.

A time to cast away stones, and a time to gather stones together; a time to embrace, and a time to refrain from embracing.

A time to get, and a time to lose; a time to keep, and a time to cast away.

A time to rend, and a time to sew; a time to keep silence, and a time to speak.

A time to love, and a time to hate, a time of war, and a time of peace.

What profit hath he that worketh in that wherein he laboureth?

I have seen the travail, which God hath given to the sons of men to be exercised in it.

He hath made everything beautiful in his time: also, he hath set the world in their heart, so that no man can find out the work that God maketh from the beginning to the end.

–Ecclesiastes 3: 1–11 (KJV)

‽ ‽ ‽

BAD TIMES, GOOD TIMES

5-16-89

Dearest Julie,

My heart is heavy this rainy Tuesday morning as I ponder the craziness of sin. I've been much involved in the pro-life movement lately, even going to jail twice in the last 3 months for blockading the Routh Street (abortuary) an abortion clinic in Dallas. But the battle seems so impossible, almost futile, that I sometimes get the blues sometimes like today. A movie called "Roe vs Wade" showed on prime-time last night. Then Tom Brokaw coddled Fay Waddleton of Planned Parenthood (Barrenhood!) on a following discussion show. Our country has gone crazy! Any nation which countenances the killing of its young is over the edge.

But that's not all. Also, on TV last night:

1. Interview with man who was ritually abused as a child by his parent in a Satanic cult.
2. A profile piece on Hugh Hefner of the Playboy empire singing his praises.
3. Geraldo Rivera interviewing a clergy group which in promoting a "sexual bill of rights" is calling for legalization of porn and prostitution and complete license for sexual promiscuity of all kinds.

It's just crazy! Can't people see that all of this is killing us? No. Sin is illogical. It values gratification over the truth. God help us.

Julie, sometimes the battle just seems hopeless. But perhaps these times of almost-despair are really good times, for they force us to depend on our all-capable God for encouragement, strength, and power.

Love,
Dad

P.S. (2021): Despairing of our own strength in the bad times leads to the good times of leaning wholly on God's strength in all times.

You, O Lord, keep my lamp burning; my God turns my darkness into light. With your help I can advance against a troop; with my God I can scale a wall.

–Psalm 18: 28–29

જી   જી   જી

COMMITMENT

1-4-90

Dearest Julie,

As you can see, I've been preoccupied the last few months. How subtly time slips away. Never underestimate the force of your mortality!

These have been good months for you, months of incredible growth in maturity both physically and intellectually. You were in your first play as Sarah in The Miracle Worker, demonstrating real initiative and, dare a father say it, talent! You're somethin' else, kid! I was so proud of the commitment you made and kept in being involved in this way.

Let me challenge you today with the importance of making commitments to God. People who care for one another make commitments to each other constantly. Some of these are short-term and easy: "I'll meet you for tennis at 4" or "I'll help you move that piano Saturday." Others are long-term and hard: "I take Thee as my wedded husband till death us do part" or "I will pay for your college education."

The point is that committing ourselves to specific actions is part and parcel of any relationship of significance, especially with the Lord. We don't have to make specific commitments of action in order to be saved. But should we? I believe so. Why? Because we love God and following through on actions of commitment is a natural way of expressing that love.

Look at Ps. 66:13: "I will... fulfill my vows to you..."

David made certain promises to God, some even under duress. But he was sincere in these and determined to follow through. That's good. It's good to commit ourselves to the Lord in specific ways, even if only for specified times. Some commitments will be short and easy. "I'll speak to my neighbor tomorrow about Jesus." Others may be long-term and hard. "I'll read your Word 15 minutes a day for the next year."

The beautiful thing is that the Lord has made His own "vows" to us (in the sense that His promise is His Word and His Word is unbreakable). Again, in Psalm 16:9, 12, and 19 ...

> ... He has preserved our lives and kept our feet from slipping,
>
> ... He has brought us to a place of abundance,
>
> ... God has surely listened and heard my voice in prayer.

It's a joy to commit ourselves to One Who is so unconditionally committed to us!

With Much Affection,
Dad

P.S. (2021): Making commitments to one you love is a joy and a privilege.

వ   వ   వ

SEEING THE UNSEEN

4-24-91

Dearest Julie,

I see it's been far too long since I sat down to write you. These last months have been real "stretchers" for your dad. The Church is growing and bringing great pressures to bear on me. I'm on a constant struggle to maintain balance. But I'm encouraged to finally be implementing some changes that will help me tend better to priorities. I have a feeling that your experience will soon reflect the same challenge: the urgent is always the enemy of the best. But it's very difficult indeed, even knowing this, to say "no" to the urgent!

In this last year, you have continued to just blossom. Your piano skills have grown. The Casa Manana theatre school has sharpened your acting, and now you're in the Irving Academy for the Performing Arts. You're reading voraciously. I can't tell you what a joy it is for me to watch you become a powerful woman that God will use mightily!

Julie, I was reading through Acts when I was struck by the reality of unseen spiritual events. In Chapter 11, we see the Lord sending Peter a vision. In Chapter 12, an angel comes to release Peter from prison. Also, an angel strikes Herod dead for accepting praise as a god. I find these accounts challenging. Though I say I believe in the supernatural, I don't usually take the reality of angels, etc., into account in my daily life. Perhaps you don't either. I wonder—would we be more motivated, more faithful, more on track if we made it a point to meditate often on such things? Walking in the flesh is so natural, so easy. But walking in the spirit is foreign, difficult! Yet, it is to a heavenly, as-yet unseen kingdom that we are called.

Go today looking over your shoulder, sweetheart. You may glimpse an angel keeping an eye on you! And if you do, how might that alter the way you live?

All My Love,
Dad

P.S. (2021): God and his angels are watching, so remember to look over your shoulder!

For our light affliction, which is but for a moment, worketh for us a far more exceeding and eternal weight of glory; while we look not at the things which are seen, but at the things which are not seen: for the things which are seen are temporal; but the things which are not seen are eternal.

—2 Corinthians 4:17–18 (KJV)

ൽ   ൽ   ൽ

WHAT MAKES YOU HAPPY

9-19-91

Hi Julie!

Last night you came to church with Mom and your siblings looking all grown up and mature. You even wore a pink top that belongs to Alice! Ah yes—my little girl is turning into a stunning young woman. And you do make me proud!

These are stretching days for me as the ministry—the focal point of all my training and effort in life—is finally beginning to blossom. We've completed major building and renovation projects, initiated new ministries, and brought on a total of 11 full or part-time paid staff. Our single's, children's, and youth ministries are growing, as is the whole church. Money is really tight but that's to be expected at this stage.

In short, it's beginning to happen, and you know what? Such external success, though welcome and nice, does not make me happy. Only a sense of personal integrity and conviction that I'm in and doing the will of God as a righteous man growing in love—only that inner assurance makes me happy. I see now the futility of looking to achievements or accolades for meaning in life which only come by learning what God has made you to be and do, then being it and doing it!

Consider 1 Jn 2:15-17 (NIV):

Do not love the world or anything in the world. If anyone loves the world, the love for the Father is not in him. For everything in the world—the cravings of sinful man, the lust of his eyes, and the boasting of what he has and does—comes not from the Father but from the world. The world and its desires pass away, but the man who does the will of God lives forever.

Julie, set yourself above all else to know God, know His will— and do it. His promise is that you'll never, ever be disappointed that you did.

Excited to see how Jesus Blesses Your Life!

Dad

P.S. (2021): Happiness is located at the center of God's will.

       ള   ള   ള

HOW GOD DIRECTS OUR PATHS

1-9-92

Dearest Julie,

Last night you were full of questions as we drove home from church. You wanted to know about college: how do we get the money to pay for it, what are the entrance exams like, what are the really good colleges, are they hard, etc. With Elizabeth at your side, our conversation moved from the van to the kitchen table to the bathroom sink while I took out my contacts! It was a rare and wonderful time as we talked of the future and how to approach it.

I felt as if I were speaking to a little adult. Julie, you're maturing so fast. Just back from your New York trip, you seem so much more insightful and sophisticated—not in a stuffy sense but grown up with a delightful innocence and youthful enthusiasm preserved.

As we spoke, I sensed that you were really tuned in. We met, shared hearts and minds, in a word—communicated—at a level heretofore unknown. I believe this was but a foretaste of the fellowship you and I will enjoy through the years to come, and I'm so blessed just at the thought of it.

You're a special person, Julie. God has given you a unique winsomeness in your personality that just shines. My words to you last night were to learn wisdom and character and that, having pursued Christlikeness, you could depend on the Lord to see you triumphantly into the future. I know this is true (Prov 3:3-6) and so here I repeat it. Can't wait to see the unique impact God is gearing up to make on our world—through you!

Love and Friendship,
Dad

P.S. (2021): To the humble and obedient God's guidance is crystal clear.

Let not mercy and truth forsake thee: bind them about thy neck; write them upon the table of thine heart:

So shalt thou find favour and good understanding in the sight of God and man.

Trust in the Lord with all thine heart; and lean not unto thine own understanding.

In all thy ways acknowledge him, and he shall direct thy paths.

-Proverbs 3:3-6 (KJV)

         ဆ   ဆ   ဆ

THE WISDOM OF TOMBSTONES

5-7-92

Dearest Julie,

Hollywood legend Marlene Dietrich dies

Provocative style made sensuous actress a star

By Philip Wuntch
Film Critic of The Dallas Morning News

Marlene Dietrich, whose smoky voice and provocative manner made her a legend in film, died Wednesday at her home in Paris, where she had lived in seclusion for more than a decade. She was 90.

One of the most photographed of stars, she hadn't strayed from her Paris apartment in recent years and refused to see friends and family members, though she talked with them regularly on the telephone. Such was her insistence on privacy that when Maxi-

■ Films, other highlights.   18A

milian Schell filmed his biographical study, Marlene, in 1986, she refused to be photographed, consenting only to have her still-silken voice used for the frank, unsentimental narration.

"Today the word 'myth' is overused, but it's certainly the way to describe the life and personality of Marlene," actress Sophia Loren told reporters.

A sensuous photograph of Ms. Dietrich, taken from the 1932 film Shanghai Express, was chosen to publicize this year's Cannes Film Festival, which opens Thursday.

Marlene Dietrich ... the actress is shown in a studio photo from the mid-1930s.

The poster now adorns billboards all over France.

Ms. Dietrich, always evasive. Please see LEGENDARY on Page 18A.

Dallas Morning News, 5/7/92

The passing of a famous film star is a good occasion to reflect on what we should truly value in life. Consider these words of Joseph Addison (The Spectator, p. 83):

When I look upon the tombs of the great, every emotion of envy dies in me; when I read the epitaphs of the beautiful, every inordinate desire goes out; when I meet with the grief of parents upon a tombstone, my heart melts with compassion; when I see the tomb of the parents themselves, I consider the vanity of grieving for those whom we trust quickly follow; when I see kings lying by those who deposed them, when I consider rival units placed side by side, or the holy men that divided the world with their contests and disputes...I reflect with sorrow and astonishment on the little competitions, factions, and debates of mankind. When I read the several dates of the tombs, of some that died yesterday, and some six hundred years ago, I consider that great day when we shall all of us be contemporaries and make our appearance together.

I'd boil all this down to a single statement: a worthy life is one lived in the light of eternity. We must never allow the temporal issues and pursuits in our world to obscure the truly important—the eternal.

Julie, as you attain success and esteem in the world, remember these things! Live today so that you'll have no regrets when your life comes to an end.

Love Always,
Dad

P.S. (2021): A worthy life is one lived in the light of eternity.

ॐ ॐ ॐ

... then, of course, there is this treasured comment ...

A TOUCH OF GRACE

7-21-92

Dear Julie

I was remembering a "touch of grace" in my life that I hadn't thought of for years as I sat at my desk this morning.

When I was about 12 or 14 in Eufaula, Alabama, I used to go out in the summers to play golf—usually alone. One day I saw a couple of old geezers each in a cart predating the Civil War, teeing off on the first hole. Alone, I walked up and one of them invited me to join them.

I did. I loaded my clubs (pull-cart and all) on the back of one of my new friends' old green cart (it had a stick to steer, not a wheel!). Julie, I can't remember his name, only that everybody called him the "Colonel." I can't even remember his voice. But I do remember his eyes, his face, his spirit. He was tall and lanky, bronzed by the sun, and possessed even at what must have been 75 years of age, a golf swing to make most men envious.

The grand old gentleman of few words let me play with him that day, and on many days to come. We became friends. He instructed me and encouraged me—even watched me hit practice balls and set up sticks in the ground around my swing to straighten it out.

He was there when I hit a high eight-iron into #7 at the Eufaula Country Club to birdie the hole and go on to break 40 on nine for the first time (38!) in my life. I also remember one day starting off w/ a dentist and his two friends who were just taking the game up because I hadn't seen my friend up ahead). The Colonel looked back, saw me saddled for a long day with 3 duffers, and intentionally left his ball on the green so I'd pick it up and have an excuse to go over to their foursome—and stay!

Why am I recalling all this about my friend—bespeckled and wearing a straw hat and with a love for golf—whose name I can't even recall? Because I'm grateful to him. He didn't have to take an interest in a snot-nosed golf course bum, but he did even to the point of allowing me to tool around with him in that old green jalopy.

Did he change my life? Not really. But he gave to me a touch of grace which moves me to tears as I remember him these 27 years hence.

I hope that I too can be a dispenser of grace—quietly, peacefully, joyfully, brightening the way for others with surprising gestures of grace.

Here's to my long-gone Friend in The Green Cart,
Dad

P.S. (2021): The fruit of the Spirit is a conduit for touches of grace which not only make memories, but also shape souls.

But the fruit of the Spirit is love, joy, peace, forbearance, kindness, goodness, faithfulness, gentleness, and self-control ...

—Galatians 5:22-23

ని ని ని

JOY

5-23-94

Dearest Julie,

Forgive me for neglecting your journal for nearly the last two years. Time is more relentless in its passing for me now than ever before. "Busyness"–the tyranny of the urgent–is my main enemy these days. Perhaps, that's why I was so struck by Bill Hybel's words in his chapter on joy from Descending into Greatness. Let me treat you to some choice morsels:

Joy is ... something that refuses to be bought."

–p180

Joy ... is a gift from God that takes us by surprise. When is it most likely to surprise us? When we are striving, with all our heart and each passing breath, to live like Jesus did: to lay down our lives freely for others, to live selflessly, without thought for our rewards.

–p181

[in the Bible] ... Joy is framed in the positive: be, do, trust, risk, love. From the Biblical perspective, joy is not defensive, but rather inherently offensive. Barriers are to be broken down, not erected. Instead of hiding in safe corners, we run toward life at full speed, embracing whatever it offers. Life in its fullness demands fullness of experience ...

–p183

Experiencing the fullness of life means experiencing pain and failure... the joy [Jesus] talked about ... had little to do with satisfying short-term desires and impulses, and everything to do with pleasing God.

—p183

[Jesus] chose the thorny and lonely path that demanded everything. While others were in the bushes confusing joy with pleasure, Jesus walked the hard road with commitment, purpose, discipline, and consistency.

—p183

I have to admit my tendency is to build defensive barriers on the premise that joy (pleasure) is something to be protected by avoiding pain. Wrong. Joy is a serendipity arising from the relentless pursuit of an eternally worthy purpose. Joy then rises above pain, for pain is inevitable. Yet, though inevitable, pain is not insurmountable. It merely drives home the worthiness of your purpose and steels your resolve to carry on. Thus, does joy often surprise us by tapping us on the shoulder in the midst of our most difficult trials. The key is to make sure those trials arise from our pursuit of Christ, not the pursuit of the flesh.

Julie, I wish you joy, even though I understand that's not synonymous with an easy or safe life. It is synonymous with a full life, though, and I'm looking forward to eternity when we can swap stories about what God did while we were down here!

All My Love &
Highest Regards,
Dad

P.S. (2021): Pain doesn't kill the joy of the Lord; it just intensifies it.

ເຂ   ເຂ   ເຂ

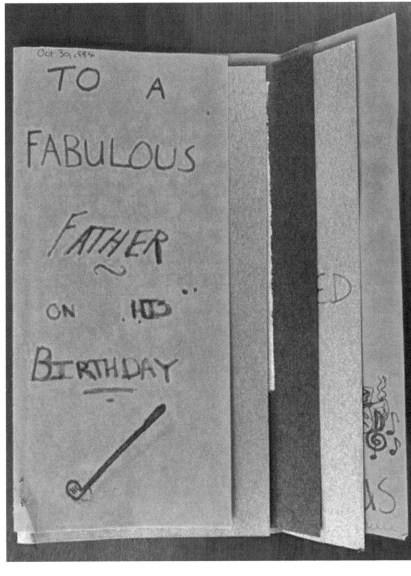

WORDS

11-2-94

Dearest Julie,

How quickly you have moved from being a little girl in a pretend world to being a mature young woman in the real world. It's almost as if one day you decided to grow up not only in wise insight (which God has given you so early) but also in the verbal skills to express your wisdom articulately.

If you continue to use your exceptional gifts for God, He will use your life powerfully for His Kingdom Sake. Of this I am so confident!

Follow Him Always,
Dad

P.S. (2021): Spirit-taught words create new worlds of wisdom.

This is what we speak, not in words taught us by human wisdom but in words taught by the Spirit, explaining spiritual realities with Spirit-taught words.

–1 Corinthians 2:13

ဆဝ   ဆဝ   ဆဝ

BANKRUPT WITHOUT LOVE

1-8-97

Dearest Julie,

I can't believe (once again!) so much time has passed since I wrote. In these two years, you've turned into a mature, godly, talented, disciplined, and beautiful young woman. When I see you walk into a room, I marvel at what a gift God gave me in allowing me the privilege of being your dad!

A reading from Eugene Peterson (A Long Obedience in the Same Direction) captured my imagination and I wanted to share it with you. Dismissing the old adage that "love is blind," Peterson asserts just the opposite in this profound thought:

> It is hate that is blind. It is habit, condescension, cynicism that are blind. Love opens eyes. Love enables the eyes to see what all along has been there but was overlooked in haste or indifference. Love corrects astigmatism so that what was distorted in selfishness is now perceived accurately and appreciatively. Love cures short-sightedness so that the blur of the distant other is now in wondrous focus.

In the words of Paul, "So, no matter what I say, what I believe, and what I do, I'm bankrupt without love." (1 Cor. 13:3)

I'm struggling right now to love a good-hearted person who aggravates me to no end and yet whom I must work with regularly. Peterson's words convicted me of a spirit of condescension and cynicism that have kept me from loving well. His words have also encouraged me to continue the quest. I hope they do the same for you, dear one.

Love Always,
Dad

P.S. (2021): Hate is blind, but love has 20/20 vision.

                               ɞ   ɞ   ɞ

FAITH

11-5-97

Dear Julie,

Two huge benchmarks ... you won a spot on the All-State-Choir and got your braces off within the last 3 weeks-CONGRATS! You're really something-kid!

I was reading the "Faith Chapter"-Hebrews 11-this morning. Note the description there of those who live by faith.

> They admitted that they were aliens and strangers on Earth ... They were longing for a better country-a heavenly one. Therefore, God is not ashamed to be called their God, for He has prepared a city for them.
>
> —Hebrews 11:13,16

Really living, in other words, requires faith-walking, pursuing that which is not yet seen, sacrificing for that which is not yet possessed. Faith is trading now for then, hope for having, fulfillment for complacency. No wonder the world considers people of faith certifiable! We're eager to trade what they so eagerly seek for that which they so dismally overlook: "stuff" for spirituality. Sounds crazy, but it's not. Faith is the stuff of life. It's what lifts human living out of the animal kingdom. Julie-welcome to the great adventure

> ... for he was looking forward to the city with foundations, whose architect and builder is God.
>
> —Hebrews 11:10

Love,

Dad

P.S. (2021): Faith never gives up the search for the City built by God.

⊗   ⊗   ⊗

a lot of people think. (We understood that [...] and still not hear [him] say, [when I stand before him] ... "Well done, good and faithful servant."

What, then, is success according to the Scripture?

1. First, *success is faithfulness that flows out in obedience to God's Word.* We discovered that nowhere in Scripture does it say that we're called to be successful per se. Success will be mentioned as a result of something, but it doesn't say we're called to be successful. We did find a passage however, that says *servants are required to be faithful* (see 1 Cor. 4:1). So I understood that if I was going to have any success in God's eyes, I had to be rooted in faithfulness. Then I began to think about the concept of faithfulness.

There's a wonderful story in Numbers 20 where the people of Israel, after the 40 years of wilderness wandering, were rebelling against Moses because they wanted water and food. They had done that 40 years earlier when God had told Moses to smite the rock and produce water. This time, God said, "I want you to speak to the rock." And Moses, in his great agony of soul and his anger at his people, instead struck it twice. Water poured out of the rock, and all Israel was supplied.

Moses was the great hero of the day, because he gave the people exactly what they wanted. But that's earth's point of view. From heaven's perspective, it was the day of Moses' greatest failure. Because he didn't honor God as holy and obey His word, Moses didn't enter the Promised Land. He didn't get his heart's desire, even though he appeared to be immensely successful to the people.

Barbara and I came to understand that you can be heralded as successful—people can be singing your accolades, you can be giving them the Word, your church can be growing—but from heaven's point of view you're not a success because you're not being faithful to God and His Word. So we understood that success is rooted in proceed and obedience to the Lord and the Bible.

What's great about the idea of success as faithfulness is true, *anybody* can be faithful! You don't have to be gifted or talented. No matter who

COLLEGE

8-17-98

Dear Julie,

As you prepare for college, I thought I'd give you a head-start by sharing the twenty-year-old entry in my own personal journal concerning the things my college experience taught me:

From Dale's Journal

5/12/78 Fischer Hall, Wheaton College (Graduation imminent):

As I write to the Lord's background music of a wonderful Chicago-spring thunderstorm, my thoughts are on endings and beginnings. Staring at my dorm-room bookshelf and its contents from the last four years, I am amazed that Wheaton is, for me, almost no more. It is an amazing ending I guess because when I started, I never visualized actually finishing! But now that I am, gratefulness for all that I've learned is overtaking me. Here are a few thoughts. At Wheaton, I've:

1. ... learned how fast I forget the Lord when life is predictable and easy and how contentedness without godliness is great loss.

2. ... experienced the frenzy of cramming, the frustration of forgetting, and the futility of half-hearted effort.

3. ... known the joy of achieving goals that I had to work my tail off to realize.

4. ... struggled with my propensity to impatience with others and gained insight into what it truly means to love.

5. ... been privileged to see the mind and heart of Christ incarnate in many of my professors and friends who have been unfailing sources to me of personal inspiration.

6. ... felt the stab of feelings of inferiority in the shadow of so many superbly talented peers as well as the joy of thanking God for them and praying for their success.

7. ... learned what it means to minister to and care for my friends, and also to humbly and gratefully receive their ministry and care in return.

8. ... gained an unlimited vision for ministry in this world as well as the conviction that, through the power of God, that vision is eminently reachable.

9. ... discovered that, no matter how trying the circumstances, I can make it or learn it or write it or get it done if I stick with it tenaciously to the end.

10. ... learned that God and people are infinitely more valuable than books and tasks.

11. ... found that a person can be lonely in a crowd and satisfied in solitude.

12. ... seen God's uncanny ways in which He moves me into unexpected experiences which, upon completion, prove essential to completing my overall, planned experience.

13. ... learned that there is no problem so dire, no hurt so painful, and no frustration so unsettling that a little faith and effort cannot overcome it.

14. ... known my anger and pride to pounce, my lust to flair, and my selfish heart to clutch.

15. ... experienced the grace of God in generous measures to defeat the above mentioned and ongoing challenges time and time again.

16. ... experienced times so hectic that I longed for escape, but never times so dead that I was ever bored.

17. ... came to the understanding that knowledge is only worthwhile if it resides in my heart as well as my mind.

18. ... found that no matter how many obstacles we overcome, there will always remain obstacles ahead and so we must choose not to allow future uncertainties to rob our joy in present verities.

19. ... found and tested a faith and values which I do believe will enable me to live a happy and fruitful life wherever God takes me in this world.

20.... been utterly blessed and forever made grateful by the privilege afforded me."

I hope Texas A&M University is appropriately excited about the imminent matriculation of one of the greatest students ever to darken their doors (you)!

I Love You!
Dad

P.S. (2021): At school, the wise learn many important things from books but many even more important things from life.

৪০   ৪০   ৪০

NOTHING IS WASTED

Friday, 13 Nov. 1998

Dearest Julie,

I've watched you weather some serious disappointments this year as Vanguard Academy has gone through painful decline. As a senior, you'd hoped for a glorious last year of high school. Well, it has been memorable, but not in the way you'd anticipated! But through it all, I've observed God doing His work in your heart. Being in a tiny class w/ no close friends has taught you to be at home with yourself, independent from others in finding worth and self-esteem. Being in obscurity, a small school with no real stage or spotlight anyone to showcase your formidable talent, has taught you humility. And being in a difficult situation which is beyond your control to change has taught you reliance on God. My what an education! Not pleasant, perhaps, but profound! Armed with the character and faith you've gained this year. I see you going forth to college and life beyond to conquer! God has a marvelous future staked out for you, and everything that has happened this year is a part of that plan. Nothing is wasted. All is purposeful. I love this assurance Joseph gave to Israel as he was about to die, and they were about to endure 400 years of slavery in Egypt.

> I am about to die. But God will surely come to your aid and take you up out of this land to the land He promised ....
>
> —Genesis 50:24

Though at times it seems so complicated, life is really a simple proposition for us as believers: live in obedience, walk in faith, and leave the rest in God's hands.

I love you, and I'm proud of you,
Dad

P.S. (2021): There is no human circumstance that can ever thwart God's promise.

 C3   C3   C3

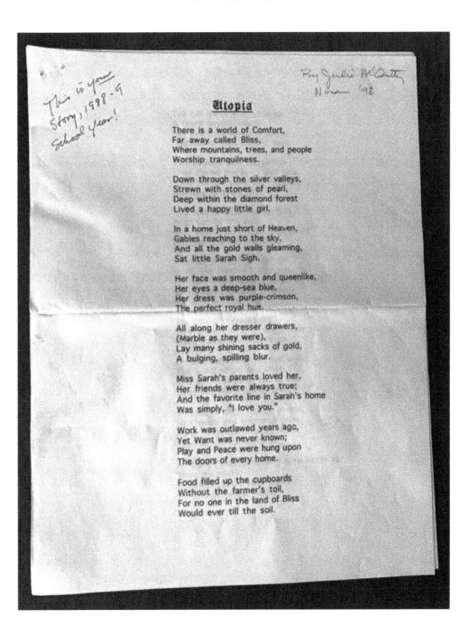

This is your Story, 1998-9 School Year!

*By Julie McCarthy
Nov. '98*

Utopia

There is a world of Comfort,
Far away called Bliss,
Where mountains, trees, and people
Worship tranquilness.

Down through the silver valleys,
Strewn with stones of pearl,
Deep within the diamond forest
Lived a happy little girl.

In a home just short of Heaven,
Gables reaching to the sky,
And all the gold walls gleaming,
Sat little Sarah Sigh.

Her face was smooth and queenlike,
Her eyes a deep-sea blue,
Her dress was purple-crimson,
The perfect royal hue.

All along her dresser drawers,
(Marble as they were),
Lay many shining sacks of gold,
A bulging, spilling blur.

Miss Sarah's parents loved her,
Her friends were always true;
And the favorite line in Sarah's home
Was simply, "I love you."

Work was outlawed years ago,
Yet Want was never known;
Play and Peace were hung upon
The doors of every home.

Food filled up the cupboards
Without the farmer's toil,
For no one in the land of Bliss
Would ever till the soil.

LEAVING

Dec. 22, 1998

Dearest Julie,

It's been an eventful end of the year for you. First, Vanguard Academy bit the dust, closing its doors Dec. 18. Then, our quest to fulfill your heart's desire to finish your senior year at MacArthur High School was denied. Though we appealed all the way up to Jack Singley, the IISD Superintendent. That's why I thought of you when I read those words by Frederich Buechner:

> Whether the things that we leave are pleasant or unpleasant, peaceful or unpeaceful, we never stop leaving them for other things. That is what life is.

I've enclosed his chapter for you, "To be a Saint." Perhaps by the time you read those words, you will better know how God is using the MacArthur disappointment to make you a saint! Sooner or later, He will!

Much Love,
Dad

P.S. (2021): Life in this world is one big leaving, and in Heaven one big homecoming.

∞   ∞   ∞

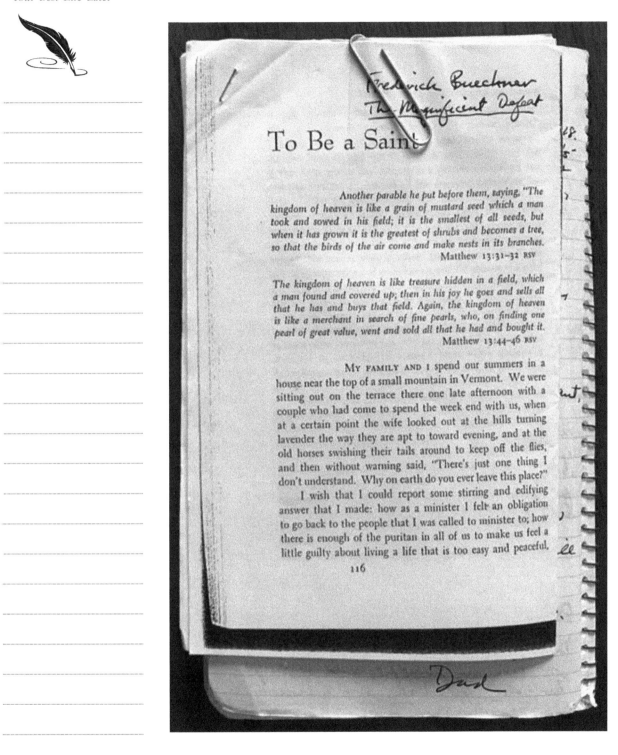

Fredrick Buechner
The Magnificent Defeat

To Be a Saint

Another parable he put before them, saying, "The kingdom of heaven is like a grain of mustard seed which a man took and sowed in his field; it is the smallest of all seeds, but when it has grown it is the greatest of shrubs and becomes a tree, so that the birds of the air come and make nests in its branches.

Matthew 13:31–32 RSV

The kingdom of heaven is like treasure hidden in a field, which a man found and covered up; then in his joy he goes and sells all that he has and buys that field. Again, the kingdom of heaven is like a merchant in search of fine pearls, who, on finding one pearl of great value, went and sold all that he had and bought it.

Matthew 13:44–46 RSV

MY FAMILY AND I spend our summers in a house near the top of a small mountain in Vermont. We were sitting out on the terrace there one late afternoon with a couple who had come to spend the week end with us, when at a certain point the wife looked out at the hills turning lavender the way they are apt to toward evening, and at the old horses swishing their tails around to keep off the flies, and then without warning said, "There's just one thing I don't understand. Why on earth do you ever leave this place?"

I wish that I could report some stirring and edifying answer that I made: how as a minister I felt an obligation to go back to the people that I was called to minister to; how there is enough of the puritan in all of us to make us feel a little guilty about living a life that is too easy and peaceful,

116

Dad

SIMPLE DIRECTIONS FOR THE GREAT ADVENTURE

6-24-99

Dearest Julie,

Being in Ireland with you was a joy. I guess you know when your children are adults when you start thinking of them as friends and colleagues. That's how I felt on our travels—friends having a grand adventure together!

As you prepare to go off to Texas A&M in the fall, I am confident that you are ready. The wide world awaits you, and you will do excellently well upon entering it in your own right. Never forget that life with God is an adventure, nothing ever remains the same (and that's nothing to fear), and that the wise person is one who is teachable and constantly learning. We are cursed for a time with a sin nature which makes constant adjustment to principles of wisdom necessary. Keep a pure heart, a clean conscience, and a sincere faith, and God will shepherd you through whatever you may face.

I clipped the segment from Ben Stein for you because I thought his insights and vulnerability were admirable: (next page).

I Love You,
Dad

P.S. (2021): Pray humbly, walk uprightly, and trust God for every step along life's way.

[Again!]

Trust in the Lord with all your heart
and lean not on your own understanding
in all your ways submit to him,
and he will make your paths straight.

—Proverbs 3:5-6

- Fear underlies all of my problems.
- I may not be much — but I am all I think about.
- My life is and always has been unmanageable without the help of God.
- God lives in the results — I live in the little baby steps.
- Ego and pride are ways to measure my distance from God.
- Envy is a way to measure my distance from God.
- I do not deserve any more than what I have.
- It's great to tell others to surrender — but it's far greater to surrender to God yourself.
- No matter who else rejects me, if I am accepted by God, that's all that counts.
- Living by my will is a quick route to insanity — living by God's will is the ticket to a quiet, peaceful world.
- Surrender admits you to the best club in town — those saved by acceptance of God's will.
- Not killing myself is up to me, not to anyone else.
- The problem is powerlessness — the solution is also powerlessness.
- Put yourself in God's hands, and go forward with your day's work — that's health.
- Faith is my map.
- You cannot lose if you are on your knees in prayer.
- I am not the boss — not of anything.
- Thank you God for my dogs, my father, my sister, my son, most of all, my wife, and for letting me be an American.
- In God's name, I must respect life — including my own life.
- There are no big deals.
- What happens to me is not very important.

And finally, three vital injunctions:

1. Love.
2. Accept.
3. Don't judge — not even yourself.

And then this coda: When the tape of self-hatred and fear of imminent doom and self-loathing plays in my head, why not take it out and put in a better one that sings, "I am in God's hands — Be Still and Know that He is God."

I read these and many more. Then I called my pal Phil DeMuth. "You're not

The American Spectator *June 1999*

> *In the third game today I felt for sure that I was going to throw up in the booth.*

the director of the show," he said. "You're just the host. God is the director."

I called Barron Thomas. He said, "Look, the show is about getting hit in the face with a pie by a young kid. You're the guy who gets hit in the head with a pie. That's what you do. That's how you pay your bills. Houses with palm trees on Crescent Drive get paid for with pies in the face. That's the way it's always been in Hollywood."

I called John Mankiewicz. "Ego," he said. "Edging God Out. Look, do you think people watching your show think you're stupid? Do you think they say, 'Hey, there's that stupid Ben Stein, that dopey guy.'?"

This is what friends are for. Spirituality. Serenity. Surrender. Friends, who are really God's messengers on earth. Sleep, blessed sleep.

THE DEFINED LIFE

7-24-99

Dearest Julie,

Taking you to A&M for conference really brought it home to me. My baby girl is all grown up and leaving home! This is a bittersweet realization. I will miss you terribly, but I'm also so proud of you and excited for the future God has laid out for you through A&M's corridors. Seize the day! I send you joyfully into the grand adventure.

Reading Cal Miller's, The Unchained Soul in which he excerpts great mystical writers. One chapter is devoted to Augustine who came to Christ from a profligate lifestyle, making him Lord. Miller writes:

> The word "Lord" makes single the eye so that our whole body can be full of light (Lk. 11:34). This passage really teaches that a healthy eye makes vision possible. An unhealthy eye creates an unreal world. Only under a single sovereignty do our many struggles who God is and what He expects of us. I haven't a clue who Peter Sellers is; says Peter Sellers. Only when Christ comes in, do we discover our own definition and why we are in the world. We are not merely saved from our own immorality. We are saved from living the undefined life.
>
> —p.15

Miller then quotes Augustine:

> Now was my soul free from the biting cares of canvassing and getting, and weltering in faith, and scratching off the

itch of lust. And my infant tongue spoke freely to Thee, my brightness, and my riches, and my health, the Lord my God.

I've quoted at length because these sentences strike me as profound concepts: Getting one's focus in life and giving oneself to it is foundational. Finding that focus in God is liberating. What's left to us is to decide. That's the challenge of life on a day-to-day basis--making moment by moment choices to keep Christ in the position of Lord in our life. Right decisions here keep us from the curse of an undefined life.

Never despair when you come to the end of a long run of poor choices and find yourself once again in the blue fog of spiritual confusion. Simply focus once again on your North Star. He never wobbles or wavers or disappears. He is a rock. He is Lord! Gratefully, He is also gracious and understanding. Blow it, but it's not blown. Our failure never diminishes His excellence. My sin doesn't nullify His Lordship. LOST? Confused? Ashamed? It's OK--just come home to Him. The undefined life can be focused again.

May you glory in His brightness, revel in His riches, and thrive with His health!

Love,
Dad

P.S. (2021): Knowing why we are in the world defines our life and sets us free.

೮೦   ೮೦   ೮೦

KEEP PRAYING

8-20-1999

Hi Julie,

As I write these words, you're off at Fish Camp. Your first taste of Aggie life is my first taste of having you gone! I admit, there is sadness in thinking that my little girl has grown up and gone, and things will never quite be the same. I know I'm not going to like leaving you at A&M when we move you in Sunday. Change is hard. Change hurts.

But what would life be <u>without</u> change? As much as your leaving home pains me, what would the alternative be? Never growing or progressing? Never reaching out for your hopes? Never stepping out to achieve your dreams? No-the pain of stagnation is far worse than the pain of change. It may provide security and stability, but it robs us of hope and the adventure of faith. So, will parting be hard? You bet. But I do it <u>gladly</u> and with excitement. This is a major positive step forward into a wonderful future for you Julie, and I wouldn't settle for anything less for you!

Let me encourage you in your discipline of prayer. Undertake by it each day to "plug in" to God. If you do, it will change your experience in college <u>dramatically</u>. The Puritan Samuel Chadwick wrote: "The one concern of the devil is to keep the saints from praying. He fears nothing from prayerless work, prayerless religion, prayerless study, but he trembles when we pray."

That's right. He trembles when we pray, because then it's no longer our meager strength he must face, but the awesome power of God. God is <u>always</u> with us. That's not the issue. How clear a channel for His work our lives will be—that's the issue. Prayer makes us powerful. So, pray, Julie, pray! And I will, too.

Much Love,
Dad

P.S. (2021): Prayer is the conduit of God's power into the lives of His children.

          ℰℭ   ℰℭ   ℰℭ

HOW GOD SEES YOU

8.22.99

Dearest Julie,

The day has finally arrived when I will finish these little musings and present them to you. I had always imagined giving this journal to you when I take you to begin your college career. Today is that day!

As I look back over these pages, I wish I had written more, much more. But I trust you will find some encouragement here, and you know I'm just a phone call (or email) away!

Last night I watched you as we spent one last family time together before you leave. We went to the IBC Summer Concert, then out for dessert at Cheddar's. Papa Eric and Dottie were there, and J. You're all grown up and ready, so ready for this new chapter in your life Julie! I asked how you felt about going, and you admitted you were a little anxious as well as being excited. But of course you are! Facing the unknown is always scary, but scary is part of the adventure of faith!

Your faith is strong, and this day, though hard on all of us for various reasons, is a <u>momentous</u> and <u>wonderful</u> day. Even so, I know there will be "down" times. We all go through them. For those, always remember the truth that Corrie Ten Boom captured when she wrote:

"I saw a man who had a very little girl, and that girl came to him crying. She had a broken doll, a very old, dirty doll. And that man said, 'But come to daddy, I will help you.' And he repaired that doll. Why in the world did a grownup man take a dirty, valueless doll so seriously? Because he saw that doll through the eyes of the little one. He cared about it, because he loved her. And so, God sees your and my problems of today through your eyes and my eyes because He loves us" (from Effectual Fervent Prayer).

Julie dear, I guess my doll—fixing days in your life are over. But God's <u>never are</u>. Always remember how much He loves you!

And Me, Too,
Dad

PS. God is there when no one else can be, as we all must walk that path alone with Him

Part 2

A Journal For Elizabeth Grace

48 entries, Aug 27, 1986–Aug 27, 2002

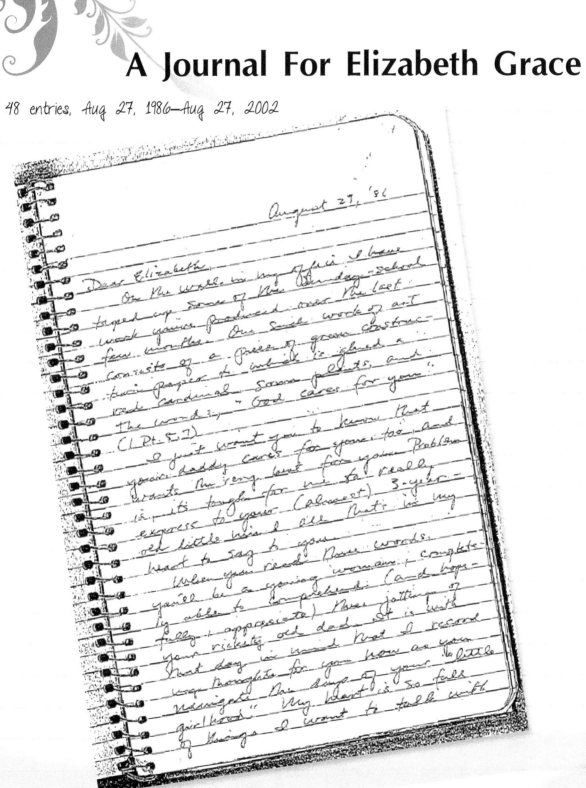

ANTICIPATION

August 27, '86

Dear Elizabeth,

On the wall in my office I have taped up some of the Sunday-school work you've produced over the last few months. One such work of art consists of a piece of green construction paper to which is glued a red cardinal, some plants, and the words, "God cares for you." (1 Peter 5:7)

I just want you to know that your daddy cares for you, too, and wants the very best for you. Problem is, it's tough for me to really express to your (almost) 3-year- old little mind all that's in my heart to say to you.

When you read those words, you'll be a young woman completely able to comprehend (and hopefully, appreciate) these jottings of your rickety old dad. It is with that day in mind that I record my thoughts for you now as you navigate the days of your "little girlhood." My heart is so full of things I want to talk with you about! Impatience has always been one of my scariest faults and in this case, it is pushing me to converse with you before you're actually able to hold up the other end of the conversation! But someday you'll be more than capable, and we'll have a grand time. In the meantime, when I have a thought (and they're rare, so I have to write each one down to save it!) to share with you, I'll just put it here for you.

I wish you could see yourself now, as I do—a blue eyed blond little beauty. I wish I could jump ahead over the years and see you as you are now ... whoops—there's my impatience flaring up again. That day: Lord willing, will come.

In the meantime, I am and will continue to be,

Your Loving Dad!

P.S. (2021): For those committed to love each other, the best
is always yet to be.

ဢ   ဢ   ဢ

TIMELY WORDS

9-16-86

Dearest Elizabeth,

The proverb says, "a word fitly spoken is like apples of gold in pictures of silver." (Proverbs 25:11) Honestly, I've never quite been sure what that meant! But I do know a "word fitly spoken" when I hear it, and I heard one this morning.

Pastor Ray P. and I met with John G., a seminary prof and former elder of our church for breakfast this morning. The first words out of John's mouth were expressions of gratitude and appreciation to Ray and me for our ministry and leadership. He had no idea what that meant to us.

You see, Ray and I lately have become aware of several people in our church who are critical and ever disrespectful toward us. We've heard some statements (especially me) which question our leadership and even qualifications. Criticism is part of any leader's life. I know this comes with the turf as Dr. Walvoord (President of Dallas Theological Seminary) said to us last Sunday. "Beware when all men speak well of you ...." To lead is to take a stand, to hold and promote a certain agenda based on certain convictions where big issues are at stake and where strong emotions will be roused and opposition surfaced. These are the facts of life.

However, it is a wonderful thing to hear words of appreciation and gratitude. It is like a fresh breeze to a sun-wearied traveler, refreshing and heartening. Perhaps that's why God asks us to "give thanks in all things." Even the Lord grows weary of perpetual complaints!

I know I'm running on, but here's my point. It is a powerful ministry to speak fit words, apt words, words of comfort, of encouragement, of appreciation. Being with John this morning picked up my spirits and gave me new courage to go on. He inspired me to want to encourage others by being a grateful person.

I hope someone encourages you this day, dear Elizabeth, and that you'll find joy yourself in bringing grace to others by your words.

Love,
Dad

P.S. (2021): Timely words of encouragement are instantly effective and forever remembered.

෩   ෩   ෩

LOVING GRATITUDE

10-16-86

Hi Sweetheart,

I see that it's been a month since I wrote to you. Sorry—it's been kind of crazy around here!

The main event came over a week ago in the person of your little sis, Bonnie Caroleen. Her arrival via C-section 2-months early caught us all by surprise and continues to wreak havoc with our lives as we now make daily visits to Medical City Hospital and ponder how to pay the bills that will be coming!

Bonnie's birth leads me to share some thoughts with you ....

First, I want you to know how special and dear you are to your mother and me. If we are successful, by the time you read these words you will know this to be true because you will have sensed and experienced it. We are aware of how hard it is to be the second child (as was your mother). You don't get the attention of the first born, and then when the 3rd child comes, you feel lost and deserted as what little attention you did get becomes whittled down and diffused. You're "sandwiched in" to the family and it's going to be hard for you no matter what we do.

Why am I writing this? Because I'm afraid of being unsuccessful—unsuccessful in giving you all the attention and regard that you will need to feel totally loved and totally important to me. I'm considering the worst scenario—that as you read this, you are not certain that we cared for you always and equally as we did for your sisters.

The truth straight from my heart is that you are greatly beloved. You are now, and you were since that Sunday evening at Medical City that I first laid eyes on you. You delight my heart and I enjoy being with you so much (even though you're just 3!).

You know what the greatest lesson I've learned to date from Bonnie's birth? Gratefulness .... I must admit that I had become presumptuous toward God before she came. Julie and you were so 'easy,' from conception to birth, you all were like clockwork! But with Bonnie, it was all different. It was some time before Alice became pregnant, but when she did, I thought we were off to the races once again. I thought I'd like a boy and I expected God to come across with all I wanted.

When we discovered Alice would have to have a C-section all of a sudden, a male child was no longer important—I just wanted a healthy baby. Then, when we discovered they would have to take Bonnie so early, a healthy baby was no longer my prayer. I just wanted a baby that would live. God has granted this so far. Bonnie is 9 days old & becoming healthier all the time! Funny how our expectations often blind us to the goodness of God. It's easy to miss His good gifts because of the ungrateful presumptions we have toward which of His gifts we want. The key thing is to become grateful for what God has given, not bitter over what He has withheld! With such a perspective one can find the silver lining in any cloud. The beauty is that that silver is sterling—the real item—and not just electroplated! God's blessings are to be found even in the deepest pits and thus gratefulness should be the chief characteristic of those who walk with God. Thus, can Paul & Silas teach us to sing praises (Acts 16) though our backs are bleeding, and our hands are fastened in the stocks!

Love You,
Dad

P.S. (2021): Sometimes God's brightest blessings arrive under cover of darkness.

୧୦   ୧୦   ୧୦

DIFFICULT PEOPLE

12-17-86

Dearest Elizabeth,

When God made man, I am certain that in His omniscience, He knew this two-legged invention of His would very shortly become to Him His chief source of delight—and heartache. And so, it is even to the present.

I believe that people are the most important factor of our existence. God made and loves people—and we are to love and minister to them on His behalf. In so doing, one quickly learns what God has always known: people are the source of our greatest blessings as well as deepest hurts.

I'm going through a time now when a couple in our church has adopted a rather bitter attitude toward me and the church over a misunderstanding generated in their own minds (as far as I can ascertain). This has caused me pain because I spent many hours discipling the man (which makes his charge that we "don't care" about him the more difficult to take!).

Such relational problems are inevitable, I believe. They will come to you, too, Elizabeth. The question is, "how do I respond?"

I think we have to search our hearts to see if we're at fault in any way. If not, then we just love 'em and leave 'em—leave them to the Lord. Never respond with acrimony or recrimination, for then you carry away a guilty conscience. Rather, do what you can to make peace and then set your face to the future, no matter what happens.

I've found that the Lord's economy is wonderfully balanced. For every Judas, there is a Peter; for every wrench in the works is a person who oils and soothes and comforts. So, don't lose heart! Accept the problems with the grace of knowing God has given you people who love you and believe in you and would lay down their lives for you.

I Know I Would,
Dad

P.S. (2021): Difficult people we'll always have with us and, by God's grace, encouraging people too.

ဆ ဆ ဆ

A FATHER'S TEMPTATION

1-13-87

Dear Precious Elizabeth,

Your joyous 3-year-old spirit brings us such joy-joy which is growing as you grow. The privilege of having you born to us is exceeded only by the delight of seeing your personality and gifts blossom. As I write these words, I'm trying to imagine what you'll be like when you read them: mind-blowing!

Last night our neighbor, Jack, helped me move a deck and chair to the church with his pick-up. With him was his 28-year-old son, Mike. Mike has long hair (over shoulders), plays in a rock band, and was wearing a "Playboy" t-shirt. Quite a contrast to His dad who, as an old-fashioned country Baptist farmer, seems to have produced in Mike his exact opposite in morals and lifestyle.

I do believe Jack has produced Mike, though Jack would be horrified to hear me say such a thing. Let me explain.

In the ten minutes the three of us were together, Jack succeeded in embarrassing Mike and me with his petty criticism and fault-finding with Mike. Mike didn't know how to tie the load down properly; Mike had scraped the side of the truck; Mike had failed to clean the truck headlights! (Mike had been borrowing Jack's truck). Their whole relationship was characterized by Jack ordering Mike around—"Do this ... do that ..." and being highly critical of him at every stage. I could tell Mike wanted to please his dad and was making an effort to get along. But he finally just couldn't take it and, at one point blurted out, "Dad—do you

think I'm a fool?!" Later as Jack and I drove to church, he continued to cut Mike down and criticize him for small things.

Part of the problem is that Jack has an older son, Mark. Clean cut, a high achiever—all that Jack wanted out of Mike. I'm certain Mike has felt the pressure of these expectations all his life as well as the disdain of not having met them. Jack put the screws on Mike expecting him to be like Mark. In so doing, he denied Mike the right to be himself and drove him away. He's still driving him away unless Jack changes his attitude and accepts and loves Mike for what he is, they will never have peace.

Elizabeth, Jack scared me last night. In him, I see the tendency of any father to become blind to the needs and feeling of his children because of his high hopes for them. I saw the devastating consequences of inter-sibling comparison. I saw the heart-breaking marring of a relationship—even a life—by the insensitivity of a parent. I saw the incredible importance of Col. 3:21: "Fathers do not exasperate your children, that they may not lose heart."

I just want to say that I have set a goal for myself to allow each of my children to be who they are, not what I think they should be (w/in Christian parameters, of course, though I really have no power to create conformity there either, do I?). I will not compare you to your sisters or communicate subtle rejection to you over unfulfilled expectations. I will love you and accept you without condition. God help me to achieve these goals.

I do so want the highest and best for you, Elizabeth. If I think you're making a mistake or being misled in any certain situation, I will say so freely. But God help me to do so in ways which attribute dignity and respect to you as an individual.

May I never employ disdain or rejection as a weapon to force compliance, for I know this only results in rebellion (and justifiably so). God help me to trust you and honor your decisions and feelings always. And if you ever sense that I'm not, please tell me, and I will stand rebuked.

I love you and I never intend to have with you or any of my girls the adversarial relationship I witnessed last night. Rather, I just want to be ...

Your Father and Friend,
Dad

P.S. (2021): The greatest encouragement a dad can offer is appreciative applause for the uniqueness of each one of his children.

ജ ജ ജ

WHOM TO PLEASE

2-5-87

Dearest Elizabeth,

Two facts about human nature cause confusion and frustration due to their inherently contradictory nature.

1. People want the be liked and accepted by others.
2. What a person says and does will never be liked or accepted by all people.

You'll find yourself in an ongoing "catch-22" if you make acceptance and popularity with people a priority. This being the case, the prudent question then becomes: "Since I can't please everyone, but I can please someone, whom is that someone that I'd be smart to try to please?" You see, you can bear the calumny of some people if you know you're doing so in an attempt to please another group of people (or person) that is more significant in your life. What you're doing is making a conscious trade-off, choosing a particular course which may offend some, but which will also please another. The important issue, then, is not whom we will offend, but whom will we choose to please.

It's clear in the Psalms whom David considered the object of his effort to please:

> Let my judgment come forth from Thy Presence; let Thine eyes look with equity! Thou hast tried my heart; Thou hast visited me by night; Thou has tested me and dost find nothing; I have purposed that my mouth will not transgress ... my steps have held fast to Thy paths.

> —Psalm 17:2-5 (KJV)

Why did David choose to please the Lord rather than men? What made God the most significant person to David?

> For it is Thou who dost bless the Righteous man, O Lord;
> Thou dost surround him with favor as with a shield.
>
> —Psalm 5:12

Elizabeth, you will find great liberty and satisfaction in choosing to please God over men. This decision will spare you unnecessary heartache (but not difficulties or trouble) and it will put you in a position of receiving God's greatest blessings.

Gloria Soli Dei,
Dad

P.S. (2021): Pleasing God first is the priority of the wise.

જી   જી   જી

MAKING THE MOST OF IT

3-5-87

Dear Sweetheart Elizabeth,

When I got home last evening you proudly related your mud pie flinging battle against "evil enemies ...." Your zeal for truth was confirmed when you said grace over supper and beseeched the Lord "... for righteousness." (we've been studying "hunger... for righteousness" in our wisdom times!). I'm proud to have a 3-year-old prophet for a daughter!

I've begun visiting the folks each Wednesday morning at Silver Leaves Nursing Home here in Garland. When I went in with Bob A yesterday, we talked w/ Mrs. E and with Harold and Harvey. Mrs. E is alone in the world, and all she has is displayed in one corner of her drab, antiseptic room. Harold and Harvey are 89 and 91 respectively; they seem happy but sit all day in their room with literally nothing to look forward to but death. I was touched by our visit and wanted to jot you some thoughts.

These people were once my age. As time has passed and brought them to eternity's threshold, so will it happen for you and me. None of these folks are wealthy (or they wouldn't be stuck where they are now). But even if they were, what good would money be to them? No good. At the end of one's life, true value lies in what one has done, not what one has accumulated.

Loneliness and old age are a devastating combination. Thank God for family and friends. May we never take them for granted!

And the moral of this story is live each day for the Lord with all your might! When you come to die, this alone will be your joy.

I Love You!

Dad

P.S. (2021): Start living your life early on in such a way that you can smile at the end.

      ଓ   ଓ   ଓ

BUILDING A MARRIAGE THAT LASTS

4-23-87

Dear Elizabeth,

There are many dangers in this life I can protect you from, and many that I cannot protect you from. Some pain can and should be avoided; some pain is unavoidable and can only be vanquished by experiencing it. One of the dangers of the former category—pains that should be avoided at all costs—is the danger of divorce. With all my heart I pray that the Lord would protect you from this tragedy, and never allow you to know the hurt and despair which this great evil brings.

My good friend CP has fallen in love with a beautiful and talented Christian girl (he's 31, she's 30)—finally! —only to progressively discover deep emotional and mental wounds inflicted upon her by a prior divorce. Divorce is a great evil which tears lives apart and, when children are involved, wrecks families. That's why God hates divorce (Malachi 2) and we should too as we do all in our power to avoid it.

Elizabeth, my counsel to you is as follows:

1. Begin immediately to view marriage as God designed it to be—permanent. Don't allow yourself to entertain the thought of divorce as an "escape hatch."
2. Allow your high view of marriage and its permanence to guide you as you set standards for whom you will marry. Don't settle for second best, especially in the spiritual area. If marriage is for life, you'll want to date and marry only someone you can see yourself with for life.

3. Purpose not to marry rather than to marry someone about whom you're not sure. It is far better not to marry and deal with the challenges of godly singleness than to marry unwisely and have to deal with the soul-shredding pain of divorce. Never assume that your ultimate happiness lies in any person. It doesn't.

4. Never "put up with" major character or spiritual flaws in a dating relationship, thinking that you'll "change" him after you're married. Growth and change are possible (thank God!) but should never be assumed! What you see is what you get. The divorce ledgers are packed with disillusioned women whose husband's "just wouldn't change."

If all this sounds pessimistic and a little bit scary, that's good. I've just seen too much pain from divorce to do any less than strive to warn you in this area. The point is, I want you to marry and enjoy all the richness and fullness God has for you in this magnificent institution. By getting you to "put your guard up," I hope I'm ensuring that you will.

All My Love,
Dad

P.S. (2021): A marriage that lasts is founded upon wise choices and life commitments made before that marriage even begins.

        ⇛   ⇛   ⇛

FEAR

5-19-87

Hi Sweetheart Elizabeth,

You are so precious to me. I feel rather bad this morning because I made you cry last night. For the bedtime story, Julie wanted me to tell about "Sir Lancelot and the Mysterious Old House" (she's taken to giving me the raw material for my stories lately). At any rate, I apparently did too good a job of spinning a scary yarn. Right at the climax (when Lance's candle blew out in the cellar of the old house), you burst out into sobs. My heart just smote me! How could I frighten a tender-hearted little girl? So sorry, sweetheart!

It makes me think about the subject of fear, however, and how different fears assail us at different stages of our lives. Right now, your greatest fears are the monsters of the mind invented by your Dad's overactive imagination. But when you read these words, you'll be facing very real fears involving living in a changing, threatening, and fallen world, fears about your future with all of its challenges and complex relationships.

The other night when I scared you with the story, I quickly wrapped you in my arms and rocked you, quickly whispering reassurances and comforting you for all I was worth. But someday soon, perhaps I won't be there to do that for you as you face fears that are real and genuine. I want you to know in that hour that you're not alone, however. Read Psalm 27 to see what I mean: "Though an army besiege me, my heart will not fear; though war break out against me, even then will I be confident." (Psalm 27:3) The reason the Psalmist, and you, can be so confident in the face of very real threats is found in verse 1: "The Lord is my light and my salvation ... the Lord is the stronghold of my life ...."

Therefore, do not fear, my precious, even when your Daddy gets carried away with his scary stories. The Lord is there for you always!

Love,
Dad

P.S. (2021): God's presence dissipates the fears of God's children.

ஐ   ஐ   ஐ

PRESSURE

7-8-87

Dearest Elizabeth,

Sorry I've been so long in writing for you. It's been a packed 2 months. The main focus for your mother and me has been the process of candidating for the senior pastor position at Irving Bible Church. We've had interviews with their search committee and elders, and now they've asked us to come and meet the entire congregation and preach a candidate message (2 of them) on July 19. I want you to know—I'm scared to death!

I'm scared of going over there to preach because I don't want to fail and be rejected. But I'm also scared of doing well and being called because I'm totally unsure that I can handle that kind of responsibility. What a dilemma, eh?! I guess you could say I'm excited and anxious—elated and terrified—eager and reluctant. Talk about schizophrenia ...!

What this is all doing to me is, however, a mighty positive thing. It's forcing me to come to grips with my own foibles and inadequacies and to rely truly on the Lord. Truth be told, we always need the Lord in everything, and should rely on Him, even in areas we think we have under control. But we don't—at least I don't. I have this compunction about "going it alone" whenever possible, and that's a horrendously arrogant attitude when one gets right down to it.

That's why the following verses mean a lot to me right now: "such confidence ... is ours through Christ before God. Not that we are competent in ourselves to claim anything for ourselves, but our competence comes from God. He has made us competent as ministers of a new covenant ...." (2 Cor. 3:4-6a) I'm seeing in my weakness and fear that it is not only when I think I need help that I need help! I'm competent only as the Lord gives me competence—at all times and in every place.

What pressures and fears do you face today, sweetheart? Don't resent them but receive and face them in a spirit of trust in the Lord. Only good things can come of being driven to a deeper dependence upon God.

Much Love,
Dad

P.S. (2021): Spiritual competence that comes from God is the only competence that truly matters.

ɞ   ɞ   ɞ

MOTIVES

10-10-87

Hi Elizabeth!

I'm writing to you from my new office at Irving Bible Church. Amazing the change that can occur in just 3 short months! Tomorrow morning is my first sermon as pastor of this church, and I must admit that I'm anxious about it. First impressions are crucial—and all that. I've chosen to preach a simple gospel message from John 7:37—39, "The Water of Life." My struggle at this point is, as usual, in the realm of motives. I ask myself, "what do you hope to accomplish in this message?" I respond, "To lead people to Jesus." But then I have to be honest and recognize that what I want more than that is to make a favorable impression on my new congregation and do well in the pulpit for my own sake.

Why do we do the things we do? Will it not always be the case that human motives are an admixture of noble and selfish—honorable and dishonorable? Perhaps the goal this side of Heaven should be to accentuate the noble and diminish the selfish in our motives as much as we can, recognizing that will never be totally pure in this life.

I'm going to try and focus my thoughts on the utter lostness of a person without God and try to imagine what it would be like to be alone in this universe with no one to trust or worship. I'm going to meditate on the horror of an eternity in Hell and on the desperate emptiness even in this life that people suffer without Jesus.

Perhaps this will help me preach the gospel with compassion and more purity of motive.

Love You Muchly,
Dad

P.S. (2021): Take care not to do spiritual things for selfish motives.

෨ ෨ ෨

MOTIVES II

Oct 20, 1987

Dear Elizabeth,

It's such a temptation to fool ourselves into believing we're pure when actually we're living and doing out of selfishness and pride. I know I do it and only occasionally do I wake up long enough to allow the Holy Spirt to shine His spotlight into my soul to see what's really there. God isn't interested in our external acts and lifestyles if these spring from wrong motives.

I read a verse this morning which motivates me to have a pure heart and right motives—Prov 16:7: "When a man's ways are pleasing to the Lord, He makes even his enemies to be at peace with him."

God looks beyond our deeds to what we do in light of why we do them. If we please God with our ways, He will spare us the opposition of those who would normally react to inconsistencies in our lives. I don't think anyone wants trouble with people. To me, "people conflicts" are painful and distasteful. So, I want to have peace—and that motivates me to "bare my soul" to the Lord and seek genuine purity.

Hope you have a great day Liz and that your enemies will be at peace with you!

Love,
Dad

P.S. (2021): Pure motives on display promote peace and not war.

∞   ∞   ∞

CHEATING

11-13-87

Dear Elizabeth,

"The integrity of the upright guides them, but the unfaithful are destroyed by their duplicity." (Proverbs 11:3) "He who pursues righteousness and love finds life, prosperity, and honor." (Proverbs 21:21) I'm facing a couple of situations now in which these verses are key. Northeast Bible Church is paying $200/month toward Bonnie's hospital expenses on our behalf. Now that we're moved, however, we could assume these payments, though it will not be easy.

Dilemma: do we allow them to continue, or do we shoulder the burden? Another situation. The "mouse" on my computer broke yesterday. I called a technician at a computer store and found it would cost me $52 to get it fixed. However, he offered to swap a mouse for mine and charge it to the repair shop if I'd give him $15. Dilemma: do I save $37 and lose a clear conscience?

I think you know where this is leading. God is very clear. He wants His people to do right and then trust Him to provide. That's what I'm going to do, no matter how much it costs. I'd rather lose money and live on a cramped budget with the blessing of God than to gain money in questionable ways and thereby forfeit God's blessing. You see, cheating only makes sense in a godless universe. There, if you've fooled people, you are scot free because there is no higher accounting. But if God lives (and He does), then cheating is silly and foolish. It only delays grief which, when it comes in judgment, is far harsher than any temporal discomfort resulting from honesty. Also, it denies the cheater the joy of trusting God, experiencing His provision, and living with a clear conscience.

For your own joy and happiness and success, Elizabeth—never cheat! Looks like I'm making $200/mo. payments and giving $52 for a mouse!

Love,
Dad

P.S. (2021): Cheating creates momentary gain at the great cost of a guilty conscience.

෩   ෩   ෩

GET IT DONE

12-4-87

Hi Elizabeth Sweetheart!

It's Friday morning and I'm behind again. I barely have an idea of the message I'm preaching Sunday and I have to get the next week's message done, too, since I'm working with AD—a musician—in a special service. A feeling of quiet desperation swept over me as I lay in bed after awakening. "I'll never get it all done!" I know these deadlines are more common in my line of work, but you'll have times when things pile up and you find yourself behind the eight-ball. How do you handle times like that?

I have 3 suggestions.

1. Pray: just relax and talk to the Lord about it. This gives you perspective ("I won't die because of this") and divine help.
2. Prioritize: determine what you must do and break down the task into objectives. Tackle these first and refuse the encroachment of distraction.
3. Persevere: start (even though you don't feel like it!) and hang in there (though it's like pulling teeth). You'll find that momentum will build, and the job gets easier as you approach completion.

Guess I better go practice what I preach or else, come Sunday, I won't be preaching at all!

Love,
Dad

P.S. (2021): Accomplish wearisome tasks through prayer, making priorities, and perseverance.

୬୦ ୬୦ ୬୦

THE PERIL OF PRIDE

1-27-88

Dear Elizabeth,

Among the "seven deadly sins" identified by churchmen in the Middle Ages, pride takes first place on the list. The older I get, the more I understand why this is so. Pride is not only a sin in itself which is displeasing to God, but it is a sin which leads to many other sins. Perhaps its greatest destructiveness, however, lies in its ability to harden us to the very things which we need—the grace and forgiveness and freedom of God.

I know a man named B who is heavy on my heart. B is a middle-aged man in our church who carries a lot of guilt over his divorce and remarriage. He was a Baptist preacher before this happened, but now works in construction. I say he feels guilt over this, and I know it's true because of his extreme defensiveness about what he has done. He feels shut out of ministry at our Church because of his divorce. By ministry, he means preaching. I think he feels that's what he should do, and no other ministry is worthy of him. B has left our church (and his wife and kids) to attend another church and is unresponsive to my calls. I'm really afraid this is going to threaten his second marriage because his present wife and kids love it at IBC.

This is where pride comes in. B is a proud man, and his pride has kept him from resolving his marital failure and getting freedom to serve God once again. In refusing to humble himself and take responsibility, he goes around taking offense at the smallest slights and blaming the church and others for his own spiritual ineffectiveness. He will never be free, never be happy, never be effective, until he humbles himself and repents and gets right. But his pride stands in the way by chaining him to old bitterness and resentment.

Why do we do such things to ourselves? Why would we make ourselves miserable just so we can preserve foolish human pride? I don't know. I do this to myself all the time. You see, Elizabeth, a lot of my problem with B's pride is a direct function of my own pride—a commodity of which I have a goodly supply. I've noticed that pride in others is most odious to those of us who are proud. My pride is like a Geiger counter to the pride of others. In observing B's poverty of spirituality due to pride, therefore, I am in a sense betraying my own. (See 11/1/91 for a happy ending to this story)

How much better to have a humble and open spirit, free from resentment and judging and condemnation! Lord help us to grow humbler and more joyful as we lose ourselves in the Lord Jesus. I hope B, by God's grace, recovers; and that I, by God's grace, will love and pray for him in all humility. And I hope you will never allow the vines of pride to grow up around your heart, my sweetheart, there to choke out your love and joy and freedom.

Blessed are the poor in spirit, for theirs is the kingdom of Heaven.

—Matthew 5:3 (NIV)
Love You!
Dad

P.S. (2021): Pride kills joy by trying to get it the wrong way.

A PROSPEROUS WAY

3-17-88

Dearest "Livvy",

I'm amazed that time has slipped by so rapidly since I last wrote. Ah—but life is fleeting. Why are we always so surprised at the obvious? I've been reading the life of Dawson Trotman, founder of The Navigators and the journal of Jim Eliot, martyred missionary. What an inspiration to see how completely "sold out" these two were for the Lord and how the Lord took their sacrifice and multiplied it into worldwide ministry that spans new generations. As one man (I think D.L. Moody) put it. "The world has yet to see what God can do with a man who is totally dedicated to Him."

In Eliot's journal, he notes in the Feb 2 entry after reading of Jehovah's "presence" with Joseph in Genesis 39:

> Lord, I know Thou art with me, but I fear that because my life is barren for Thee so much of the time, that you gain little glory from being with me. I pray Thee, make my way prosperous, not that I achieve high station, but that my life may be an exhibit to the value of knowing God. Vindicate Thy self through me.
>
> —p.20 Eliot's Journals

That seems a worthy prayer, doesn't it? To ask God's blessing not for selfish gain or a life of ease, but as a way to reflect glory back to Him is in harmony with the Lord's Prayer. "Hallowed be Thy Name." God's name is Jehovah Jireh, the "God who provides". As God provides for us, then, His name is exalted in the eyes of men. A powerful and prosperous Christian is that man or woman who humbles their heart to the point of seeking God's honor in all things, even in the granting of their good.

Much Love Always,
Dad

P.S. (2021): Christians' lives should be exhibit A to the value of knowing God.

ℬ   ℬ   ℬ

DILIGENCE

7-27-88

Hi Liz,

The months have rolled on and you are growing so rapidly. I feel some desperation as I realize how little I've written you and how much I want to say! Realistically, I know I'll never be able to communicate all that is in my heart for you and that you will live your life and successfully discover God's wisdom for yourself. My hope now is to be able to steer you around some initial potential obstacles. I do love you so!

I do believe that one sine qua non of a fruitful life is diligence. As I am approaching my middle years, I'm seeing that the difference in effectiveness of various people lies in their diligent effort & discipline as they pursue their life goals. I'm having to face the dismal truth that if I do not reach my God-given potential, it's going to be due to slothfulness. The constant temptation we face in a modern, free country where leisure time is abundant is to indulge ourselves in too much leisure. Recreation and fun are essential, but it can be a destroyer if carried too far. It will destroy in the sense that potential achievement is blocked by selfish, lazy, indulgence. The possibility is real that we might exchange sports, parties, games, TV, videos, telephones, and novels for books we might write, discoveries we might make, ministries we might build, and lives we might touch.

Elizabeth, always evaluate your time and how you spend it. I am constantly convicted by my lack of discipline. I goof off too much! I know I have to get with it if my life is to count. My desire for you is that you develop patterns of diligence in your priorities of life early in your experience. If you do, the impact of your life will be maximized.

What priorities? Meditating on God's Word, prayer, creative thought given to building God's Kingdom through serving, and obedience. Those are a few for starters! Prov. 12:24 notes: "Diligent hands will rule; but laziness ends in slave labor."

Sounds strong, right? But it's true. Liz, you have such a willing heart, an eye for detail, and a penchant for truth. (You're always calling me down, even at age four, for perceived inconsistencies!) Use your natural instincts in these areas and build on them. Determine to make your life count and pay the price of diligence to achieve that end!

I Love You,
Dad

P.S. (2021): Diligence creates its own opportunities.

∞   ∞   ∞

BOLDNESS

11-10-88

Dear Elizabeth,

Our church has been through a capital campaign to raise money for building a Christian Education Complex at IBC and it's stretching my faith big-time. This week the results are rolling in. So far, they're not encouraging. We needed to raise $650,000 but so far only 25% of our people have responded for a total of $280,000. We've said we will not borrow to build, and it's possible that either we'll never build or that it will be several years before we build. Neither scenario is the least bit attractive.

Of course, it's also possible that substantially more will yet be pledged and given than what has already been turned in. The point is that life often calls upon us to launch out in faith. We face doing things the outcome of which is uncertain at best. In short, faith involves risk. There's no way around it. Yes, when we launch out into uncharted territory, we could fail and sometimes do. And yet, is the risk of launching out into some bold new venture of faith more dangerous than remaining static, fossilized, monolithic, reactionary, and inflexible? Isn't it better to fail while striving valiantly than to fail by sitting passively? I believe so.

Elizabeth, you will undoubtedly face decisions of faith as you move through life. My best counsel to you is to face them courageously. Don't allow fear to paralyze you. "For God did not give us a spirit of timidity but a spirit of power, of love, and of self-discipline." (2 Tim. 1:7) As you approach the decisions of your life with a desire to honor the Lord with your life, you can believe the Lord will honor you. But you must draw on His power by faith, walk in love, and exercise self-discipline. God does not coddle the self-indulgent!

Will the $ come in for this building? Will we fail? Will the people's confidence in my leadership deteriorate? Will strife and disunity be engendered in the church? I don't know. But Elizabeth, I'm not worried. I'm just praying this thing through—for God's glory and our good. I believe God will provide, that our faith will prevail, and that the risk will have been worth it.

By the time you read these words, I'll have the whole story. Why don't you ask me about it?

Much Love,
Dad

P.S. (2021): Bold action is not born of certainty, but of faith.

৪৩ ৪৩ ৪৩

CHRIST'S SOLDIERS

3-1-89

Dearest Elizabeth,

What a beautiful and special little person you are, capable already of asking penetrating questions and making insightful observations. As your spirit grows stronger and God opens your eyes yet more and more to the world around you, you will see many things wrong with our world. Evil and rampant sin will confront you, and you will be grieved in heart. Then, you must decide. You must decide where you stand, whom you serve, and what you'll do. That will require faith and courage. Moreover, it will require sacrifice. God terms us "soldiers." (2 Timothy 2) A soldier's commitment is simple: his reputation, fortune, and very life is on the line for the cause of Christ.

I am feeling the string of criticism and opposition for my stand against abortion in being arrested for blocking the infamous Routh Street abortuary two weeks ago. I'm receiving veiled threats and I'm the object of scorn in some minds. I am learning by experience what I already knew by precept: taking a stand comes with a price tag. The stronger and more confrontive the stand, the hotter and more vicious the resistance.

But you know, there is a certain joy to be had only in the heat generated by acting on one's convictions. I wish this for you, Elizabeth—not that you be scorned, but that you be strong for right. In that is life because in that is purpose and

meaning. Better to suffer for right than live a life of ease by winking at evil. Those who do are fully alive.

Love Overflowing,
Dad

P.S. (2021): The spiritual cost of taking a stand for Christ is always less than not taking a stand for Christ.

🙝 🙝 🙝

A PURE HEART

1-3-90

Hi Elizabeth!

Remember me? Sorry I've failed to write you for so long! I'm amazed at your growth in these months. You have such a sharp power of observation and an uncanny knack for seeing through veneers. At only age 6, you ask the perceptive questions that force me to watch my step! Just the other night, you nailed me for watching a news program at the dinner table after I had said you couldn't watch "The Cosby Show" at the dinner table just a few nights before. Thanks for keeping me honest Liz! Perhaps God has this special role for your future—to keep justice before people in a prophetic sort of way.

If that's true and God really has given you a special penchant for truth and justice and consistency, then He will use you mightily in restoring conscience to our world. But before any prophet can be a conscience, they must have a conscience. Proverbs 17:3 says: "The crucible for silver and the furnace for gold, but the Lord tests the heart." The ultimate test is not whether we impress others, but whether we impress God. He's not interested in our ability to bring truth and conviction to others if we haven't faced and dealt with the skeletons in our own closet. Be pure, Elizabeth! Seek to walk uprightly before God in the inner sanctuary of your heart. If you speak truth in your own soul, God will use your gift to speak truth to the many.

Much Love & Affection,
Dad

P.S. (2021): Pure hearts produce searching questions.

෨ ෨ ෨

A HOLY LIFE

8-9-91

Dear Elizabeth,

I hope this day will be a great one for you. I'm convinced that we have a lot of control over such things. Good times come because we choose to make them happen by our words, attitudes, and actions. Plant seeds of faith, love, and sacrifice, and it will grow up a harvest of joy.

I'm trying to do that these days in my life. I'm under a lot of pressure in my work from finances and staff decisions. And I have seen the gaping hollowness in my soul that results from trying to live and minister in my own strength. I'm attempting to get my life in order through renewed disciplines both spiritual and physical. This is to demonstrate to the Lord my awareness of needing Him, of wanting Him to be my Lord.

That's why I was challenged by Oswald Chamber's comments (My Utmost for His Highest) on 1 Pet. 1:15-16, "Be holy, Because I am holy." Chamber's writes:

Continually restate to yourself what the purpose of your life is. The destined end of an individual is not happiness, not health, but holiness... He did not come to save people out of pity. He came to save people because He had created them to be holy.

Livabeth (a term of endearment, EAW), being holy should be a priority in our lives because it is Our Father's purpose for our lives.

I Love You,
Dad

P.S. (2021): A holy life results from daily decisions to be holy.

℘   ℘   ℘

LAUGHING AT LONGINGS FULFILLED

11-1-91

Dearest Elizabeth,

In Genesis 18 we read the story of Sarah laughing when she heard the Lord's messenger announce she would bear a child at age 90. It was a bitter, cynical laugh born out of frustration of knowing this promise for a child had remained unfulfilled for years. But let's not judge Sarah's response too harshly. In similar circumstances, I'm sure I'd have done the same—or worse! The point is, however, that God did His miracle in spite of Sarah's laugh. To the incongruity of His promise He added the surprise of His grace.

I think about God's dealings w/ Abraham and Sarah and wonder if He doesn't long to do the same for you and me. He made them a promise—a wonderful promise of a child but one nonetheless for which they would have to wait in faith for years. They waited, sometimes up and sometimes, as here, down. And in due time, the Lord made good on His promise.

I think God's richest promises and most wonderful gifts are those that come to us after the longest waits and deepest trials. Hasty gratification of our deepest longings would not build our character and maturity deep within our souls that Christ wants there. But gratification is not forever delayed. All good things come to those who wait!

Elizabeth, how big a dream can you dare to dream for your life in Christ? I pray you can trust Him for truly marvelous and incongruous things in your life! But remember, the more marvelous the dream, the more strenuous the wait. We've got to be in this faith for the long haul, hanging on to God's promises through thick and thin if that faith is to prevail. Dare to dream.

Determine to persevere. If you do, someday you'll be laughing, too. Not the bitter, cynical laugh of broken dreams, but the delighted, joyful laugh of miraculously fulfilled longings.

Much Love to One Who Is A Miraculously
Fulfilled Longing to Me,
Dad

P.S. (see the entry in this journal from 1-27-88) Liz, let me tell you again about BR. In the summer of 1988, he was at Horn Creek family camp w/ our church group. RP was speaking and made some comment against racism. B, who among other things was extremely prejudiced, walked out. The next day, he left Horn Creek and drove all the way to Texas alone. That's the last I heard of B for a long time. He drifted back to church in 1989. I didn't know it, but God was working in B's heart. That's why I was so surprised when he signed up for a ministry trip to Haiti I was leading in the summer of 1990. On that trip, B became a new man. One evening we were visiting in a T.B. ward full of pathetic little Haitian children. I watched as B picked a little girl up out of her wheelchair. She put her head on his shoulder—and that's when I think it happened. The pride and bitterness of the past just evaporated, and the racism died. B returned from Haiti a new man. He joyfully attends church now, hugs me and tells me he loves me, and generally has a whole new outlook and attitude. And guess what? B just got back from a second trip to Haiti (Sept, '91). When I saw him recently, know what I did? Just laughed and laughed! People can and do change by God's grace (even me)! P.T.L.

P.S. (2021): The last laugh is always worth the wait.

❧   ❧   ❧

SOWING SEEDS

2-18-92

Dearest Elizabeth,

Never underestimate the power of a seed! One of God's most powerful and oft-over- looked miracles is that of a tiny seed, dead and buried, coming to life w/ the energy to push through packed earth and stone as it becomes a fruit-bearing plant. The delight of the seed is that you thought it was dead and gone. You thought you'd seen and heard the last of it. But with the passage of time, what you thought had flowed past in the river of time suddenly crops up as part of the present and future.

It is the wise person who understands the way of the seed. Such a one knows never to grow weary in the planting of seeds, to never scoff at investing time and energy in that which has no immediate return. Eventually, they know, the fruit will come. But only after patient sowing and diligent waiting.

Elizabeth, I have always struggled w/ the seed principle. Impatient and impulsive by nature, I find it difficult to be satisfied with the mundane chore of planting seeds. Oh, when the harvest is ready, call me. That's my forte (but who's forte isn't it?)! But I've learned that the harvest depends upon sowing faithfully (profound, huh?!). Never underestimate the power of a seed! "Peacemakers who sow in peace raise a harvest of righteousness" (Jas 3:18).

How do we sow seeds? Kind words and deeds, acts of service and sacrifice, choices that reflect godliness and excellence. We sow seeds of peace when we stand for the right, reflect Christ's compassion, and exercise self-discipline. Most times, you'll think nobody notices or cares when you do such things. That's how it is planting seeds. They seem buried, dead, and gone. But they're not. Life comes from seed-planting. Never underestimate the power of seed-sowing!

It works the other way, too. "Whatsoever a man sows, that he shall also reap," (Galatians 6:7) Seed-sowing is powerful, but unfortunately so is weed-sowing. Bad habits, negative attitudes, little compromises along the way sow seeds that produce a bitter harvest. What goes around comes around and what we sow we reap—for good or for ill.

I love you, Liz! Sow good seeds today!

Affectionately,
Dad

P.S. (2021): Sow in such a way that you'll welcome the harvest you inevitably reap.

෪   ෪   ෪

GENEROSITY

6-3-92

Dearest Elizabeth,

How beautifully you sang "Sentimental Journey" in front of 200 people at your grandparents 40th anniversary party! Your confidence and sparkle shone through, hinting at how God has gifted and will use you. I'm proud of and excited for you!

I want to teach you a principle which is hard to learn but utterly worthwhile: Long after the money's gone, the memories remain. I get this from Mark 14:1-11 where Mary's and Judas' attitudes toward money and priorities so starkly contrast. Mary lavishes on Jesus a costly perfume to anoint Him for burial. Judas promptly objects, protesting this extravagance as a waste of money. But was it? Wasn't it worth the money to make the memory? These 2,000 years later when both Mary and Judas are both long dead and buried and their money and possessions long gone, we see how stingy and short-sighted Judas was to sacrifice a worthy generosity to momentarily preserve wealth that would soon perish.

Mary, on the other hand, joyfully gave what she could not keep (wealth) to gain what she could not lose (memory, honor, love). Perhaps Judas was more fiscally responsible. But who was wiser? Remember, sweetheart, you never lose when you give. Generosity is always a good investment for long after the money is gone, the memories remain.

Your Loving Father,
Dad

P.S. (2021): It really is more blessed to give than to receive!

હ્ય   હ્ય   હ્ય

OBEDIENCE

8-28-92

Sweetheart Elizabeth,

What a joy you are to me. I marvel at the depth and clarity of your insight into people at the tender age of eight. As I've noted in these pages before, that's a gift with you. Some would say you are streetwise! I'd just say you have a natural grasp of how people think and act. Use your gift to keep your own soul in line and thus help others do the same!

I was reading Exodus 15:22-27 this morning—the story of the bitter waters at Marah. Here are some observations: God tested Israel w/ thirst only three days after their great victory at the Red Sea. Trial often follows closely on the heels of spiritual highs. Beware! Obedience was the way to Israel's health. When Moses obeyed God and threw the tree into the bitter water, it became sweet. When we set our hearts to obey God, He will make our lives sweet, as well. But the real test of obedience is not in good times, but hard times. God wants our allegiance to His word when we're up or down, feeling strong or weak.

The best thing you can do, then, is obey—when you're hurting, confused, or disappointed. Remember, the Lord specializes in making the bitter, sweet. I can't help but think of another "tree" in scripture which, when thrown into the flow of human history, made the bitter, sweet. That's the tree of Calvary, the cross of our Lord Jesus Christ. That tree took the bitterness of sin, death, and despair and made possible faith, hope, and love for all who "obey" the gospel by believing in Jesus.

Liz, the older I become, the less it seems I know. That's why simple truths like this become so precious. I don't have to understand life. I just have to obey the Lord who created life. He will take care of the rest. Count on it!

With Love,
Dad

P.S. (2021): I don't understand then obey; I obey then understand.

⁃⁃⁃   ⁃   ⁃

D-DAY EVERYDAY

5-30-94 Memorial Day

Dear Liffy,

I see that I've taken nearly two years off from this journal. Sorry about that! I certainly haven't taken any time off from being totally impressed by and in love with you!

On June 6, 1944, Capt. Joseph Dawson was among the first infantry soldiers to hit the Omaha beach off Normandy in the famous D-Day invasion of World War II. Over 2,000 men would die on the sands of that beach within the next few hours. I want you to have 2 statements Capt. Dawson later made:

> All the many weapons of war seemed to be concentrated on that naked, exposed bit of sand, and the miracle of it all was that I still cannot tell just how I crossed it, or how we managed, but we did. Though many fell as we moved through the storm of steel, they didn't falter for an instant but came on without stopping.

> As God is my witness, the men of my company lived, fought, and died in true glory.

Elizabeth, you probably wonder why I'm recording these words for you. It is not because I think war is neat or want you to join the army! Rather, it's because Captain Dawson's actions and attitudes on D-Day 50 years ago exemplify principles by which we all ought to live all the time:

- Never give up. Is opposition tough? Is there danger? If you're in the right, don't falter but come on without stopping.

- In all things, live honorably. Never compromise your integrity. Do right no matter the cost.
- Live and, if necessary, fight and die, with true glory. You will have all eternity to celebrate your faithfulness. So, will I!

Your Loving Father,
Dad

P.S. (2021): Glory is not easily won, and that is why it's not ever forgotten.

৪৩   ৪৩   ৪৩

TIME FLIES

11-2-94

Dearest Elizabeth,

Thanks so for your powerful reminder of the brevity of life! (See attached hand drawn birthday card) We are like leaves of grass as the scripture says. The wind blows across us, we wither and die so quickly—yet the love of God (and our souls) last forever (Psalm 103: 15-17).

I can scarcely believe I'm 39 and you're 11. Liz, one day soon, you'll be 39, too (I know that's hard to believe, but it was for me too and look what's happened!). So goes life. The lesson to be learned is this: don't fear the passing time. Rather experience it fully and invest it wisely, always with the Heavenly fields in view. This is not our home—we're only passing through!

Love,
Dad

P.S. (2021): No one can slow time's passage so we may as well go joyfully with the flow.

∞   ∞   ∞

Happy. BIG. HUGE,
GIGUNTIC.oooo
39th

BIRTHDAY

Just imagin...ooo 11 more
years and you'll be .. 50
on top of the hill, then 60
half way down the hillooo
then you'll be... DEAD at the age
(just a joke I love you of 100 Q G
I read 2 over

love, Elizabeth

SELFISH OR SELFLESS

1-15-97

Dearest Elizabeth,

What a long time since I've written in these pages! And how much you've grown! Now in your second year at Lexington Academy (7th grade), you've blossomed into a great student, athlete (BB and softball) and trumpet player. More than that, you've matured in both physical and spiritual beauty. I'm so proud of you when I see you. I can scarcely believe God has given me the privilege of being your Dad!

I was challenged greatly by a passage I read in Eugene Peterson this morning. I'd been having one of "those days" when everything goes wrong and my plans are completely disrupted. Generally, I don't handle aggravations well. I just let them get me more aggravated!

Then I read,

The self, if it is to become itself, must find a larger house to dwell in than the house where everyone coddles us and responds to our whims. The passage from leaving home to entering marriage is the archetypal transition from the comfortable, cared-for self to this strenuous, caring-for self.

Self-love is obsessed with keeping what it has and adding a little more of the same. That is why it is so boring. There is never anything new to say, nothing new to discover.

Self-love assesses its position by what it has and is panicked at the thought of losing any of it. Forced into new relationships, into new situations, its first consideration is not of the new fields for love but of the appalling prospects of loss. So, it clings. It holds and it whines.

—Living the Message, Eugene Peterson, p. 49.

Ouch! He nailed me. Allowing myself to whine about "things not going my way" is not only selfish, but wasteful as I'm allowing a chance "to dwell in a larger house" to slip away. What a more wonderful experience we have in life when we receive its surprises, not as intrusions, but as opportunities to experience love at a higher (and more joyous) level.

Love,
DAD

P.S. (2021): Self-love never has anything new to say, but selflessness always does.

෮   ෮   ෮

... it all comes out when you play the game.

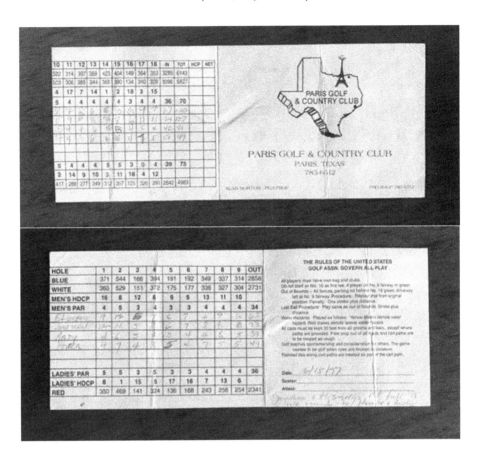

FAITH OR FEELINGS

12/30/97

Hi Liz,

For Christmas this year, you gave Mom and me matching gold crosses/chains. To earn the money for these beautiful gifts, you worked weekends in a jewelry store. I am moved by your love, generosity, and industry, and I will wear this cross until it or I completely wear out!

(N.B. added 6/99. Dear Liz, on our trip to Ireland. I wanted to honor my cousin Elizabeth—your namesake! —— w/ a special gift for her graduation from Bible School. My most valuable possession was the gold cross you gave me and which I was wearing. I gave it to her as I told her you had given it to me, and she was so blessed! I hope you'll see this as my honoring your gift to me, because that's what this meant to me.)

I came across (again in Living the Message by Eugene Peterson) a profound and helpful definition of faith which I believe can make us more powerful believers:

> When we define faith as a feeling—of belief, or of piety—what we're actually measuring is not faith but an emotion. Faith is not a feeling. It is simply an act of assent, of openness, and often doesn't feel like much at all. Faith has to do with what God is doing, not with what we are feeling.

When you were about 10, we were at "Wet and Wild" and you wanted to go down the huge slide. Remember? But when we climbed all the way to the top, you had second thoughts (me too!). Looking down that precipitous drop, you no longer felt like taking the plunge. But you acted on faith. Ignoring feelings of fear, you shoved off and I watched your little blond head shoot down that slide like a bullet, hair streaming out behind you! That was "an act of assent, of openness..." You acted based on faith instead of retreating based on fear.

It's the same in your spiritual life, Liz. God is there. Believe in Him. Trust Him. No matter how you may feel, act in faith. And enjoy the ride!

Love,
Dad

P.S. (2021): Faith is the choice to act on our beliefs and not our doubts.

෪   ෪   ෪

NEW CHALLENGES

8/27/99

Dearest Elizabeth,

You are such a blessing to my heart! Ted and Tracy were over last night with you and Alex. You've become good friends w/ them as youth sponsors, and through them you've become inspired in your walk w/ the Lord. Every day you're up before dawn, reading your Bible and praying. You've taken up the guitar because you love worship music and you're getting quite good on it. The resulting spiritual maturity in your life is obvious. You've become more expressive of your faith. When I drive you to school, I love to ask what God taught you that morning in your quiet time. You always have an answer! Lately you've been studying Philippians. I just want you to know, I'm proud of you!

I went with you on your first day at R.L. Turner High as a 10th grader. It was so intimidating! As I watched you getting your I.D. picture taken in the library, I could only pray that God would protect and help you as you "break in" to a whole new situation. We searched all over for your locker, finally found it and practiced opening it all the while me wishing I could stand by your side all day. But I couldn't. I left you, but you went bravely on, and the Lord was with you.

Now you've joined the softball team & select choir and you're making friends and doing well. I know your faith has been a major aspect of your courage in "going for it." I'm just proud of you! Even when things go wrong, you keep it together. Yesterday, I was supposed to pick you up after school, but totally forgot! You waited 1:15 hour in the heat. Yet, when mom got you and then you saw me, you were forgiving. Wow! Thanks Liz! I'm amazed at your patience.

I'm excited for your future, Liz. I hope you will be too. Never let self-doubt diminish your faith in what God can and will do in and through you! Here's what Bill Hybels says:

> Vision is the God-given ability to catch a glimpse of what God wants to do through your life if you dedicate yourself to Him. God delights in using foolish people to confound wise people. He loves to use weak people to amaze strong people. And He'd love to use you if you'd just believe all things are possible.
>
> —Who You Are, pp. 44-45

Believe it, Liz! All things are possible if your faith is in God. You've got a great start on the grand adventure. Never let up.

With Anticipation and Love
Dad

8/28/99 P.S. Hi Liz, I took you to "detention" at RLT this morning. Your infraction? Tardy (due to being in the restroom and not hearing the bell). For this, you had to be there on a Saturday morning from 7:30-9:30, doing busywork they assigned you in a "tardy-packet." What a drag! Yet, you kept your good nature and took it all in stride. I'm sure learning a lot from you!

P.S. (2021): The path to fulfilling God's vision for our lives runs right through new challenges in our lives.

෬   ෬   ෬

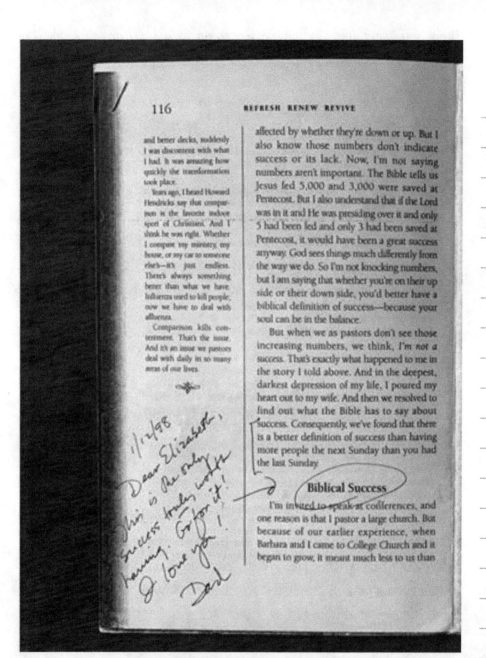

116   REFRESH RENEW REVIVE

and better decks, suddenly I was discontent with what I had. It was amazing how quickly the transformation took place.

Years ago, I heard Howard Hendricks say that comparison is the favorite indoor sport of Christians. And I think he was right. Whether I compare my ministry, my house, or my car to someone else's—it's just endless. There's always something better than what we have. Influenza used to kill people, now we have to deal with affluenza.

Comparison kills contentment. That's the issue. And it's an issue we pastors deal with daily in so many areas of our lives.

affected by whether they're down or up. But I also know those numbers don't indicate success or its lack. Now, I'm not saying numbers aren't important. The Bible tells us Jesus fed 5,000 and 3,000 were saved at Pentecost. But I also understand that if the Lord was in it and He was presiding over it and only 5 had been fed and only 3 had been saved at Pentecost, it would have been a great success anyway. God sees things much differently from the way we do. So I'm not knocking numbers, but I am saying that whether you're on their up side or their down side, you'd better have a biblical definition of success—because your soul can be in the balance.

But when we as pastors don't see those increasing numbers, we think, *I'm not a success.* That's exactly what happened to me in the story I told above. And in the deepest, darkest depression of my life, I poured my heart out to my wife. And then we resolved to find out what the Bible has to say about success. Consequently, we've found that there is a better definition of success than having more people the next Sunday than you had the last Sunday.

Biblical Success

I'm invited to speak at conferences, and one reason is that I pastor a large church. But because of our earlier experience, when Barbara and I came to College Church and it began to grow, it meant much less to us than

1/12/98

Dear Elizabeth,

This is the only success truly worth having. Go for it! I love you!

Dad

a lot of people think. We understood that I could pastor a large church and still not hear from Him (when I stand before Him), "Well done, thou good and faithful servant."

What, then, is success according to the Scriptures?

1. First, success is faithfulness that shows itself in obedience to God's Word. We discovered that nowhere in Scripture does it say that we're called to be successful per se. Success will be mentioned as a result of something, but it doesn't say we're called to be successful. We did find a passage, however, that says stewards are required to be faithful (see 1 Cor. 4:1-2). So I understood that if I was going to have any success in God's eyes, it had to be rooted in faithfulness. Then I began to think about the concept of faithfulness.

There's a wonderful story in Numbers 20 where the people of Israel, after the 40 years of wilderness wandering, were rebelling against Moses because they wanted water and food. They had done that 40 years earlier, when God had told Moses to smite the rock and produce water. This time, God said, "I want you to speak to the rock." And Moses, in his great agony of soul and his anger at his people, instead struck it twice. Water poured out of the rock, and all Israel was supplied.

Moses was the great hero of the day, because he gave the people exactly what they wanted. But that's earth's point of view. From heaven's perspective, it was the day of Moses' greatest failure. Because he didn't honor God as holy and obey His word. Moses didn't enter the Promised Land. He didn't get his heart's desire, even though he appeared to be immensely successful to the people.

Barbara and I came to understand that you can be heralded as successful—people can be singing your accolades; you can be giving them the Word; your church can be growing—but from heaven's point of view, you're not a success because you're not being faithful to God and His Word. So we understood that success is rooted in profound obedience to the Lord and the Bible.

What's great about the idea of success as faithfulness is that anybody can be faithful! You don't have to be gifted or talented. No matter what

BOAST ABOUT THIS

8-9-00

Dear Elizabeth,

It's obvious from the date that I've really fallen down on the job—almost a year since I last visited you in these pages! In that time, you completed your sophomore year at R.L.T. You played left field and lettered on the varsity girls' softball team. You held jobs at the UA Cinema and at Chili's Two. You got your new guitar at Christmas and have been studying with Barry and leading worship at youth group on Sunday nights. You went to the shores at Pine Cove. And today, you begin your junior year of high school.

Just last night, I did a memorial message for Chad (John and Sue's little special needs boy who passed away). You knew Chad for years—so enthusiastic and happy and full of praise for God. I spoke for Chad from Jeremiah 9:23:

> Let not the wise man boast of his wisdom, or the strong man boast of his strength, or the rich man boast of his riches, but let him who boasts boast about this: that he understands and knows Me, that I am the Lord who exercises kindness, justice and righteousness on the earth, for in these I delight, says the Lord.

Chad was anything but wise, strong, or rich in the world's eyes. He died at 23 with the intellect of a 4-year-old. He still wore diapers. He was totally dependent on others for everything. Yet he loved God. He knew and understood God! And he taught us all that true wisdom is trusting God whole heartedly, true strength is loving life authentically, and true riches & wealth consist of loving people unconditionally.

Liz, remember Chad sometimes. He was a gift from God to help us all remember that life is not the province of the powerful and strong, but of those who know God and humbly walk with Him.

Much Love,
Dad

P.S. (2021): Of all your achievements, let the greatest be knowing and understanding God.

        ଓ   ଓ   ଓ

CARPE DIEM

New Year's Eve '00

Dearest Elizabeth,

Tonight, Alex is a very fortunate young woman not only because she came through major surgery successfully, but because she has a faithful, loyal friend named Liz McQuitty. You spent the night in her hospital room last night to keep her company, and that's where you are tonight. I have always been impressed by your care for others, Elizabeth. May you always have friends worthy of you!

At midnight we will welcome a new year, a new decade, a new century, and a new millennium. Wow—how many people in the history of humanity have the chance to experience such milestones! But we do. I try to imagine you at the end of this decade. Maybe you'll be married with children, a college degree, perhaps pursuing a career or building your home. Whatever path you choose, pursue it with all your heart, Liz. Go for your dreams. Why? Because life is a vapor and time is fleeting. Seize the day! Before you know it, I predict you'll be giving the same advice to your own kids.

Love You Much!
Dad

P.S. (2021): An old year passing is a great reminder to live one day at a time.

୫୦ ୫୦ ୫୦

149

NAME: Stan

DATE: 9-16-00

THREE WAYS I'D LIKE GOD TO USE ME IN MY LIFETIME

DAD	LIZ	BON
1. Continue to lead a godly family	Raise godly children	Use abilities to impact people + glorify God.
2. Leave a vibrant, healthy church	Use my talents to impact people for God.	Good role model for young people
3. To Encourage others to follow Jesus.	To show God's love to others.	Work with others to accomplish something worthwhile for God.

GOOD ADVICE

1/24/01

Hi Liz,

The article clipped here has some great advice from a great man to his daughters. Wish I'd thought of it first, but I didn't, so here it is! (Charley Reese, "The Remarkable Robert E. Lee", Dallas Morning News, Jan 15, 2001).

Love,
Dad

The remarkable Robert E. Lee

JANUARY 15 — Robert E. Lee, whose birthday (Jan. 19) is celebrated this month, is one of the most remarkable men America has ever produced.

While Lee waited in Richmond, Va., after the war to learn if he would be arrested, two Confederates in tattered uniforms appeared at his door. Their 60 comrades had chosen them because their clothes were the least tattered. They had found a farm in the mountains, reachable only through a narrow pass, and if Lee and his family would come there, the Confederates would defend them with their lives.

LEE WAS MOVED to tears by their offer but declined it. A day or two later, there was another pounding on the door, and when Lee's sons opened it, there stood a grizzled Union sergeant with a boy holding a big basket of food. This man had served with Lee on the Western frontier before the war, had heard that Lee was hungry and wouldn't stand for that.

Lee, who heard the commotion, assured the man that they had plenty of food but finally said he would accept the gift if the sergeant would agree that it be sent to the hospital for use by the wounded. Before Lee's sons could stop him, the sergeant grabbed Lee in a bearhug and planted a kiss on his cheek. "Goodbye, Colonel! God bless ye. If I could have got over in time I would have been with ye."

What was it about Lee that provoked such loyalty and affection

CHARLEY REESE

among common soldiers? Lee was always reserved and dignified, was tightly disciplined and almost never showed his emotions. But one of Lee's subordinates said of the Confederate soldiers, "As a military leader, they respected Lee, but as a man, they loved him."

THE ANSWER IS Lee's character. He was indeed a hero, an outstanding soldier, but first and foremost, he was a Christian. He never took credit for victory and never blamed anyone else for defeat. In fact, he never publicly criticized anyone or answered any of his critics. He wore a plain uniform, rarely carried a weapon and invariably passed gifts of food or clothing directly on to his men.

Alexander Stephens, the Confederate vice president, said of Gen. Lee, "What I had seen General Lee to be at first — child-like in simplicity and unselfish in his character — he remained, unspoiled by praise and by success."

At the end of the war, Lee was world-famous. Lucrative offers poured in. One English lord offered him an estate. But unlike modern generals of far fewer accomplishments, the thought of profiting from the death and misery of war was unthinkable to Lee. He wanted to be useful and finally accepted the presidency of Washington College, which was on the verge of bankruptcy.

His character is revealed in his letters. In writing to one of his sons, he said: "You and Custis (the oldest son) must take great care of your kind mother and dear sisters when your father is dead. To do that you must learn to be good. Be true, kind and generous, and pray earnestly to God to enable you to keep his commandments."

In a letter to a daughter visiting friends, he reminded her that it would not be becoming of a Virginia girl to be fine or fashionable. "While her people are suffering," she should practice self-denial and show her sympathy in their affliction."

TO ANOTHER DAUGHTER he wrote, "I hope you will also find time to read and improve your mind. Read history, works of truth, not novels and romances. Get correct views of life, and learn to see the world in its true light. It will enable you to live pleasantly, to do good, and, when summoned away, to leave without regret."

CHARLEY REESE
Copyright 2001 by King Features Syndicate

P.S. (2021): Recognizing good advice is a prerequisite to giving it.

∞   ∞   ∞

SPIRITUAL NUTRITION

12-12-01

Dear Elizabeth,

I don't quite know how to explain my long absence from this journal. I could offer all the usual excuses—busy, preoccupied, yada, yada, yada. The truth is I've just been on a spiritual side-track of listlessness. Combine that with laziness (I hate this old flesh!) and you've got the recipe for a guy who not only has little to offer his daughter, but little also to offer his own soul.

It's an irony that Pastors often commit spiritual bulimia while preparing messages to feed and encourage others! Anyway. I'm making a concerted effort at least to put myself back in the way of God's blessing. I surely can't force it. But that's unnecessary when God's grace is always flowing. You don't have to "try" to get wet in a summer rainstorm. Just go outside! That's my plan in these days. Go outside my own little interior world of thought and opinion and pride and fear and let God's thoughts rain down on me.

I'm learning that God's Word is powerful even when I'm bored with it. The worst thing I can do when spiritually dry is what my flesh wants me to do—isolate myself from the Word and prayer. We go to God every day of our lives not from a sense of duty or obligation but of love and life. We eat because we're hungry, sleep because we're tired, and drink because we're thirsty. Our souls get hungry, tired, and thirsty, too. We go to God because we need Him, and wise are those who do not deny their desperation.

I've been so proud of you in these days. A wonderful leader in the Fellowship of Christian Athletes, you played guitar and sang for Jesus with your friends at the Turner H.S. Talent show. As a senior, you are taking Emergency Medical Technician training and bravely riding the ambulance on regular shifts. It gives me joy to see your strength, independence, and leadership.

Always remember that the source of all true strength is the Holy Spirit, and that God gave you great gifts for serving Him. Use them for that purpose, and you'll never be disappointed.

(PS: This is a prayer-guide we used in a special IBC Staff retreat. Thought it might help you at some point...SEE SCRIPTURE READING AND PRAYER SHEET ATTACHED).

All My Love,
Dad

P.S. (2021): When you least desire spiritual food is when you most need to eat.

ℨ ℨ ℨ

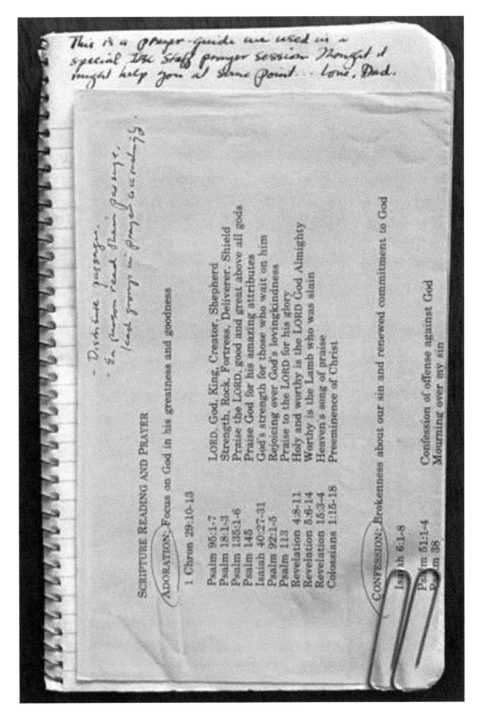

This is a prayer-guide we used in a special TDF staff prayer session. Thought it might help you at some point... Love, Dad.

- Distribute passages
- so everyone reads their passage
- close group in prayer accordingly

SCRIPTURE READING AND PRAYER

ADORATION: Focus on God in his greatness and goodness

1 Chron 29:10-13

Psalm 95:1-7	LORD, God, King, Creator, Shepherd
Psalm 18:1-3	Strength, Rock, Fortress, Deliverer, Shield
Psalm 135:1-6	Praise the LORD, good and great above all gods
Psalm 145	Praise God for his amazing attributes
Isaiah 40:27-31	God's strength for those who wait on him
Psalm 92:1-5	Rejoicing over God's lovingkindness
Psalm 113	Praise to the LORD for his glory
Revelation 4:8-11	Holy and worthy is the LORD God Almighty
Revelation 5:6-14	Worthy is the Lamb who was slain
Revelation 15:3-4	Heaven's song of praise
Colossians 1:15-18	Preeminence of Christ

CONFESSION: Brokenness about our sin and renewed commitment to God

Isaiah 6:1-8	Confession of offense against God
Psalm 51:1-4	Mourning over my sin
Psalm 38	

DEATH MOTIVATES

12-13-01

Hi Liz,

Among other things, what made Jesus' life so compelling was His sense of destiny. Every moment on earth, He was aware of why He had come, what He would accomplish, and the difference it would make. How would it impact the way we lived our lives if only we had the same awareness?

I was reading John 2 today. After turning water to wine at the wedding in Cana, Jesus cleanses the temple (celebration-consecration). Challenged by His enemies to give a sign validating the authority to do such a thing, Jesus replies: "Destroy this temple, and in three days I will raise it up." (Jn. 2:19)

What amazes me about this clear prediction of His own death and resurrection is when it came—at the very beginning of his ministry! 3 years from this point Jesus would preach and teach and heal, all in the shadow of constant awareness that death waited at the end of the road.

Barring Jesus' return, Liz, death waits at the end of our road, too. What urgency, what focus, what seriousness that fact should inspire as we spend our days, not to make us morbid, but determined. Jesus began His ministry by predicting His own death, then led the most powerful life ever lived! Liz, we won't be here long, either. Let's make it count!

Carpe Diem,
Dad

P.S. (2021): For the spiritually skeptical, death terrifies; for the believing faithful, death motivates.

ဆ   ဆ   ဆ

THE LONG VIEW

12/14/01

Dear Elizabeth Grace,

It's wise to take the long view. Patience is not exactly a McQuitty trait. We generally like to go for something and get it quickly, or study something and understand it easily or stand for something and be vindicated swiftly. But most of the really important things in our lives play out over decades and I don't have to remind you that eternity lasts a long time!

So then, it's just wise to take the long view. If you don't, you'll get depressed, discouraged, and cynical. When injustice prevails, you'll be disillusioned. When your own flesh is weak and fails, you'll be ashamed. When what you believe in seems to let you down, you'll be disappointed. The enemy, Satan, wants you to take the short view. "Turn these stones to bread; leap from the temple; accept these riches" (Luke 4). Jesus rebuffed him, and so must we. Satan is threatened by those who take the long view, who commit for the long haul, who stay the course persistently and relentlessly.

We always overestimate what can be accomplished in a year, and underestimate what we can accomplish in ten years. So, take the long view. Today's failures and setbacks can be overcome in time. No failure is final, but neither is any success.

"The Lord is king forever and ever..." (Psalm 10:16). Forever and ever is a long time, so Liz, take the long view!

Love You,
Dad

156

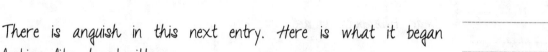

P.S. (2021): Impatience short-circuits the deep and powerful
work God wants to do over time.

∞   ∞   ∞

There is anguish in this next entry. Here is what it began
looking like, handwritten:

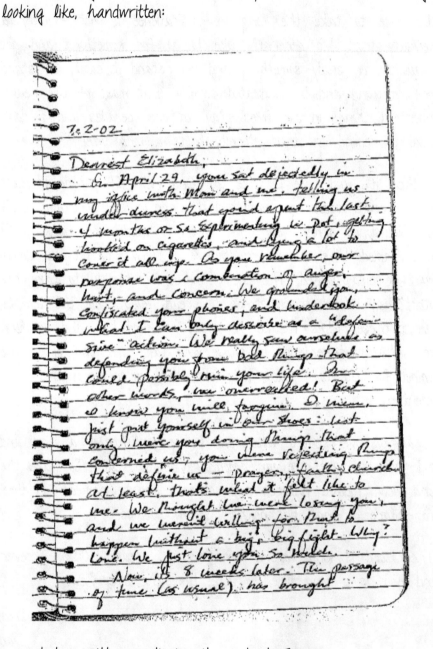

… and typewritten, continuing it as best I can:

LEAVING THE NEST

2-2-02

Dearest Elizabeth,

On April 29, you sat dejectedly in my office with Mom and me, telling us under duress that you'd spent the last 4 months experimenting with pot, getting hooked on cigarettes, and lying a lot to cover it all up. As you remember, our response was a combination of anger, hurt, and concern. We grounded you, confiscated your phones, and undertook what I can only describe as a "defensive" action. We really saw ourselves as defending you from bad things that could possibly ruin your life. In other words, we overreacted! But I know you will forgive. I mean, just put yourself in our shoes: not only were you doing things that concerned us, you were rejecting things that define us—prayer, faith, church. At least, that's what it felt like to me. We thought we were losing you, and we weren't willing for that to happen without a big, big fight. Why? Love. We just love you so much.

Now, it's 8 weeks later. The passage of time (as usual) has brought perspective and (hopefully) deeper wisdom. In that time, I've thought about you and prayed for you more than any time in your life—except maybe when you were a baby! I want to tell you where I've come both to encourage you in your own parenting someday and to sort out my own thoughts:

1. This isn't about me, it's about you babe. Take it on faith, parents have a hard time separating themselves from their kids! I had to realize that if you choose a different path or conviction than me, it doesn't necessarily mean that I've failed or that I'm a bad father. It could mean that, but it doesn't have to. I just had to stop thinking in terms of

158

what your choices say about me and just let them be your choices!

2. We can disagree and still love. Liz, my biggest fear was that the precious relationship we've always had would be lost. It has not been and knowing that loving each other as a value transcends any other value has given me the ability to relax. If I know I'm not going to lose you, I don't have to pick a fight with issues that set us at odds.

3. You are moving, not defecting. In everyone's life come "moments of truth" when we've got to forge our own convictions. You can't live on your parent's faith or weather life's storms with your friend's values. Your faith needs to be yours. You need to own your own values. But how do we build faith and own values? By living, observing, searching, and experimenting for ourselves. You're on the grand quest, Liz, of calibrating your own internal spiritual compass. That's a good thing! I deeply believe that truth is consistent and undeniable and pervasive and that those who objectively and honestly seek it, find it. I'd rather have you moving than stand still—and you are. Only good things can come of your search, and they will.

4. My role now is no longer to tell, but to advise. It's a funny thing to be a dad. You want your kids to grow into strong, independent adulthood while still remaining your kids! I love the adult person you've become, Liz. Confident, personable, winsome, beautiful! But there's a sadness in realizing my little girl with the cow lick is no longer little and, in the sense of authority, no longer mine. You will, I hope, forgive me in those weak moments when I just don't want to let go. I'll get over it eventually! I'll understand that I can no longer tell you what to do or believe. You're grown, and you will do what you choose. Hopefully, you will yet want my advice or counsel from time to time. I promise I will endeavor only to offer it when asked!

To sum up, I love you. I'm here for you. In just a few weeks, you'll be off to A&M as a freshmen bio-med major. As you go, I'm entrusting you to the Great One pictured on the opposite page. This portrait of Aslan hangs in the Wade Collection at Wheaton College. The

Lion of the Tribe of Judah is not visible, but He is always present. He is not safe, but He is good. Beyond our understanding, He comprehends us intimately.

I Love Him, and You,
Dad

P.S. (2021): A parent's greatest fears and greatest joys are all wrapped up in the independence of their newly adult children.

                                     ଔ   ଔ   ଔ

CHARACTER

July 3, 2002

Hi Sweetheart,

I've been reading some great stuff lately and wanted to share a few highlights with you. Indulge me? Thanks!

From David McCullough's John Adams:

Adam's wrote affectionately to his second son, "you have in your nature a sociability, Charles, which is amicable, but may mislead you. A scholar is always made alone. Studies can only be pursued to good purpose by yourself. Don't let your companions then, nor your amusements, take up too much of your time."

–p. 365

Liz, you also have an "amiable sociability" in your nature! That's wonderful, but heed Adam's last line!

To his grandson, Adams wrote:

Have you considered the meaning of that word 'worthy?' Weigh it well ... I had rather you should be worthy possessors of one-thousand pounds honestly acquired by your own labor and industry, than of ten million by banks and tricks. I should rather you be worthy shoemakers than secretaries of states or treasury acquired by libels in newspapers. I should rather you be worthy makers of brooms and baskets than unworthy presidents of the United States procured by intrigue, factions, slander, and corruption.

–p. 609

I love that. No amount of success or notoriety is worth sacrificing your integrity or good name. Peace of mind and a clear conscience are life's great treasures. Never exchange them for cheap imitations!

All My Love,
Dad

P.S. (2021): Never Exchange a Clear Conscience for anything at any price

Better is little with the fear of the Lord than great treasure and trouble therewith.

–Proverbs 15:16 (KJV)

જી જી જી

Peace I leave with you; my peace I give you.
I do not give to you as the world gives.
Do not let your hearts be troubled and do not be afraid.
—John 14:27

DRY SPELLS

7-10-02

Dearest Liz,

Faith is the substance of things not seen. And since things not seen are quite insubstantial, faith is elusive. That's why ...

> Sometimes we experience a terrible dryness in our spiritual lives. We feel no desire to pray, don't experience God's presence, get bored with worship services, and even think that everything we ever believed about God, Jesus, and the Holy Spirit is little more than a childhood fairy tale.
>
> That's when it is important to realize that most of these feelings and thoughts are just feelings and thoughts, and that the <u>Spirit of God dwells beyond our feelings and thoughts.</u> It's a great grace to be able to experience God's presence in our feelings and thoughts, but when we don't, it does not mean that God is absent. It often means that God is just calling us to a greater faithfulness. It is <u>precisely in times of spiritual dryness</u> that <u>we must hold on to our spiritual discipline so that we can grow into new intimacy with God"</u>
>
> —Henry Nouwen, Bread for the Journey, 7/02
> (underlining added by me, EAM).

Over the years, I've been through many seasons of dryness spiritually. My reaction sometimes has been petulant anger toward God. "If you won't be more real to me, then I won't believe in you!" Big whup. It has dawned on me that God isn't at all threatened by the possibility of my unbelief. He will go on being real and powerful in the universe whatever I do. The loser in that scenario isn't God. He's totally unaffected by my defection.

No, the loser of the petulant anger game is always me. Living like God is irrelevant merely deprives me of the benefit of His leading and protection and the joy of His presence.

It's much better then in times of dryness to follow Henri's advice. It prevents us from cutting off our nose to spite our face. And it deepens us to a new level of faith. I think sometimes God sends us into a dry spell to move us past the shallow end of the pool into the cooler depths of the deep end where we find time to grow past the wrong expectations and selfish wants of the early stages of our relationship with God.

That may feel like God is rejecting us. He's not, He's just pushing us out of the nest so we can fly higher and farther. Do you feel dry? God still loves you, still exists, still is close. Keep reaching out to Him, and you'll find Him. And when you do, He will be a grander and more wonderful Father than the One you wrongly thought you'd lost.

Love Always,
Dad

P.S. (2021): Greater faithfulness grows through seasons of honest doubtfulness.

ജ   ജ   ജ

DON'T TRY, TRAIN

7-18-02

Hi Sweetheart,

How to be transformed as a person to be more like the Lord Jesus—that's the question. Some believers never grow deep. Others try to change, fail, and quit in discouragement. These people substitute conformity with true inner change. The problem with both of the above approaches is that they're based on unrealistic expectations. It's unrealistic to think God could ever bless someone who just wants "fire insurance" and not a life of devotion. But it's also unrealistic to believe we can will ourselves into a transformed life.

As John Ortberg and Dallas Willard have pointed out in their writings, the key to transformation is not in trying, but training. Put me in a marathon tomorrow and try as I might, I couldn't finish. But let my train for 6 months, and I could. Put me in Moscow tomorrow, and try as I might, I couldn't speak Russian. But let me train for a year, and I could. The thing that discourages us spiritually is attempting things by trying that can only be accomplished by training.

Patience, love, discipline, faith, etc., come from training. We train by addressing our weaknesses. If I'm weak, I hit the weight room. If short-winded, I run laps. In the spiritual life weakness has been categorized into two basic divisions: sins of commission, and sins of omission. The classic spiritual disciplines (silence, solitude, meditation, service, etc.) address both types of sin with corresponding initiatives of engagement and abstinence. Hence we battle Sins with Disciplines. We battle stinginess (omission) with generosity and gossip (commission) with silence.

I believe that to be transformed, we must diagnose our own issues and design a training regimen that is personal and purposeful. That's how we stop rowing ("try") and stop drifting ("quit") and start sailing (transformation!) (Rom. 12:1-2)

Love You, Babe.
Dad

P.S. (2021): Trying harder is no substitute for training longer.

                                               ജ   ജ   ജ

SELF-REJECTION

7-19-02

Hi Liz,

It was fun yesterday going with you on the motorcycle to the mall, eating BBQ for lunch, and talking about home mortgages. I predict that someday you'll be a real estate mogul if you can find time in your medical practice!

In my reading this morning, I came across 1 John 3:19-20:

> This then is how we know we belong to the truth, and how we set our hearts at rest in His presence whenever our hearts condemn us. For God is greater than our heart, and He knows everything.

Guilt is the great "distancer" from God. We avoid His presence because we fail and then we fear. We assume that, since we can't feel good about ourselves, surely God can't either. We project our own self-rejection and disgust on God and allow shame to sever fellowship with God. In other words, our "hearts condemn us."

But God is greater than our projection, prejudices, assumptions, and pettiness. He knows everything, and marvel of marvels, loves us still. Our hearts are powerful in condemnation. But God is even more powerful than our hearts in His redemption. Here is how we can set our hearts at rest in His presence-realize we can always come home because His love is greater than our sin.

We put Rembrandt's Return of the Prodigal on our IBC art wall as a constant reminder that no one need ever stay in the "far" country.

P.S. (2021): Never allow your heart to condemn you when God, who is greater than your heart, doesn't.

‰   ‰   ‰

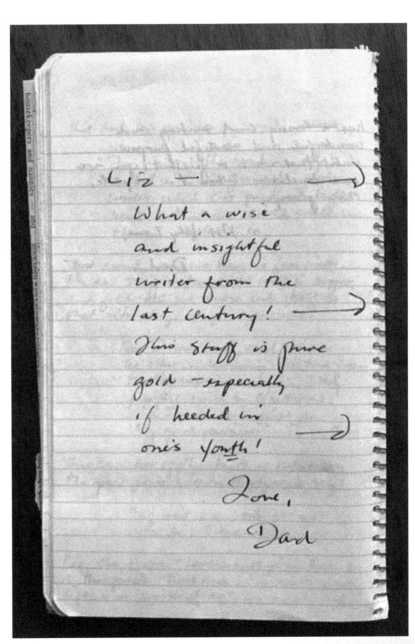

Liz —

What a wise and insightful writer from the last century! This stuff is pure gold — especially if heeded in one's youth!

Love,

Dad

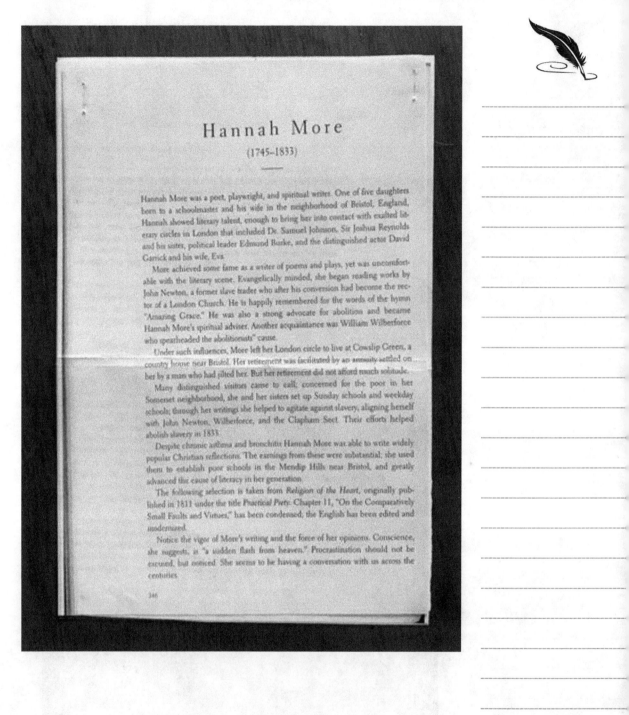

Hannah More

(1745–1833)

Hannah More was a poet, playwright, and spiritual writer. One of five daughters born to a schoolmaster and his wife in the neighborhood of Bristol, England, Hannah showed literary talent, enough to bring her into contact with exalted literary circles in London that included Dr. Samuel Johnson, Sir Joshua Reynolds and his sister, political leader Edmund Burke, and the distinguished actor David Garrick and his wife, Eva.

More achieved some fame as a writer of poems and plays, yet was uncomfortable with the literary scene. Evangelically minded, she began reading works by John Newton, a former slave trader who after his conversion had become the rector of a London Church. He is happily remembered for the words of the hymn "Amazing Grace." He was also a strong advocate for abolition and became Hannah More's spiritual adviser. Another acquaintance was William Wilberforce who spearheaded the abolitionists' cause.

Under such influences, More left her London circle to live at Cowslip Green, a country house near Bristol. Her retirement was facilitated by an annuity settled on her by a man who had jilted her. But her retirement did not afford much solitude.

Many distinguished visitors came to call; concerned for the poor in her Somerset neighborhood, she and her sisters set up Sunday schools and weekday schools; through her writings she helped to agitate against slavery, aligning herself with John Newton, Wilberforce, and the Clapham Sect. Their efforts helped abolish slavery in 1833.

Despite chronic asthma and bronchitis Hannah More was able to write widely popular Christian reflections. The earnings from these were substantial; she used them to establish poor schools in the Mendip Hills near Bristol, and greatly advanced the cause of literacy in her generation.

The following selection is taken from *Religion of the Heart*, originally published in 1811 under the title *Practical Piety*. Chapter 11, "On the Comparatively Small Faults and Virtues," has been condensed; the English has been edited and modernized.

Notice the vigor of More's writing and the force of her opinions. Conscience, she suggests, is "a sudden flash from heaven." Procrastination should not be excused, but noticed. She seems to be having a conversation with us across the centuries.

146

DECISION-MAKING

7-25-02

Hi Liz,

Wise are those in life who seek to act, not react, to choose, not be forced; to take initiative, not be manipulated. Most people are driven to attitudes and choices by forces they can't see and don't understand. But believing themselves autonomous, they flaunt "freedom" while remaining slaves.

For example. A girl raised in a dysfunctional home with an abusive father moves out as soon as possible. She throws off Christ and scripture and shacks up with serial lovers. She is "free." No longer bound by stupid rules, she's the master of her own fate. Or maybe not! Maybe her sexual aggressiveness springs from the well of a wounded heart. Maybe she's not driven into the arms of men who will love her and leave her by choice, but by need. She thinks she's choosing, but really, she's just losing. She's not acting, but reacting, and on the road to disintegrating. This is why I've found it instructive to answer a few questions to myself before making important decisions:

1) Why am I doing this? Lonely, want to fit in? Insecure, want to impress? Lazy, don't want to try? Hurt, trying to forget? Bitter, want to get even?
2) What are the long-term effects of my doing this? On me? On my friends/family? On people who observe me?
3) Where is God in all of this? Is He leading me, or am I trying to lead Him? Is He part of this, or like Jonah am I fleeing Him? Can He bless this?

Liz—don't be driven. Don't serve forces you're not even aware of! Instead, sit before the

Lord and listen to His Word. Then joyfully do what He says. Choose. Decide. Live!

Love,
Dad

P.S. (2021): The wise admit they have no control and joyfully submit to the Only One Who does.

❧ ❧ ❧

I'M SORRY

7-26-02

Hi Elizabeth,

This has been one of those days I wish I could do over. I got out of bed and into trouble immediately. Flew off the handle at the boys for losing some parts to a saw while cleaning up—something I had asked them to do! Then got in a big debate at lunch w/ some staff overpay issues. Came away from that feeling like an ogre. Now it's occurring to me, maybe I am an ogre! This I know—I am a sinful man constantly in need of the forgiveness of God, others, and myself (That last can be the toughest!).

Based on my being reminded today of that unpleasant fact, I want to apologize to you for all the times I was a selfish, impatient, demanding ogre with you. It is my earnest desire to have you know I deeply love you, and that I hope that truth will balance out somewhat those many lapses when you wouldn't have known it from my words and/or actions.

This parenting gig is a slippery, sobering thing. I hope that by the time I really get the hang of it, it won't be too late.

Affectionately,
Dad

P.S. (2021): No one can move past unacknowledged failures.

₮ ₮ ₮

A DISCIPLINED PERSON

8-6-02

Dearest Elizabeth,

Why do we make walking with God seem like such a pain, when its meant to be a joy? Somehow, the message comes through that a "spiritual" person is one who rigidly follows rules to earn brownie points with God. We have to do a bunch of things we don't want to do so God won't do a bunch of things we don't want Him to do. Capisce?

Here's a great definition: "A disciplined person is one who can do the right thing at the right time in the right way with the right spirit." In other words, a spiritual discipline is any activity that helps us live like Jesus. And the ultimate measure of spirituality is our capacity to fully love God and people. Let's lighten up, love, and LIVE!

Affectionately,
Dad

P.S. (2021): Self-discipline is not a possession, it's a pursuit.

෨   ෨   ෨

FINISHING WELL

8-13-02

Sweetheart Elizabeth,

Opal Core died at 12:30 PM last Friday, completing 90 years of living to the hilt. She was faithful to the end. My last conversation with her was all about seeing the Lord Jesus and finally getting to go to Heaven. She wasn't just resigned to crossing over from this life. She wanted to. She was excited to!

Opal meant a lot to me because she accomplished a rare feat in this world. She finished well. Many years ago, she started out her life of faith determined to live a life of goodness and service to God. I only got to see the last 15 years of that journey, but it was impressive. Opal prayed for hours every day. She prayed for you, Elizabeth, by name, everyday (she loved and prayed for our whole family).

At IBC, she set aside her personal preferences regarding music/ministry style and encouraged us to do whatever it took to reach young people. So unselfish! She always remembered people who were sick or hurting with cards and cakes. And she did all of this alone (her husband died 41 years ago) and often in pain (she had lupus). We released balloons at Opal's funeral to signify the celebration the angels were undoubtedly throwing for her in Heaven.

Liz, it's easy to start well. But good intentions alone do not constitute success. A good life is one that ends as well as it started. It's not how we begin the race that's ultimately the measure, but how we finish. Someday soon, Liz, you will perhaps look back over 90 years of your life and pause to reflect. I pray that the choices and commitments and disciplines and values you embrace now will enable you to say then, "I am finishing well too!"

Love,
Dad

P.S. (2021): It's highly unlikely that a poorly run race will finish well even if the start was great.

୫   ୫   ୫

REAL BODIES IN A SPIRITUAL WORLD

8-19-02

Hi Sweetheart,

Today your mom and I celebrated 24 years as husband and wife. Apart from my redemption, no gift from God has been more precious or wonderful to me than Alice. I pray that someday the Lord will similarly bless you, Liz. In her poem A Christmas Carol, Christina Rossetti offers this stanza:

> Angels and archangels may have gathered there,
> Cherubim and seraphim thronged the air.
> But only his mother in her maiden bliss
> Worshipped the beloved with a kiss.

Herein, Liz, lies the glory of being human. This tactile world of touch and emotion and action was made for our habitation. While we are alive in it, we have the freedom and power to respond and touch and act and express. Unlike spirits and angels whose home is not this world, we are not restricted or bound. The archangels were present at Jesus birth. But only Mary kissed Him.

What a powerful privilege we're afforded by God's gift to us of bodies through which we can act in this world and make a difference! What a lamentable waste if we squander this power. As another poet has said:

> Only one life, 'twill soon be past.
> Only what's done for Christ will last!

Again, Rossetti captures the key to our making the most of the time God grants to us on this earth. In her last stanza of *A Christmas Carol*, she wonders:

What can I give Him, poor as I am?
If I were a shepherd, I would bring a lamb,
If I were a wise man, I would do my part
Yet what can I give him?
Give my heart.

Love you, Liz. A whole lot!
Dad

P.S. (2021): Give God your heart while you still can.

       🙿   🙿   🙿

POIEMA

8.20.02

Hey Liz,

One of the greatest sources of assurance we have as Christians is the biblical doctrine of the sovereignty of God. It simply says that God is King. He rules over all things. Job says: "I know that you can do all things and that no purpose of yours can be thwarted." (Job 42:2) If that's true, and it is, then our lives are part of His purpose. We're not just thrown into this world to make the best of things as best we might. Rather, we are sent into this world to accomplish a specific purpose that God has for us. "For we are His workmanship, created in Christ Jesus for good works, which God prepared beforehand so that we should walk in them." (Ephesians 2:10)

That doesn't mean we have no free will. We do. It's just that God's will is bigger and folds all we choose into itself so that ultimately, His plan prevails. "For I am God and there is no other ... declaring the end from the beginning ... saying, 'My purpose will be established, and I will accomplish all my good pleasure.'" (Isaiah. 46:9–10)

The conviction of this truth is what led the great pastor Henry Martyn to say: "If God has work for me to do, I cannot die." Liz, the word "workmanship" in Ephesians 2 is "poiema," poem. Your life is a work of art for which God has a loving and exciting and wonderful and beautiful purpose. Until that work is finished, you are indestructible. When it is complete, then glory.

All My Love,
Dad

P.S. (2021): Beautiful lives are God's poems.

ဆ   ဆ   ဆ

GOODBYE FOR NOW

8-27-02

Dear Elizabeth,

Tomorrow I will help you move into your dorm room in Mosure Hall at Texas A&M. My little girl is all grown up and stepping out from home. As I finish this little journal on the occasion of your leaving home, I want to write you again the words I first wrote on these pages 16 years ago. "I just want you to know that your daddy cares for you... and wants the very best for you."

If anything, that is even more true today than when I first wrote it! You are an exceptionally talented, beautiful, intelligent young woman. More than that, Liz, you are a leader. People pay attention to you; they listen to what you say. So, my encouragement to you is to maximize your gifts and opportunities.

If you discipline yourself and work hard, there is no limit to how far and high you can go. God will honor and bless you as you seek His face and walk faithfully before Him. "Let not mercy and truth forsake you; bind them around your neck, write them on the tablet of your heart, and so find favor and high esteem in the sight of God and man." (Proverbs 3:3-4) That's the key to building respect and a good name. But that's not all! "Trust in the Lord with all your heart and lean not unto your own understanding; in all your ways acknowledge Him, and He shall direct your paths." (Proverbs 3:5-6) That's the key to divine help and guidance.

Liz, as your earthly father, I will do all I can to help you. But your Heavenly Father can do infinitely more than I ever could, and He wants to do so! As you leave home, I'm transferring immediate care, protection, and oversight now of my Elizabeth to the Heavenly Father. The Lord Jesus is closer than your very breath, Liz. Talk to Him every day! He loves you always, as I do,

With All My Heart,
Dad

P.S. You don't need to talk to me every day, but please do talk to me a lot!

P.S. (2021): We can trust the Great Shepherd with those we love the most.

෩   ෩   ෩

Part 3

A Journal For Bonnie Caroleen

48 entries from Nov 3, 1986, to Aug 18, 2005

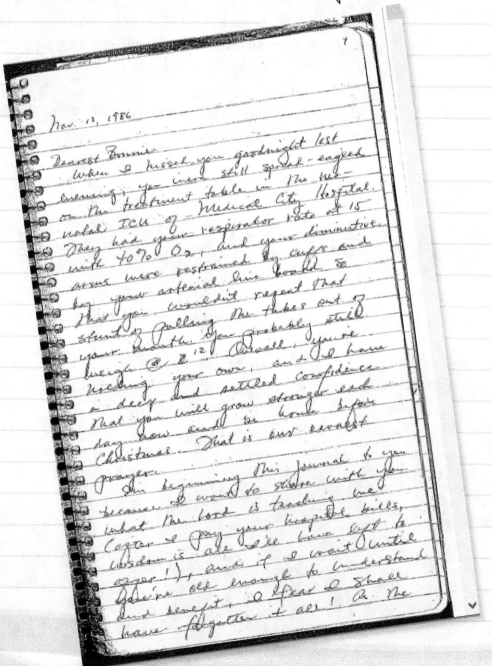

IN GOD ALONE

Nov 13, 1986

Dearest Bonnie,

When I kissed you goodnight last evening, you were still spread-eagled on the treatment table in the neonatal ICU of Dallas' Medical City Hospital. They had your respiratory rate at 15 with 40 O2, and your diminutive arms were restrained by cuffs and your arterial line board so that you wouldn't repeat that stunt of pulling the tubes out of your mouth. You probably still weigh @ 2 pounds, 12 ounces. Overall, you're holding your own (what a fighter!), and I have a deep and settled confidence that you will grow stronger each day now and be home before Christmas. That is our earnest prayer.

I'm beginning this journal to you because I want to share with you what the Lord is teaching me (after I pay your hospital bills, wisdom is all I'll have left to offer!), and if I wait until you're old enough to understand and benefit, I fear I shall have forgotten it all! As the years pass, I know that I will have much to say to you—many thoughts for and about you that could be appropriately recorded only on these pages. So please be patient and indulge your doting dad some time to read what he has lovingly recorded for you here.

I want to tell you one of the primary lessons that God has taught me through your rather dramatic arrival (will you always have a penchant for the sensational?!). God wants us to trust Him alone—not our abilities and talents, not our friends and family, not our money or investments—just Him alone. As we have seen you through the first 5 arduous weeks of your life, we have experienced 5 arduous weeks ourselves. We've realized our weakness and ability to do anything on a physical level to help you. We've experienced fears and anxieties and difficulties that cannot be assuaged by even the most well-meaning people. We've seen our financial resources gobbled up and digested before our very eyes.

In short, the Lord has caused us to realize that He alone can meet our needs. He alone can give purpose to our troubles. He alone is to be trusted.

I hope to provide well for you, Bonnie. But if you ever find yourself in difficult straights and especially if you find yourself in a comfortable situation—please allow yourself to place your trust and security in nothing or no one but the Lord alone. He will be there when all else is gone. Thus, we must sometimes lose all things to gain the one thing worth having--a fulfilling and intimate spiritual walk with the God who made us.

Don't ever forget this wonderful truth which you have yourself taught me!

Love,
Dad

P.S. (2021): Gratefully receive help from friends and family, but ultimately put your trust in God alone.

         ଛ ଛ ଛ

STRESS

12-17-86

Dear Bonnie Caroleen,

You're really amazing to an awful lot of people! In the last couple of weeks, you've decided to get on with it and grow! You now weigh in at a hefty 4lb. 3oz., and you breast-feed like a champ. Will you always be so precious, Bonnie?

In your dramatic debut, you have inspired much joy. You've also precipitated a lot of stress (quite unpremeditated, I know!). Alice has been especially hard hit, and it's building on her as she anticipates getting you home right in time for Christmas and all the family who is coming.

Stress is an intriguing force. Completely unseen and intangible, it is yet so powerful and real that it is credited for causing a high percentage of heart attacks. It's not something that hits you from outside in. Rather, stress is a corrosive force that stirs and seethes and inflicts its damage from within. But we don't have to allow it! The stress a person feels is actually controllable by that person. It's said of Hudson Taylor that he could sit still and listen to alarming reports from his 1800 missionaries on the Chinese field (late 19th century) without batting an eye or losing his peace. He had learned how to handle stress. Bonnie, you're going to deal with stress as well. May I give some suggestions on how to do so?

1. Examine your heart and soul: was I wrong? Have I done my best?
2. Confess any sins and ask forgiveness as needed.

3. Having cleansed your heart, place yourself in God's hands by consciously committing yourself & your problems to the Lord.
4. Pray specifically and often.
5. Having prayed, purpose to live one day, one hour, one minute at a time with your thoughts fixed on the Lord.
6. Be grateful. A thankful spirit guarantees that your burdens will bear fruit.

Much Love,
Dad

P.S. (2021): Stress plus grateful prayer equals peace.

Don't worry over anything whatever; tell God every detail of your needs in earnest and thankful prayer, and the peace of God which transcends human understanding, will keep constant guard over your hearts and minds as they rest in Christ Jesus.

–Philippians 4.6-7 (JB Phillips)

ৰ৹   ৰ৹   ৰ৹

AMBITION

1/28/87

Dearest Bonnie,

Your mother and I (but especially your mother) are bleary-eyed from going about 3 weeks without a solid night's sleep. We have this little "noisemaker" in our room now that produces a loud racket about every 3-4 hours. I won't mention any names (we do love you so...!).

I want to warn you about a pitfall that will tempt you greatly, a subtle assumption natural to most people which insidiously robs them of God's best:

"My true happiness lies in the pursuit of personal prosperity and life fulfilment."

Most people, even Christians, operate subconsciously on this premise. The problem with the premise is that it denies what Jesus teaches. "What good is it for someone to gain the whole world, and yet lose or forfeit their very self?" (Luke 9:24, NIV)

I believe Jesus is referring to His vision of personal prosperity and fulfilment by the words "very self." In essence, He's saying that genuine fulfilment and lasting joy emanate from relinquishing my personal agenda and embracing God's. To the extent I let go my personal concerns in lieu of God's priorities, I will find ultimate joy.

I'm wrestling with this issue as I consider various opportunities for ministry in my first pastorate. I find myself limiting what I am willing to do by such factors as the size of the community (I've grown accustomed to the city with its amenities and don't want the limitations of a small town), the size/success of the church, the future potential of the church (cast in terms of my personal ambition, not God's glory).

In short, I'm seeking personal peace and prosperity and not remaining open to the possibility that God may want me to "lay my life down". I'm not "seeking first His Kingdom and His righteousness. (Matthew 6.33) In so doing, I fear I'm sabotaging the potential for genuine fulfilment in my life.

I believe that God will give me the grace to do right, but oh, what a battle it is! I'm sure you will face this battle in your life as well, Bon. Just wanted you to be,

Forewarned & therefore Forearmed,
Dad

P.S. (2021): Prioritizing God's will ultimately produces the greatest fulfilment in our lives.

છ   છ   છ

NEVER QUIT

3-5-87

Hi Bonnie Sweetheart!

You now weigh in at 8'8" and are a whopping 22" long! You've become more aware of your surroundings and have begun to smile delightfully. We still think you're mighty special—and always will!

Just wanted to urge you—never be a quitter. Life will throw you some curve balls for sure, but never quit! When pressures and setbacks and disappointments and heartaches come, never quit!

I was playing a racketball match the other day against a fellow who'd lost to me 1 out of 1 match. He's quite proud and evidently wanted revenge. As we played, he realized he was not doing too well and was headed for another defeat. Result? He quit. Walked off the court and took his ball with him like a 3-year-old might do (no offense, Bon!).

That made quite an impression on me and I've thought about it a lot since. Here's what quitting really says:

1. I wasn't really committed in the first place.
2. Doing the cowardly thing and taking the easy way out is more honorable than losing honestly!
3. Winning is more important than my personal integrity.
4. Losing reflects, not on my athletic skill, but on my character.

When we quit in this way, we reveal our true character. Losing after giving a sincere effort bears no shame; it's quitting rather than lose that heaps dishonor on a person. I can respect someone who fights and loses infinitely more than someone who quits to avoid losing. The truth is that such a one ultimately loses far more than a game.

Much Love,
Dad

P.S. (2021): Play to win but never run from a loss because you never need be ashamed or afraid to lose.

ʊ ʊ ʊ

OUR LAST DAYS

3-25-87

Dear Bonnie,

Heard Dr. Ralph Winter, a well-known missiologist, say a provocative thing. "Whether the world is in the last days is a moot point, since we know that each of us as individuals is in his or her last days." The world may continue for another millennium, but what concerns me is what happens in the relatively few years I have left in that world.

This morning I was visiting in a local nursing home and I spoke to an 88-year-old woman named Jean. Jean cries a lot. She's lonely and crippled and nearly blind. Doesn't have much to live for (she does know the Lord, however). All too soon, my Bonnie, you too will be 88, though I pray in much happier circumstances (and I'll be there even sooner than you!).

So, seize the time; use it well. Live and do today what you will be glad you did when your life is over! That will be joy indeed—to see Jesus having lived well.

Love you,
Dad

P.S. (2021): Time is short so do your best!

℥ ℥ ℥

LAUGHTER

5-26-87

Hi Sweetheart!

You have recently learned a delightful and endearing new skill—how to laugh. What a joy to hear you burst into a peal of laughter—you whose little brow has been knit in an apprehensive furrow virtually since the day you were born! I would not be surprised to discover, given our Lord's sense of proportion, that you of all my children have the keenest sense of humor and lightest spirit. You already have suffered so much more than many do in a lifetime!

Much Love,
Dad

P.S. (2021): God gives the oil of joy for mourning to His beloved.

"God has brought me laughter, and everyone who hears about this will laugh with me." (Genesis 21.6)

ᔆ   ᔆ   ᔆ

HUMILITY

7-13-87

Hello Bonnie Dear!

It's been quite a while since I've written you, and as I reflect back, I see that it's been a momentous 2 months. Our church where I am associate pastor (Northeast Bible Church) has been going through some growing pains, much of which culminated in the worship service yesterday. It's not important to know a lot of details (some new elders on our board harbored resentment against old elders and the senior pastor. Last week we had 2 long meetings totaling 12+ hours to work this out).

I want to share one really important principle with you that I've learned through these events. It's clearly stated in Proverbs 11:2: "When pride comes, then comes dishonor, but with the humble is wisdom." Human nature naturally tends to this idea that to admit fault or weakness causes others to draw back in disrespect. We somehow think that we have to convince others of our perfection though both we and they know it's not true!

God says just the opposite: "The fear of the Lord is the instruction for wisdom, and before honor comes humility." (Proverbs 15.33) To gain true honor, we must first be honest, transparent, and vulnerable. Others see this and because they're human and know how hard it is to do this themselves, respect you for it.

Yesterday in church, all our elders stood before the congregation in humility as I read a statement which expressed the truth about our conflicts as elders, our repentance to each other, our unity. It was risky. Ray (the Sr. pastor) and I feared that people would react negatively or lose confidence in the Board. But just the opposite happened. People poured out love and appreciation to us. As a result, I feel our church is now stronger than it's been in 2 years.

I say all that to say this: never fear to be open and honest with others by admitting mistakes and humbling yourself to ask forgiveness. There is power and grace in this. And you never will fear to do this if you're sincerely walking with the Lord and attempting to grow in your areas of weakness. The proud tend to be those who know their weakness and are unwilling to rectify it. That necessitates the cover-up of arrogance.

Have a wonderful day!
Love,
Dad

P.S. (2021): Pride is disrespected but humility is honored.

ॐ ॐ ॐ

WORRY'S ANTIDOTE

10-11-87 Sunday 7:28am

Dear Bonnie,

Since I wrote last, the Lord has answered our prayers for leading and brought us to Irving Bible Church. It's a great church with a rich tradition of Bible-teaching, and I'm honored and privileged to be here.

I'm also scared half to death! Last Sunday was my installation service, and in just a few hours I'll be preaching my first message as senior pastor.

That's why I'm writing—to share a further thought with you about facing scary experiences. I thought it would be more pertinent now since I'm facing one!

Here's the thought: time will propel us through scary experiences and inevitably deliver us to the other side. The way to get by hard experiences is to project through them and view them from a past perspective. Then we can ask, "How will I have wished that I handled this situation?" Such perspective will make a difference. It will help you relax and even enjoy yourself. Don't worry: few scary things in our lives are potentially fatal!

We celebrated your first birthday Friday night! At the party were Steve/Julie/Blair/Lee /Bob & Jane. We had chicken casserole & cake and sang to you and your sisters helped you rip open presents. I think you had a good time—especially playing "play dough" with your first piece of cake!

Much Love,
Dad

P.S. (2021): Commit to living like Jesus and He will shepherd you through the scary times of your life.

"Do not be anxious about anything, but in every situation, by prayer and petition, with thanksgiving, present your requests to God."

—Philippians 4:6

଼   ଼   ଼

IMMATURITY

11-4-87

Hi Bonnie!

Last night I went on a visit to a family that's dropped out of our church for various reasons. I just listened as they recited a litany of "concerns" which had led them to leave. As I sat there, my ire began to rise up. I was incensed at the self-centered myopia of these people. It seemed they thought things should revolve solely around their thoughts and ideas, and they were hurt because they felt ignored. In short, I was put out with these folks because they were immature. Like babies, they were central in their world and screamed when others failed to share their perspective!

Later on, though, I began to come under conviction. Who am I to grow impatient with others for the sin of selfishness? Who am I to label others "immature"? For is not my reaction to their selfishness a product of my own selfishness? Is not my defensiveness a manifestation of immaturity in wanting to be recognized, appreciated–vindicated? I think it is.

Perhaps the highest maturity is seen in a response of love, patience, and compassion for the immature in our midst. When you can truly love and accept selfish people, then maybe you can think that you've made inroads in your own battle against self.

Obviously, I've a long way to go!

Love,
Dad

P.S. (2021): Human nature is to criticize the faults of one's own soul when seen in others.

                                                ဢ   ဢ   ဢ

GOD SO LOVED

11-25-87

Dear Bonnie,

How great is the love of the Father, that He should have given His Son to die for us! I just read Genesis 22, the story of Abraham's faith in taking the son of his old age—Isaac—to sacrifice him in obedience to God. I pictured Abraham's grief when, going up the mountain, Isaac asked where the sacrificial animal was. I visualized the instant when, the firewood having been laid and preparations made, Abraham's eyes locked with Isaac's and the dread realization of imminent death at the hand of his father battered his heart. I saw tears streaming down Isaac's face while his father, shaken with sobs, bound his hands and feet. I saw Abraham embrace his helpless son with a cry of anguish, holding and rocking him while his heart fairly broke within him. And then I saw Abraham lay Isaac's prostrate form on the wood and, with Isaac's imploring eyes following, reach for the knife and raise it above the heart of his son. Bonnie, I began to weep when I read this, because I saw myself as Abraham and one of my children as Isaac. I felt what Abraham must have felt, and it tore my heart!

But you know the story. God provided an animal instead, and Isaac was spared. Whew! But God wasn't. That which Abraham almost did and what I could never do, God did. "For He gave His only begotten son... (John 3:16) ... and delivered Him up for us all." (Romans 8:32) What makes me weak to think about, God did because He loves us!

And I Love You!
Dad

P.S. (2021): God's heart was broken that our hearts might be healed.

☙ ☙ ☙

CHRISTMAS EVE

12-24-87

Dear Bonnie,

It's Christmas Eve, and I'm sitting alone here at the church pondering the "reason for the season." I reread the account on Luke's Gospel of Jesus' birth, and was touched by the special invitation given the shepherds. Why did God send His glorious angels to announce the birth of His Son, especially to these poor, unlettered men? Why the personal invite to shepherds to "come and behold Him, born the King of Angels?"

Did God invite them because they were the only ones awake at that hour? Or was it because they were conveniently nearby? Did God invite them because they were bored and had nothing better to do? Perhaps God invited these poor men to spite the wealthy and proud. I don't know!

One reason, however, that the shepherds were personally invited was to symbolize to the world what the Bethlehem Babe Himself would be. They were poor in spirit and meek, and so would be Yeshua. They were shepherds and, as such, diligent watchers over the flock. So would the child be. In fact, Jesus is called "That Great Shepherd of the sheep." And so, it would only be fitting that shepherds be there when the Greatest Shepherd made His debut. Perhaps this is the most poignant picture of Christians—God coming to care for those who could not care for themselves, the Lord of the Universe entering the company of sheep and cows and men to shepherd them spiritually through time and into eternity.

"The Lord is my shepherd; I shall not want..."

Merry Christmas,
Dad

P.S. (2021): Christmas was when a lowly band of shepherds were first to welcome the Greatest Shepherd of all.

ॐ　ॐ　ॐ

PRESUMPTION

3-3-88

Hi Sweetheart!

Been a while since I've written. Sorry! My life has been a rush lately. This week I'm doing my first solo funeral and wedding-in addition to preaching and everything else. I thank God for the privilege!

Psalm 19:13 says: "Keep back thy servant also from presumptuous sins; let them not have dominion over me." Presumption is essentially bypassing the Lord-assuming we don't need Him or that His will doesn't come to bear on what lies ahead of us. This is a deadly mistake! Scripture shows that we bypass God at great peril. We should never grow so complacent or confident that we fail to submit every decision to His guidance.

In Joshua 9:14, we find that presumption led to the debacle of the Gibeonite deception. "The men of Israel sampled their provisions but did not inquire of the Lord." As a result, Israel became obligated to defend rather than defeat one of her enemies.

Let's don't feed the sharks! There are false prophets and false philosophies and false values and ideas in our world. They're all waging a subtle war for our hearts and souls. Only the Lord can guide us through this mine field. Let's always ask before we leap!

Love you,
Dad

P.S. (2021): When we bypass the Lord, we also bypass His blessings.

MATERIALISTIC MARRIAGE

6-24-88

Dearest Bonnie,

You've been walking now for a whole week and a half, and I've never seen a child so pleased with herself! And well you should be because you've overcome tremendous odds to get where you are.

When you read these words, you will be struggling to learn a different kind of walk—walking with God. Here also you will find yourself up against formidable opposition. Serving God whole-heartedly in our day is like making your way through a minefield. It's no Sunday stroll!

As you make your way in the world, one of the most crucial choices you will make is that of a life mate. Based on some painful recent experiences with bad marriages, may I exhort, urge, and emphasize one point to you regarding marriage? It is this: refuse to settle for anything less in the man you marry than ...

1. Proven character (dependable, honest, diligent, hard-working, humble) and
2. A growing devotion to Jesus Christ (seeks to be obedient to the word, sensitive to God's leading, tender conscience for his own sin, eternal values).

Bonnie—please hear your father: don't be infatuated by a guy's good looks, popularity, athletic prowess, neat sense of humor, intellect, promising future, fine family background, fancy sportscar, or wealth if he has not proven character and a growing devotion to Jesus. If you do get hooked on the surface bells and baubles and wind up married to a proud, materialistic, self-centered man, you will suffer no matter if you live in a mansion or drive a Rolls-you will suffer.

Sweetheart, this is not to scare you away from marriage, just away from a bad marriage.

From A Loving Heart,
Dad

P.S. (2021): Spirituality is the first casualty of a materialistic marriage.

ဆာ   ဆာ   ဆာ

FAITH-FILLED GENEROSITY

9-27-88

Dearest Bonnie,

I want to share a story with you about my good friend, Pastor Ray. Two years ago, Ray and Marlene (his wife) made a pledge to give $10 thousand to the Northeast Bible Church Building Fund. Times since then have been hard. They've had financial setbacks. Also, their car died. As a result, they weren't able to do much about their pledge.

Ray did have $7500 of stocks. When their car died, he sold the stock to buy a new one. But then he thought, "I told the Lord I'd give this money to the church, and I haven't done it."

Result? He and Marlene gave all that money, which was all they had, to the church instead of getting the car they needed. Truly the "widow's mite" revisited!

I am challenged by such sacrifice for conscience sake before God. I can't help but believe God is very pleased. Can you?

Love.
Dad

P.S. (2021): Generosity is the measure of a Christian's faith and integrity before God.

℘   ℘   ℘

TAKING A STAND

2-22-89

Sweetheart Bonnie,

Last Saturday, your daddy acquired a police record by blocking the entrance to an abortion clinic after police ordered us to leave. I left when they physically carried me off to jail. We believe some babies were saved that day, so it was well worth it.

I want you to know that I experienced great joy in what I did. It was truly one of the only actions I've ever taken for conviction sake that really cost me something. I'm convinced that many Christians don't have the abundant lives God wants for them because they are fundamentally disobedient. Oh, they walk the straight and narrow on a personal basis but ignore God's concerns when it comes to social conscience.

Bonnie, be a warrior for God. It'll cost you, but it'll keep you humble, keep you trusting, keep you joyful, and keep you powerful. There's no other way to live!

Love,
Dad

P.S. (2021): The acid test of conviction is action for conscience' sake, i.e., taking a stand.

⋈   ⋈   ⋈

WEAK, STRONG

6-28-89

Dear Bonnie,

Some recent tests show that you are significantly behind developmentally at this stage in your growth. We're being encouraged to get you into a program for special help.

I don't know how long you will have to struggle to compensate for the effects of your premature birth. Perhaps you'll be all caught up in just a few years. Perhaps you'll always have to work just a little bit—or maybe a lot—harder than others. But what I want to say is, that's OK! Why? Several reasons...

1. 1.God made you, and He knows what He's doing. We must not resist His will but approve it by showing it to be good and pleasing and perfect. (Romans 12:2) You do this by maintaining a positive, can-do attitude which is justified by Romans 8:28 (NIV), "And we know that in all things God works for the good of those who love him, who have been called according to his purpose."

2. God often gives burdens to those specially selected to do a significant work for Him. Remember Paul's "thorn"? Read 2 Corinthians 12:9-10 to see how extra burdens keep God's servant humble and thereby a candidate for God's grace!

3. The very character and self-discipline required to overcome a handicap in one area leads to extraordinary achievement in others. "Normality" is often this bane of significant achievement because it sometimes implies that greatness is within the reach of average effort. Not so. The struggle to accomplish even "normal" things that come easy to others creates a momentum which will carry you through the mundane into the magnificent.

"Therefore, I will boast all the more gladly about my weaknesses, so that Christ's power may rest on me. That is why, for Christ's sake, I delight in weaknesses, in insults, in hardships, in persecutions, in difficulties. For when I am weak, then I am strong."

Bonnie, I anticipate great things in your future through Jesus!

Lovingly,
Dad

P.S. (2021): Surrendered weakness is an opportunity for God to show Himself strong in our lives.

ଓ   ଓ   ଓ

GODLY HATE

2-16-90

Sweetheart Bonnie,

This old world presents us with an awful lot to hate ... injustice, cruelty, selfishness, and oppression. Indeed, we ought to hate such things with a holy hatred! I have come to hate the slaughter of unborn children—euphemistically termed "abortion"—with an intense hatred. I can truly understand (though never justify!) the impulse of those who firebomb these killing centers. I have vented my rage by blocking a few of their doors—and going to jail for it.

The question is not: "Are there things we should hate?" But rather, "Where will we allow our hatred to lead us?" I'm coming to see that we must recognize our hatred of evil as a first step. Don't repress or deny it. But having recognized it, we must move through it. The end result for Christians must be love. But not a spineless, idealistic, or gushy love. The love which grows from hate is tough as nails and brutally realistic. When we experience such love, truly we have become mature.

Eugene Peterson explains this powerfully in his book Answering God, pp 102-3:

> Our hate is used by God to bring the enemies of life and salvation to notice, and then involve us in active compassion for the victims. Once involved, we find that while hate provides the necessary spark for ignition, it is the wrong fuel for the engines of judgement, only love is adequate to sustain these passions. But we must not imagine that loving ... our enemies ... is a strategy that will turn them into good friends. Love is the last thing that our enemies want

from us and often acts as a goad to redoubled fury. Love requires vulnerability, forgiveness, and response; the enemies want power, control, and dominion. The enemies that Jesus loved and prayed for killed Him.

Love You!
Dad

P.S. (2021): Wisdom is loving what God loves and hating what God hates.

   ဢ   ဢ   ဢ

STEADY ON

8-13-91

Dearest Precious Bonnie,

In just two months you'll be five. I don't know of any other five-year-old whose life has been quite as dramatic, full, or welcome than yours! 1 Peter 2:6 says, "See, I lay a stone in Zion, a chosen and precious cornerstone, and the one who trusts in him will never be put to shame." As someone commented, "Steady. In-destructible. Immovable. Jesus was all that. And now He calls you to be the same."

When life's circumstances get you down, when disappointment burdens you and anxiety bends you and discouragement barrages you, just remember the rock. Trust in Jesus, honor Him with your life. Turn your cares over to Him. The storms will pass, but Jesus will remain. Problems come and go. But He is faithful. Depend on it! He is there for you if you will only go to Him!

P.S: I'm going to Him big-time these days!

Love,
Dad

P.S. (2021): Jesus is the Cornerstone; steady is the life founded upon Him.

◊◊   ◊◊   ◊◊

TIME IS PRECIOUS

11-7-91

Dear Bonnie,

Amy Harris died yesterday of cystic fibrosis. She was just 18. Amy was the salutatorian of her graduating class. She loved to drive around in her Ford Escort which she bought with money  earned by working at a Snow-Cone stand. The people in Wills Point (TX) loved her so much that they'd raised $300 thousand to pay for the lung transplant surgery which would have saved her. But the lungs never came available, and Amy died. Amy was interviewed often on T.V. during her last few months. She had a sweet spirit and courageous disposition. I think she knew the Lord and is with Him now.

Bonnie, I don't know why the Lord took Amy at such a young age. I wept when I heard she was gone. But her death does remind me of 2 facts:

Life is short
—and—
Time is precious.

Robert Louis Stevenson wrote: "Young or old, we are all on our final voyage." Amy died early. But she would have died eventually as we all will. The question is not whether our time on earth is unlimited. It's not. The question is whether we'll use the limited time we have wisely.

Bonnie, your very life is a gift. God brought you through a shaky start in miraculous ways. Every moment you breathe is His good gift! Let's both remember that OK? And when we're tempted to complain or waste time, let's think of Amy.

Much Love,
Dad

P.S. (2021): It's always a wise use of time to contemplate the brevity of our life on this earth.

୫୦ ୫୦ ୫୦

SUCCESS

3-19-92

Dearest Bonnie,

First Samuel 18:14 gives us the key to success in life: "In everything he [David] did he had great success, because the Lord was with him." The greatest asset you or I could ever hope to have in our life is the blessing of God.

If God's blessing is with us, we'll have strength that will empower us, wisdom that will guide us, and protection that will shelter us. If God is with us, all that we set our hands to, will be successful. The question, then, is how do we bring God's blessing upon our lives?

Perhaps the answer is back in 1 Samuel 16:7. "The Lord does not look at the things man looks at. Man looks at the outward appearance, but the Lord looks at the heart."

Bonnie, I want you to find fabulous success in all you do. But I can't make you successful. Even you can't make you successful. Only God can, and He will if you truly give your heart to Him— serving Him from the inside out. Then, you will have a "heart after God's own heart." (1 Samuel 13:14)

You are a special gift from God. I know He has a unique plan for you, Bonnie. Seek His best and you'll fulfil the plan.

Ecstatic for Your Future,
Dad

P.S. (2021): The greatest asset in life is the blessing of God.

৪৩ ৪৩ ৪৩

AUTHENTICITY

Dear Bon, the Won,

When you had your tonsils and adenoids out a month ago, Dr. Frank Theilen said it would help you grow! And it has. You're breathing better, eating better, and seem to have taken a real leap ahead. The other night Julie featured you as her co-star in one of our in-house McQuitty productions. You played a compassionate Queen. So careful and studious were you in annunciating your lines: "Where are you bound?" and even ad-libs. After Julie sneezed hard, your shook your finger and proclaimed, "No sneezing in this castle!" How we do love you, Bonnie!

Authenticity. Reality. The truth. I find it very difficult to maintain these on a day-to-day basis. I find it convenient to deceive myself with regard to motives and feelings rather than recognize crass selfishness or shallow convictions. I reflect socially and spiritually acceptable rationales publicly for attitudes and actions that may be privately shameful. And I'm not alone.

Part of our legacy as fallen human beings is the urge to justify our failures. It's just too scary to acknowledge them. Yet, acknowledgment is the only path to improvement. You cannot excise the cancer if you persist in steadfastly ignoring its existence. And you cannot experience true grace until you admit genuine need. What a predicament when we suffer for need of medicine which we reject because we're ashamed to admit an illness!

Isn't that what happened to Peter in Luke 22:33? Jesus, knowing what was truly in Peter's heart, predicted his denials. Poor self-deceived Peter, he who had sincerely believed his own

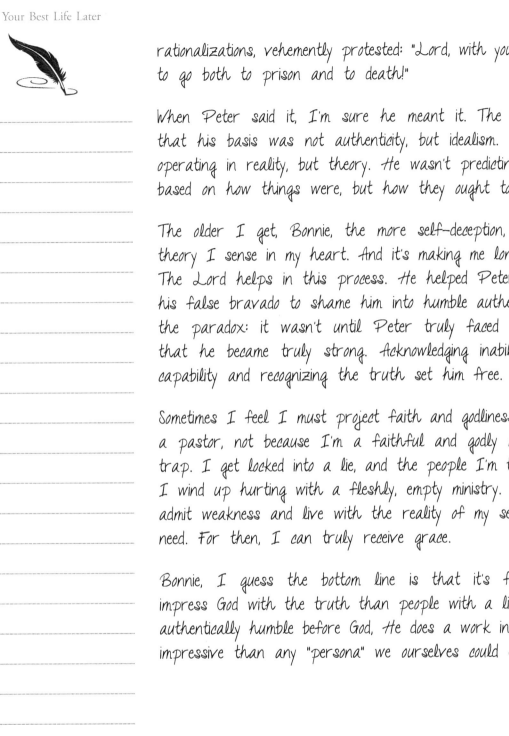

rationalizations, vehemently protested: "Lord, with you I am ready to go both to prison and to death!"

When Peter said it, I'm sure he meant it. The problem was that his basis was not authenticity, but idealism. Peter wasn't operating in reality, but theory. He wasn't predicting an outcome based on how things were, but how they ought to have been.

The older I get, Bonnie, the more self-deception, idealism, and theory I sense in my heart. And it's making me long for reality. The Lord helps in this process. He helped Peter by allowing his false bravado to shame him into humble authenticity. Here's the paradox: it wasn't until Peter truly faced his weakness that he became truly strong. Acknowledging inability gave him capability and recognizing the truth set him free.

Sometimes I feel I must project faith and godliness because I'm a pastor, not because I'm a faithful and godly man! What a trap. I get locked into a lie, and the people I'm trying to help I wind up hurting with a fleshly, empty ministry. Far better to admit weakness and live with the reality of my selfishness and need. For then, I can truly receive grace.

Bonnie, I guess the bottom line is that it's far better to impress God with the truth than people with a lie. When we're authentically humble before God, He does a work in us far more impressive than any "persona" we ourselves could ever project.

Love You!
Dad

P.S. (2021): Unacknowledged faults and failures repel the freedom of God's forgiveness

જી   જી   જી

POLITICS IN PERSPECTIVE

11/4/92

Sweetheart Bonnie,

The '92 national elections were held yesterday and I'm reeling from the results. Bill Clinton has captured the presidency and anti-life initiatives from abortion rights to euthanasia passed all over the nation. All day long, I've been depressed. I feel like an alien in my own country. How can so many millions be so deceived, or how can I be so out of synch?

Yet in the middle of this I remember that life's greatest priorities have little to do with politics or policies or material prosperity. Knowing and serving Christ and others is all that really matters. In the dark economic times that lie ahead, the church can perhaps minister in ways impossible heretofore. Thus, I must not be selfish, greedily attached to a standard of living or comfort zone that subtly keeps me from truly trusting the Lord.

Bonnie, I can't predict what kind of world you'll enter as an adult. You may not enjoy the freedoms and living standards of my generation. You may face hardships that I never did. But even if that's true, you'll have the rare and wonderful chance to trust the Lord and see His response in tangible, mighty ways. And that's what makes life truly exciting and worthwhile.

Your Loving Father,
Dad!

P.S. (2021): No matter what happens in the White House, the Lord is in His holy Temple.

୫ ୫ ୫

DOULOS

8/3/94

Dearest Bonnie,

I see that's it's been a long time since I wrote to you. I'm sorry. I've been busy, but that's no excuse. Sometimes it's easy for a person to get his priorities all jumbled up even if he means well! I'll try to do better.

I can't believe how you've grown these last two years. God has given you a very special spirit, Bonnie. It is pure and spiritually alive and more open to God than I've ever seen in anyone. How beautiful you are! And how I do love you. I recently started a sermon series on the Book of Romans. The very first line in that book really captivates me. Paul introduces himself there as "... a bond servant of Christ Jesus, called as an apostle, set apart for the gospel of God." (Romans 1:1)

The "bond-servant" (the translation of the Greek word, doulos) in Paul's day was a man bought in the agora, or market, as a slave. Paul saw himself as a slave to Jesus. The Apostle Peter also called himself a "servant and apostle," (2 Peter 1:1) and James and Jude, half-brothers of Jesus, both refer to themselves as Christ's bondservants.

These writers simply meant that they were dedicated to Jesus as their one master and that they would never leave him for another. Paul also saw himself as an "apostle"—a "sent one." He knew who he was and where he fit. Finally, Paul knew he was "set apart for the gospel" and thus embraced an all-encompassing life purpose.

Jesus had taught that the greatest of all was the "servant (doulos) of all." (Mark 9:35) As Christ's apostle and doulos, Paul was a blessed and joyful and great man because he knew whom he served, where he fit, and why he was alive.

Bonnie, Christ gives you and me the same opportunity. He will be our Master, too. He will show us we have a place, also. He will use us as part of His eternal plan as well.

But how does a Christian get started on the road to spiritual greatness that Paul the apostle walked? Obedience. That's simply recognizing the Lordship of Jesus and living out its implications: purity, prayer, study, sacrifice, service, self-denial, holiness as Christ's doulo.

Seems hard? Not really. God made us for this. Obeying Jesus is the path to joy.

All My Love,
Your Dad (and Bond Servant to Jesus Christ)

P.S. (2021): The greatest freedom is serving Jesus Christ.

      ∞   ∞   ∞

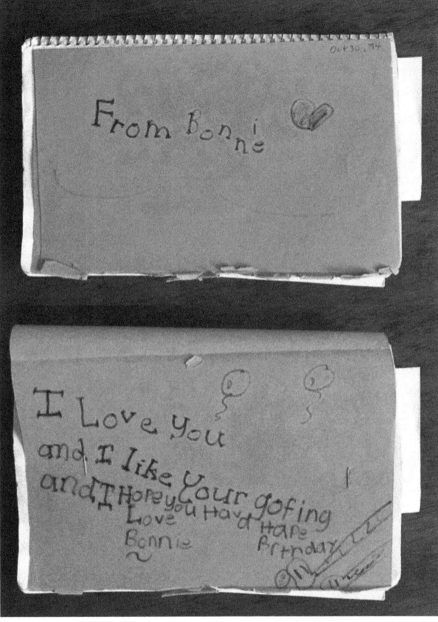

GREAT BEFORE GOD

9-3-96

Dearest Bonnie,

Wow—I'm glad to have found this notebook again; it's been so long since I last wrote! You're grown up so much, too. Such a lovely nine-year old lass! I'm so proud of you. You continue to be very serious about what you commit yourself to last Spring you were awarded The Spirit Trophy by your softball team for being the one who always hustled and gave it your best. Your coaches said they could always count on Bonnie to be the one who listened and worked and gave it her all. It's been the same with your schoolwork. You've taken great leaps in your reading skills. You always give it 110%. And your faith in God is no exception. I love your prayers—so direct, so trusting. God has His hand on you, Bonnie!

I want to tell you about a friend of mine named "George." He is from India and speaks broken English. About 40 (my age) he is married and has children. George works as a locker room attendant at the Four Seasons where I work out. He also works at a pizza place. George is special because he loves the Lord so much. His little Indian Church recently built a new sanctuary, and George was heavily involved. His only times off during the week are Wednesday night and Sunday morning. He uses these times for prayer and worship at his Church. He takes his Bible and devotional books to work to study on breaks.

Here's what touches me about George. Though he is a humble man with a family stuck in two low-paying, menial jobs (probably for the rest of his life), George is a servant of God and others and is a very happy man. Money and prestige are not important to George. Knowing and serving Jesus are!

George is a lesson to me about what truly matters in life and about what devotion as a believer means. You don't have to be prominent to be one of God's "A" players—just faith-full!

George is; I hope to be; and I encourage you, Bonnie, to join the party! Actually, I believe you already have!

All My Love,
Dad

P.S. (2021): True success is not about what you achieve, but whom you become.

ഉ   ഉ   ഉ

THE POWER OF CONTENTMENT

5-14-97

Dearest Bonnie,

I am so proud of you. There is a spirit of excellence in you which produces integrity and motivates perseverance. You are the kind of person with whom I love to work or play on a team with, because you can be trusted and counted upon. God will use this wonderful quality in your life to do great things. Never covet the more glamorous gifts of others who may have a superficial ability to impress. Your gift goes deeper and endures. You are the real thing. If I'm choosing teams, I choose Bonnie first!

Psalm 37 is a wonderful "batch" of truth that will give you much encouragement, Bon. I especially commend verses 10-11:

> A little while
> and the wicked will be no more
> though you look for them,
> they will not be found.
> But the meek will inherit the land
> and enjoy great peace.

There will always be wicked, arrogant people in this world who, in their evident "success," laugh at good, humble people and cause them to question their own value. "Why should I struggle and sacrifice to live right when those who cut corners have it so good?" Psalm 37 answers that question. A godly life always, always, always prevails in the long run. Sure, the wicked may prosper for months, years, or even a lifetime. But they have no peace in their prosperity and then they enter eternity and the judgment.

Take the long view, Bonnie. Live for it. Put your treasure in Heaven. Then not only will you, the sincere and Godly one, be first, but you'll also have "the last laugh"!

Joyfully Your Fan,
Dad

P.S. (2021): It takes a lifetime for Heaven's real winners to be identified.

"You're blessed when you're content with just who you are—no more, no less. That's the moment you find yourselves proud owners of everything that can't be bought."

–Matthew 5:5 (The Message)

ଚ୍ଚ   ଚ୍ଚ   ଚ୍ଚ

116   REFRESH RENEW REVIVE

and better decks, suddenly I was discontent with what I had. It was amazing how quickly the transformation took place.

Years ago, I heard Howard Hendricks say that comparison is the favorite indoor sport of Christians. And I think he was right. Whether I compare my ministry, my house, or my car to someone else's—it's just endless. There's always something better than what we have. Influenza used to kill people; now we have to deal with allergies.

Comparison kills contentment. That's the issue. And it's an issue we pastors deal with daily in so many areas of our lives.

affected by whether they're down or up. But I also know those numbers don't indicate success or its lack. Now, I'm not saying numbers aren't important. The Bible tells us Jesus fed 5,000 and 3,000 were saved at Pentecost. But I also understand that if the Lord was in it and He was presiding over it and only 5 had been fed and only 3 had been saved at Pentecost, it would have been a great success anyway. God sees things much differently from the way we do. So I'm not knocking numbers, but I am saying that whether you're on their up side or their down side, you'd better have a biblical definition of success—because your soul can be in the balance.

But when we as pastors don't see those increasing numbers, we think, I'm not a success. That's exactly what happened to me in the story I told above. And in the deepest, darkest depression of my life, I poured my heart out to my wife. And then we resolved to find out what the Bible has to say about success. Consequently, we've found that there is a better definition of success than having more people the next Sunday than you had the last Sunday.

Biblical Success

I'm invited to speak at conferences, and one reason is that I pastor a large church. But because of our earlier experience, when Barbara and I came to College Church and it began to grow, it meant much less to us than

1/12/98

Dear Bonnie—

Thinking of you!

Love,

Dad

BEARING WITNESS

11-13-98

Dearest Bonnie,

What a beautiful, talented, sweet-spirited little 12-year-old you are! Last Sunday, Papa Eric preached at our church on sharing the gospel with lost people. In the drama preceding, a lost man talked to several Christians hoping that someone would share good news with him. But none did! You played the role of a young Christian who almost witnessed to the man, but at the last minute decided not to do it. You were great ... got the biggest laugh from the audience!

I got a kick out of your performance because I knew you truly were acting. You love to share your faith already, and I suspect that someday God will use you to bring many to Christ. You have such a sweet spirit; people immediately trust you and love you. That's a precious gift to you from God, as you are to me.

Love,
Dad

P.S. (2021): The next best thing to hearing the Good News is sharing it with others.

಄   ಄   ಄

7/5/99

Club Rules   made by : President
                 Bonnie McQuitty

1. no going in Attic ditches or pick cotten areas.

2. don't leave without derning off the light (Jeffery don't come up without one of us).

3. Leave place clean

4. Don't bring up any furniture

5. Club members only! (keep secret)

6. Be quiet as possible when mom home

7. treat furniture with respect.

Members Sign up.

Arus Ott
Jonathan Mabry
Bonia
Jeffry

PERSEVERANCE

9-2-99

Dearest Bonnie,

As I drove you to Barbara Bush Jr Hi this morning, I told you how proud I was of you. You weren't excited about going back to public school after the fiasco year at Vanguard (which closed at Christmas) and Renaissance Academy. It was scary to you. Yet, you've been brave. Not only are your grades high, but you tried out for and made the 2nd volleyball team out of four (a real honor in itself!) only to be promoted to the "A" team right before the first game!

I love it that you did not give up on the year before it started and that, because you gave it a shot, you're discovering that things are working out better than you imagined they could. I know things aren't perfect. You told me about the unruly students in your language arts class who won't pay attention. But Bonnie, such you will always have with you not only in Jr Hi, but in life.

Let the immaturity of others not discourage you but motivate you to a higher personal standard yourself. This is leadership-living well in spite of those around you. Those who stand alone don't do so for others' sake. They lead and manage themselves, not to change others, but to fulfil their own values. Thus, even if no one follows their lead, they're unaffected because they weren't "playing the crowd" to begin with.

But don't be surprised, sweetheart, if eventually you strike out alone in doing good only to find others falling in behind you. Or maybe they won't be going your direction, but just not as fast in the opposite direction as they would have had not Bonnie McQuitty been there! There is always hope for one who perseveres! "Not only so, but we also glory in our sufferings, because we know that suffering produces perseverance; perseverance, character; and character, hope." (Romans 5:3-5)

Remember—the only set of eyes upon you which truly matter is God's. Play to that audience of One and worry about no one else. Get His blessing, and you have all you need!

I Do Love You So,
Dad

P.S. (2021): Perseverance through problems effects the greatest positive change.

      ℠ ℠ ℠

USING YOUR GIFTS

8-11-00

Dearest Bonnie,

You've been back in class at Barbara Bush for 2 days of your 8th grade year. I turned around one day, it seems, and you were suddenly this grown-up teen going to Jr Hi and acting like an adult! I'm so proud of the way you've held your own at school as a Christian. You're strong in your faith and don't back down or suck up to other kids for acceptance or popularity. You're your own person in Christ. You love reading about believers standing for Jesus—missionary biographies and books about Christian martyrs. I think God is equipping you now for a significant ministry someday in His name!

To that end Bon, keep in mind these words from the Apostle Paul to Timothy:

> For this reason, I remind you to fan into flame the gift of God, which is in you through the laying on of my hands. For God did not give us a spirit of timidity, but a spirit of power, of love, and of self-discipline.
>
> —2 Timothy 1:6-7

There are three important facts in these verses for you ...

1. You, Bonnie, have God-given spiritual gifts. They are uniquely yours and integral to the makeup of your heart and personality. These gifts are supernatural, and they are wonderful!

2. You can use these gifts, or not. They will be employed or wasted and it's all your choice. "Fan into flames the gift of God!" No fan, no flames.

3. The enablement you need to step out for God comes from the assurance that power, love, and self-discipline have been given to us. Call upon these by seeking to be strong and love well and live well, and you'll find them at your disposal. But you must call. You must try. You must use your gifts. The power doesn't activate for selfishness and triviality, just for God and His Kingdom. Fan that flame Bonnie!

Much Love Always,
Dad

P.S. (2021): An unused gift might as well never have been given.

৪৩   ৪৩   ৪৩

CHARACTER

12-18-01

Dearest Bonnie,

This week you'll finish final exams for the Fall semester. A freshman at RL Turner High School, you have done extraordinarily well adjusting to big challenges. You've made the most religiously diverse group of friends of any of our children, including a Buddhist, Jew, Hindu, and Muslim. You've pursued your walk with God, too. I took you to the mall the other night because you wanted to buy a devotional book. You got the Experiencing God workbook. You've also stepped out and become involved with your beautiful singing voice in the girls' chorus at RLT (gorgeous Christmas Concert!) and also landing a lead role in the school production of Oklahoma. I'm just really proud of you (can you tell?)!

I see a lot of your mother in you (as you know, that's a big compliment!). You are very patient, accepting, and unselfish. Oh, and I wish I had your calmness! You also have real loyalty and a desire for excellence.

From long experience, I have come to appreciate so deeply people with your gifts, Bonnie. Others may be loud, aggressive, and spotlight seeking. But steady hands and true hearts make the world work —hands and hearts like yours.

Your Biggest Fan,
Dad

P.S. (2021): The depth of your character determines the height of your achievement.

℘   ℘   ℘

MATURITY

10-09-02

Hi Sweetheart!

Monday was your 16th birthday! How can it be that the tiny, wee baby bairn that I could hold in one hand at birth is now qualified to drive me around in a car?!

We enjoyed your traditional birthday biscuits and gravy breakfast while watching you get your new comforter, lamp, etc. Then that night we took you to the revolving Antares Restaurant on top of Reunion Tower where we enjoyed top sirloin and watched the city lights of Dallas make a complete revolution around our table! What a great way to celebrate a beautiful, accomplished young lass.

It just seems to me, Bonnie, that you've truly come into your own since Julie and Liz left for college. It must be hard to grow up in the shadow of two older sisters, both lovely and accomplished in their own rights. But I see in you some character traits which that big "sister" challenge has directly produced:

1. Sensitivity to people not in the limelight. I love to see your friendships with great girls at school from all sorts of backgrounds. You are able to appreciate qualities in others which are valuable if not flashy. That's a gift and a skill, Bonnie, that will serve you well all through life.
2. A pleasing personality born of unselfishness. You are such a wonderfully unpretentious person! With some people, it's always got to be all about them, all the time. But you are interested in others, never a hogg for attention or glory, and fun to be with. Prima donnas go for glory and produce grief. But

humble, caring people serve and help and leave a legacy of love. That's you, Bon!

3. Strength. Being the middle child of 5 has made you a master of getting along with others without relinquishing your rights. You know what is appropriate and right. That means you don't grab for what's not your fair share. But it also means you don't lay down and let others walk over you. You are level-headed and firm in your convictions. How rare is that?

In short, Bonnie, your first 16 years on this planet have been well-spent, fitting you for a lifetime of success and happiness such that I would encourage you with these words from Paul to Timothy: "Don't let anyone look down on you because you are young, but set an example for the believers in speech, in conduct, in love, in faith and in purity." (1 Timothy 4:12, NIV) Bonnie, you already are!

So Proud of You,
Dad

P.S. (2021): The most compelling examples of godliness are mature young believers

∛ ∛ ∛

A SERVANT'S HEART

2-3-03

Hi Sweetheart Bonnie,

You and your intrepid company have just completed a triumphant run of Guys and Dolls at Turner High. You have put in long hours practicing and building and working, and the resulting show was wonderful. The Irish lads staying with us (Darren and Stewart) in our home were blown away. I'm so proud of you!

But I'm especially proud because you did all that work even though you didn't have a major speaking or solo role. You will one day, I'm convinced. But even though you didn't get the parts you wanted you stayed the course. You faithfully and humbly did your part and supported everyone else even though the spotlight wasn't on you. "For those who exalt themselves will be humbled, and those who humble themselves will be exalted." (Matthew 23:12) That, my girl, takes character! And you should know that my eyes, if not the spotlights, were always on you!

Love,
Dad

P.S. (2021): The Lord honors those with a servant's heart.

෨   ෨   ෨

TRUE HOLINESS

11-1-04

Dearest Bonnie,

My, my, what a derelict dad I have been about writing to you in these pages. So sorry, my dear. I could make all sorts of excuses, but I'll spare you. Just know that this season in my life has been so crazy that several important things in my life have been the victims of neglect. Hopefully, I can get things back on track. Perhaps that's what I should write you about— the uneven, often disappointing, and failure-prone but sometimes fulfilling and victorious nature of life.

I used to assume that, at some advanced stage in my life, I would achieve a sort of spiritual nirvana. I'd never struggle with selfishness and laziness and pride again but only spend my days living wisely, powerfully, and blissfully. Guess what? I just turned 49, and I feel further than ever from ever achieving the kind of moral perfection that I dreamed of when younger!

Perhaps I should have known all along that this is a pipedream. After all, God has told us in His word that our flesh wars with our spirit. Until we reach heaven's wonderful freedom from the presence and power of sin, we will always grapple mightily with it down here. Perhaps the clearest clue to this ongoing, never-ending struggle with sin on earth is Paul's self-descriptive statement, "This is a faithful saying, and worthy of all acceptation, that Christ Jesus came into the world to save sinners; of whom I am chief." (1 Timothy 1:15, KJV) If the great apostle felt that way, I suppose I shouldn't be too down on myself for feeling the same way!

All that, dear Bonnie, to say this: failure from time-to-time is inevitable but quitting never is. Don't quit. Are you down and discouraged? It's OK. Start in again. God is the Lord of second chances, indeed as many chances as you need.

Let me end with some words of Jesus that challenge me greatly. Criticizing the Pharisees' brand of religious expression, He observed: "Everything they do is done for men to see." (Matthew. 23:5) You know what God loves? Acts of love, obedience, and service to Him and others that will never be seen except by Him. Maybe that's the greatest victory of all—private, genuine, sincere expressions of love to God.

Take a Swing, Bonnie. You'll knock it out of the park!
Dad

P.S. (2021): Everything holy people do, best be done for God to see, rather than for men.

      考   考   考

Well, your getting up there! Your birthday only shows that your getting wiser and blinder everyday! Daddy, I hope you enjoy this wonderful day, be happy, eat food, ride bikes!

Happy
Birthday!

♡ Bonnie

THOUGHTFULNESS

Nov 5, 2004

Dearest Bonnie,

A quick follow up on the last entry ... for my birthday. You made me this card! Let me list the reasons I love it:

1. I got a lot of b-day cards, not only from family but also IBC staff and friends. Yours is the only hand-made one! You always take the time to add that special touch, even though I'm sure that this might have been done late at night when you'd much rather have been sleeping! But that's what makes you special.

2. I love the detail and thoughtfulness you put into it. I could make a hand-made card, but I doubt I'd take the time and effort to do what you did—make it well!

3. I love your humor (I'm not that blind yet, am I?) and your heart; you know how I love riding my motorcycle. It may not be what you'd do on your birthday, but you were considering me!

That's the heart of thoughtfulness (which is the heart of God), and I am blessed.

All that to say, you are a special, beautiful young woman—outside and in!

And I love You,
Dad

P.S. (2021): The opposite of selfishness is thoughtfulness.

છ   છ   છ

THE FEAR OF THE LORD

1-19-05

Dearest Bonnie,

You have been working so hard with your theatre friends at Turner on The Wizard of Oz. Of course, as Dorothy, you have the lead role and must work harder than others. I commend you for your poise and attitude in doing so. Yesterday, you told us that several in the cast were upset about various things. Some quit, others stomped off. But not you. It must be very difficult to keep an even keel while working around such volatile (and dare I say "needy" people). Yet ever the anti-prima donna, you pull it off with panache!

This morning, our breakfast devotional was from Proverbs 22:4: "Humility and the fear of the Lord bring wealth and honor and life." Bonnie, you are a humble, beautiful, unprepossessing spirit! You do fear the Lord and you do walk in His ways. Keep on these wonderfully wise paths, and the promise is sure: The Lord will bless you with wealth and honor and life that will last well beyond this world!

Oh, and congratulations on receiving your letter of acceptance from Ouchita Baptist U! I'm so proud of you! They are most fortunate to get you—as they will discover in due time.

Love You,
Dad

P.S. (2021): Honor is due those who persevere through trials with the fear of the Lord.

⅋   ⅋   ⅋

241

TRAGEDY

4-06-05

Dearest Bonnie,

The weather is turning mild and we're into Springtime in Texas. That can mean only one thing—The Masters Golf Tournament! (I'm sure that was you first thought, too). No really, they do play The Masters this week and I've been reading about some of the players.

For instance, Jack Nicklaus (who has won it 6 times) will be playing in his 45th Masters. His son Steve will be caddying for him. That's all pretty cool, except for this one thing which I just learned. Steve's little baby girl (Jack's granddaughter) died one month ago by falling into a hot tub. She was 17 months old. What an awful tragedy. My heart just breaks for that whole family.

Evidently, they debated about doing the golf tournament, but decided in the end it would probably be good therapy for them both. I tend to romanticize what it would be like to be Jack Nicklaus—a famous golfer revered at Augusta National. But I'd be willing to bet he would trade all his wins at the Masters, all his wealth and fame, for the life of that little girl.

I guess what I'm getting at is that as nice as money, fame, and success might be, there are far more important things in life - like, love, family, and faith. In all of our pursuit of the former, let's never forget the latter. I don't think the Nicklaus' have, and that's admirable. "The LORD is close to the brokenhearted and saves those who are crushed in spirit." (Psalm 34:18, NIV) May God see them through.

Love You,
Dad

P.S. (2021): God does not promise to spare his children pain, but to walk through it with them every step of the way.

          ಝ   ಝ   ಝ

GODLY SELF-CONFIDENCE

May 1, 2005

My Dearest Bon,

I'm sitting by the pool at Solana Marriot as I write this. I'm feeling a wee bit guilty since it's also 11:30 AM on Sunday morning. Thus, while I'd normally be preaching at IBC right about now, I am instead spending a few quiet moments writing to my daughter. I find the exchange desirable! I imagine you are also "feeling the pain" on South Padre Island with the IBC youth group senior sneak. I wonder: does my Bonnie feel guilty as I do for not being in Church right now? I've been looking forward to this little break with Alice for some weeks now. I have just preached 13 weekends in a row and needed time off. Alice also has been working so hard on writing and teaching. But inevitably, we've spent most of our time away talking about our kids! We're so excited for you to be off to college in the Fall and pray that this will be a wonderful time of discovery and confidence-building for you.

Bonnie, you've occupied the hardest slot in a family tree—middle child between 2 brothers and sisters on either end! I think that getting out of the "system" will both challenge your comfort level and afford you new freedom, and both are actually very good. Sometimes there are parts of our personalities and abilities and passions that lie dormant until a new environment with new demands and different expectations unlocks them. I can't wait to see how you blossom once free to spread your proverbial "wings" and fly!

Just remember, be who you are unapologetically. I spent personal time this week with a national religious figure who couldn't stop bragging about the people he knows and the things he's done. I was amazed at his insecurity, his evident need to be more than what he feels he is in the eyes of others. And I thought of Paul's wise words about godly self-confidence. "If anyone thinks they are something when they are not, they deceive themselves. Each one should test their own actions. Then they can take pride in themselves alone, without comparing themselves to someone else, for each one should carry their own load." (Galatians 6:3-5, NIV)

In Christ, we are free to love and serve. And Bonnie, in Christ you are so very beautiful just as you are! I always want you thereby to be strengthened with godly self-confidence.

All My Love,
Dad

P.S. (2021): Healthy self-confidence grows from an accurate assessment of God's gracious gifts.

ဆ ဆ ဆ

UNKNOWN FUTURE

5-19-05

Dearest Bonnie,

You've had your hair cut and colored in such an attractive way. What a beautiful, radiant girl you are, inside and out! I think of you often these days in your near-future new home at Ouchita Baptist University. I have predicted to your mom that you will love college for two major reasons.

First, you're just really coming into your own in these days, maturing beautifully both intellectually and socially. I think college will be a grand adventure for you as you spread your wings and fly.

Second, you will find many like-minded students there—serious about learning and doing whatever you do well as well as about having a good time. I think high school has been frustrating for you in a way because not many there have had your commitment to what is good and excellent. At Ouchita, though, you will have lots of company!

Just know always that God has made you unique as a person. Therefore, simply to be fully who you are is your greatest success and that which gives your Heavenly (and earthly!) father the most joy. Sometimes that will mean going with the crowd. Other times that means taking the road less travelled. At all times, however, it means walking close to the Lord who is always with you: "Trust in the LORD with all thine heart; and lean not unto thine own understanding. In all thy ways acknowledge him, and he shall direct thy paths." (Proverbs 3:5-6, KJV)

By the way, I was so happy for you to receive that iPod from OBU in the mail! They obviously already know they have something special in Bonnie McQuitty!

All My Love,
Dad

P.S. (2021): The unknown future is an adventure to those who are actively trusting the Lord.

ೞ   ೞ   ೞ

GET IT DONE

5-19-05

Dearest Bonnie,

I'm really supposed to be working on my sermon for Sunday, but instead I thought I'd write you! This whole week has been like that for me—feeling restless, unmotivated, unproductive, lazy, not wanting to apply myself to my duties. I'm bothered by such times because of the wise man's words: "One who is slack in his work is brother to one who destroys." (Proverbs 18:9)

These seasons in our lives are not that unusual, though, because it's very difficult to have even two weeks in a row of even-keeled emotions and experiences. Life has a way throwing us curveballs, and that affects the way we feel. I'm talking about it because, when these lulls hit you from time to time, I don't want you to get stressed out over them but know the way through them.

The key to doing well in such times despite "the blues" is to break down what needs to be done (and what you often don't want to do!) into small, manageable pieces. Then, just take the next 30 minutes and say, "I'm going to accomplish _____ in this half-hour." Don't worry about the 50 other things that also need doing! Just do that one-thing, and then you're ready to move on to the next 30 minutes' one-thing. After a few hours of this, you will have done a LOT and, by the way, will probably be feeling a lot better about yourself and the day!

Well, writing you was my 30-minute goal. Time for me to move on to the next thing. I'm feeling better already!

Love you,
Dad

P.S. (2021): Life by the yard is hard, but by the inch it's a cinch.

೫ ೫ ೫

CONSISTENCY

5-28-05

Dearest Bonnie,

You have now completed all aspects of your High School with the exception of walking the stage to receive your diploma—and that happens Sunday evening. You have done so well as a diligent student, a talented singer and actress, and a warm and personable friend! Your teachers honor you and your friends love you and your daddy is proud of you!

All of which is to say you've made a fabulous start on life. Having done so, it's important to maintain your rhythm. By that I mean you develop a certain "momentum" with discipline and commitment as you live your life. Doing good and trusting God and experiencing His blessing become ingrained so that even when you're not at your best, good things still happen.

Maintaining the rhythm of the commitment and lifestyle and attitudes and practices that bring such blessing is most important. You just can't ever "cram" for life like you might for a history exam! A steady pace of self-discipline and spiritual practice is required. Otherwise, you risk becoming like many who vacillate from commitment to backsliding, precipitously either ascending the mountain top or descending into the depth of despair but never levelling out to a healthy "regularity." Such people never really achieve anything of significance or experience consistent happiness because they're too distracted by unnecessary "drama." Far better it is to move with measured pace, not in a rush but never in a rut, seeking to know and honor God and love others in His name.

The "every-dayness" of such a mindset may not be the most exciting thing in the world, but it is most gratifying. One last thought while I'm at it! The more you can remember that life is NOT about you, the happier you'll be! Those whose pride and self-centeredness have afflicted them with the burden of selfishness, number among the most miserable people in the world. Their insatiable need to be recognized, given credit, have first place, get respect, and be honored truly sets them up for constant disappointment. No one can always be the honored one, and those to whom that's all-important will always be miserable and unhappy about something!

Miserable people do two destructive things.

1. They make foolish decisions.
2. They drive people away.

I've been dealing with a perfect example of this on IBC staff recently. Two people leading a large ministry event were asked to consult with experienced participants. This was an imminently reasonable request and would have left their leadership of the event completely intact. Unfortunately, these two believed this was "their" ministry and they should be accountable to nobody. They got an ugly attitude, had to be relieved of their duties, and both left IBC. To their consternation, the event (which you attended!) went great—without them. In summary, not only should these folks have led the event, but they should have had the joy of seeing its fruit. But their pride made them suffer alone as the world moved right on without them, because to them it was all about them! Bonnie, it's not about us, ever. Only Jesus. "He must increase but I must decrease" said John the Baptizer. (John 3:30) What a wise man he was!

Love Always,
Dad

P.S. (2021): Daily training in godliness through spiritual disciplines helps us maintain a steady pace that goes the distance.

℘   ℘   ℘

WHAT LASTS

5-31-05

My Dear High School-Graduated Girl,

Not only have you graduated from R.C Turner H.S, but you have done so in style—with a stole and a gold medal around your neck and a track record of faithfulness and achievement in your heart you've made such a great start on the rest of your life, Bonnie! You've proven the power of:

1. Being kind to people and treating them with respect.
2. Working hard and diligently at whatever you do.
3. Stepping out and involving yourself even though there are no guarantees and failure is possible. Nothing ventured, nothing gained!
4. Respecting authority and fulfilling your duty.
5. Choosing your friends wisely.
6. Above all, honoring Christ with your life and obedience. Serve Him first, and life takes care of itself! "But seek first his kingdom and his righteousness, and all these things will be given to you as well." (Matthew 6:33)

These are principles of life that will always work, no matter what stage of life you're in or what you're doing. Bonnie, I can't wait to see how God continues to bless your life as you live wisely and well for Him!

All My Love,
Dad

P.S. (2021): Only one life, 'twill soon be past; only what's done for Christ will last.
—C.T. Studd

         ಐ   ಐ   ಐ

R.L. Turner High School

93rd Commencement Ceremony

Class of 2005

Carrollton-Farmers Branch

Independent School District

Sunday, May 29, 2005
6:00 p.m.
University of North Texas
Denton

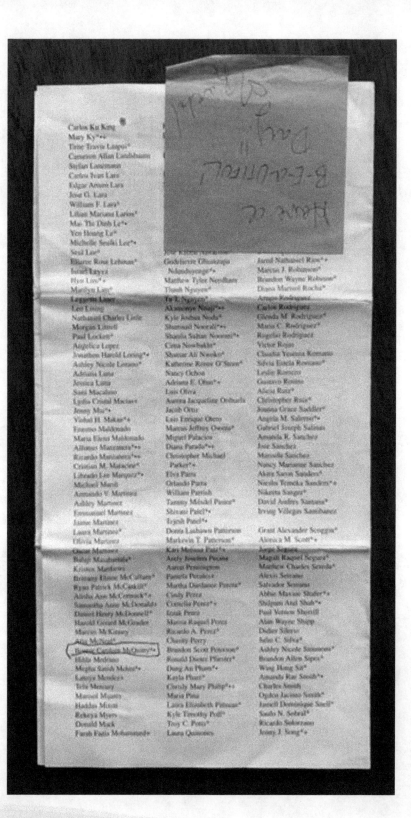

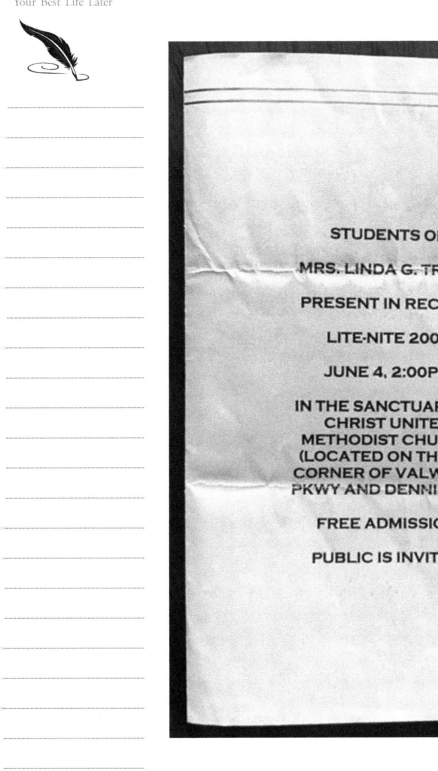

Bonnie — you were the BEST!

Dad

Presentations and Announcements
MRS. TRAUE

"No Moon"	<u>Titanic</u>
BONNIE MCQUITTY	Maury Yeston
"On My Own"	<u>Les Misérables</u>
NIKKI CAPENER	Claude-Michel Schönberg
"What'll I Do?"	
BONNIE MCQUITTY	Irving Berlin
"Softly, As I Leave You"	
NIKKI CAPENER	A. DeVita
"In His Eyes"	<u>Jekyll & Hyde</u>
SENIOR DUET	Wildhorn/Bricusse

BABY STEPS

6-21-05

Dearest Bonnie,

I find that it is disturbingly easy to "coast" in life, to get comfortable in a place and then do only what is barely necessary to maintain. The reasons for this are many. I think basic laziness accounts for most of it in me. It's hard work to move ahead in life, and sometimes I just want to take the path of least resistance!

Oddly enough, I think success causes complacency. If you attain a certain measure of it, the drive to achieve becomes diminished and you're tempted to rest on your laurels. Spiritual apathy is another cause. Our enemy wants us to be fat and sassy—i.e., complacent and self-satisfied—so that we'll fail to become and do all that God has for us.

As King David discovered when he sinned with Bathsheba, complacency of soul is a dangerous condition. It leaves us open to a variety of temptations and weakens our ability to resist them. If we don't address the problem when it crops up in our souls, God's love for us dictates that He will. But that usually means severe measures (David lost his son, his family, and his kingdom!). Far better to ride herd on our own sin-issues than to be passive and force the Lord to intervene!

So, what is to be done? Little things, faithfully. When I'm "coasting," I sometimes find myself paralyzed to act because I've concocted an unrealistic idea of what I need to do. If I've been drifting from the Word, for instance, I'm prone to assume that coming back to God means spending punishing hours reading and studying and memorizing scripture. The thought of that discourages me from doing anything, so I remain stuck.

Bonnie don't let yourself be intimidated by false requirements! Take a few baby steps toward God and be faithful. Read one verse a day and pray it faithfully back to God. That's not much but it's better than nothing! "Your word is a lamp for my feet, a light on my path." (Psalm 119:105)

God honors little stuff done faithfully. Short prayers. Small acts of obedience. Brief but sincere times in the Word. It's little stuff faithfully done that leads to the end of "coasting" and big stuff gloriously accomplished. Take some baby steps Sweetheart! They'll get you where you need to go much faster than spinning your wheels in the mud!

Love You Girl,
Dad

P.S. (2021): God said His Word is a lamp for our feet, but He never mentioned high beams.

॰৪ ৪ ৪

BOLD FAITH

June 26, 2005
(Evergreen Lodge, The Woods, Pine Cove Camp)

Dear Bonnie,

You're not here with me at Pine Cove because of your summer job selling Cutco knives. I miss you terribly, but I'm proud of you for taking on this job and working hard at it! (And you're very good at sales ... because I was your first customer, helpless before your pitch!).

I had lunch with Mario and Lynelle Zandstra today. As you probably remember, he is the president/CEO of Pine Cove Christian Camps. They have 7 children, a couple of whom are now grown. Lynelle has a debilitating, chronic disease that weakens her and often makes her feel bad. Yet despite all these pressures, responsibilities, and pains, the Zandstra's are praying about adopting another child! Not because they need more kids (obviously!), but because they've heard that there are a large group of inner-city, multi-ethnic precious kids in Dallas right now who desperately need them. Therefore, the Zandstra's are thinking of doing this unusually costly and sacrificial thing out of love for these children and in obedience to God. That's faith!

When I heard this, I secretly questioned my own heart. "Is there anything extraordinary that you're doing that can only be explained by your faith in a living God?" Sadly, I couldn't think of anything. I've grown complacent, too accustomed to the safety of the predictable, the ease of the comfortable. Faith thrives on making bold, uncommon moves. But it withers in the neglect of always choosing the easy, selfish way. "Now faith is confidence in what we hope for and assurance about what we do not see," (Hebrews 11:1)

I hope to live in an extraordinary way before I die. Mario and Lynelle have certainly given me a needed wake-up call to get busy.

Love you Bonnie!

Daddy

P.S. (2021): Stepping out in faith is always invigorating and never boring.

ജ   ജ   ജ

PEOPLE OF EXCELLENCE

June 27, 2005

Dearest Bonnie,

One of the best things about Pine Cove is the encouragement I receive observing the college-age staff in action. As you know, they serve as counsellors and leaders and workers in making this camp go and they are a servant-hearted godly, enthusiastic group. I can easily picture you among their member someday as we have talked.

The point is, young people of excellence do exist in this world, and you should never allow your life to be impacted by anyone less. The friends you choose and ultimately the husband you wed should uncompromisingly be drawn from such quality. You ARE that and you deserve that! Sometimes, we're tempted in discouraging times to lower our standards and settle for less than the best. Don't give in to that, ever! "For He will command His angels concerning you to guard you in all your ways ...." (Psalm 91:11)

God is faithful Bonnie, and you can trust Him to meet all your needs especially where friends and life mates are concerned!

Much Love,
Dad

P.S. (2021): People of excellence are one of life's great joys ... whether you know them personally or not.

౪   ౪   ౪

BIG CHANGE

July 28, 2005, Charlotte, N.C. (Airport)

Hey Sweet Bonnie,

Just talked to you on the phone about picking your mom and me up at the airport. It struck me that, in a very short time, it won't be us coming home to you, but you coming home to us! College changes lives, and not just for you who are going! There's a certain sadness that I already feel at knowing that you will be away. But at the same time, there's real joy in knowing you will have embarked on the rest of your life as an adult in this world.

I know the Lord has wonderful things in store for you, and that a bright future is a cause to celebrate. Your future is bright, and I can't wait to see all that God does in your life. Even so, there's a part of me for which you will always be my little girl!

7/28/05

I love you daddy! — thank you for being so gracious w/ your car!

Bonnie

We've had a fine time in Chattanooga, Alice and I both speaking at a conference at a big Baptist Church. I love these Baptists, but I'd never want to become one! It will be good to get (quickly) back to IBC! Just goes to show me again that God's Kingdom

261

is big and wide enough to accommodate a wide range of folks. They're calling my plane, so better run!

Love You Bon,
Dad

P.S. (2021): Don't cry because it's over. Smile because it happened.
—Dr. Seuss

    ∞   ∞   ∞

GOOD GIFTS

July 29, 2006

Dearest Bonnie,

I was so thrilled to go with you to find and buy your car this afternoon! I think it's a real good one, and I'm hoping it gives you a lot of pleasure as you tool around Texas and Arkansas in it over the next four years! "Every good and perfect gift is from above, coming down from the Father of the heavenly lights, who does not change like shifting shadows" (James 1:17). No one deserves a nice car more than you!

Love,
Dad

P.S. (2021): Life's great gifts all point to the Great Giver of Life.

෨ ෨ ෨

FORGIVENESS

August 2, 2006

Hey Bonnie,

It was a treat for me to watch you drive off to OBU on Sunday in your Acura Legend. I'm impressed by your confidence in going cross-country alone on a 4-hour trip. I guess it's really true—you're all grown up! I'm so proud of you!

Growing up is one thing, but attaining maturity is Christ in another. We achieve the former simply by breathing. But the latter is attained only by constant struggle and hard work and even then, only imperfectly. A case in point: me!

I'm meeting with a man today who's been angry with me for quite some time about issues only he knows. This has, in turn, made me angry with him! So, both of us have stayed out of each other's way, secretly nursing the conviction that "I'm right and he's wrong." Of course, the reality is that neither of us is perfect—both of us are flawed. Most likely then we're both right and both wrong at the same time!

In any case, I've been convicted of my need to forgive and be humble and seek reconciliation. That's why I set up a meeting with him today. Would you pray for me in that meeting? I know by the time you read this, that meeting will long be over. But God knows right now what you will pray then and can count it for good toward my encounter today. So, ask the Lord to tenderize both our hearts, make us each willing to hear and heal and restore our relationship.

I don't just want to be grown up. I want to be mature as well!

Love,
Dad

P.S. (2021): And forgive us our debts, as we also have forgiven our debtors ....
—Matthew 6:12

      ∽   ∽   ∽

A CLEAR CONSCIENCE

August 6, 2005

Dear Bonnie,

Thanks for praying. Though the meeting was difficult and seemingly fruitless and a great disappointment, I did my best and I'm trusting that God will yet continue to work.

This is just how life works sometimes. You pray, obey, and trust, yet there's not always a storybook ending. That doesn't mean we've failed or that God has ignored our plea. That things don't always go the way we want can have multiple possible explanations: wrong timing, stubborn human will, incomplete repentance. It can also mean simply that God is still at work and things will get better later. I am sad, but at peace because I know in my heart that I've tried.

> Above all else, guard your heart, for everything you do flows from it.

> —Proverbs 4:23

My conscience is clear, and that's the biggest thing!

Love You,
Dad

P.S. (2021): All you can do is all you can do, so do it and be at peace.

જી   જી   જી

MERCY

8-8-05 Sunday AM, my IBC office

Dear Bonnie,

I'm preaching on the forgiveness of sin today. I believe God wants us to lead lives characterized by joy, not weighed down by guilt. When people see a church where people are unburdened by grace, they may be tempted to believe that church isn't serious about sin. I like to think it's just the opposite. They're so serious about sin that they've addressed it God's way which is the most powerful way. What is that way?

> You can't whitewash your sins and get by with it;
> you find mercy by admitting and leaving them.
> —Proverbs 29:13 (Message)

Love You!
Dad,

P.S. (2021): Grace is the only efficient cleanser for sin.

℘   ℘   ℘

EMBARKING

August 18, 2005

Dear Sweet Bonnie,

As I write this last entry in a journal I began for you 19 years ago, I am so proud of you! (I think I've written that last phrase 50 times in these pages!). You've matured into a smart, capable, beautiful, godly young woman, and I'm honored to be your dad! As your mom and I launch you into the world (by taking you to college) tomorrow, we do so with the bittersweet realization that, though you're taking a huge step toward independence which will alter the dynamics of our home, you're also embarking on the adventure of your life with every prospect of success and happiness and fruitfulness for the Lord.

Since the day I watched you come (via C-section!) into the world, I've always had the sense that you are special to God, to us, and to the world. Now I get to be a spectator of the story God is telling through your future. I know you love Jesus, and that your trust is in Him. Follow Him always, honor Him in all things, and He will honor you!

Last night Julie and Gordon were over, and we all offered you some advice. That was probably a bit overwhelming! If so, I want to reiterate a couple of ideas that I believe will be important for you not just in college, but in life.

1. Be your own best self that God made you to be and never worry about comparing yourself to others. You honor Christ best by being who He made you to be, trusting Him to use you in ways unique to your personality and giftedness. There will always be people around us who are more intelligent,

beautiful, talented, etc., but do not be intimidated. The special contribution of personality and love and talent that is Bonnie McQuitty is one of a kind and unique in all the world. Rest in what God did when He made you and be who you are!

2. Don't procrastinate! The world is full of people with great potential who never fulfil it because they just "never got around to it." Whether it's work or studies or relationships or spiritual relationships, this one imperative will change your life if you make it a discipline from now on—DO IT NOW.

3. Hang in there! Bonnie, nothing worthwhile is ever easy. Success, therefore, always carries the price tag of your perseverance. You can do what is required of you always. Remember that! With God's help, nothing that you're called to is beyond your grasp if you refuse to give up. Many times, you will fail on the first or fourth attempt. But hang in there. The prize ultimately goes to those who refuse to quit!

4. Treat people right and expect the same in return. When we boil life down to its essence, we have our faith, family, and friends. That means that relationships are fundamental to happiness. So, in building relationship, be kind and truthful and loyal and forgiving and a servant. And from others, expect the same. Never settle for abuse or disloyalty from those around you. Love and forgive but don't embrace as close friends or trust those who have chronically demonstrated their unworthiness for such. Be gentle but be wise!

5. The last thing is the plaque that hangs in our kitchen at home.

"Pray hard, work hard, trust God."

Bonnie, that about says it all! You do those 3 things, and I see nothing but great things ahead for you! And since you're already doing them, I am confident that, as great as your young past has been, your future is even greater. I am humbled and honored to be your biggest fan as you embark on life's great adventure!

All My Love Forever,
Dad

P.S. (2021): The best for God's faithful children is always yet to be.

૪૦ ૪૦ ૪૦

Part 4

A Journal For Jonathan Andrew

30 entries beginning May 31, 1989, to Sep 5, 2007

The father of a righteous man has great joy,
he who has a wise son delights I him.
—Proverbs 23:24

5-31-89

Dearest Jonathan,
Welcome to the world, welcome to my life, son. You are greatly loved and appreciated — a precious gift from God, a long-expected privilege.

You arrived at 4:10 P.M. on Sun, May 21, 1989 after putting your Mom through 17 hours' labor! A strapping 9' 13⊙ and 21" long, you were absolutely beautiful: so big, so healthy, so you. When I saw you emerge, big hands and stout body and all, I just began to laugh out loud! I was going to preach on Mk 3:20-35, "Getting Ready for Rejection"—but your arrival kept me out of church. All Irving Bible Church rejoices at your birth (brace yourself: as a P.K., you have about 300 parents—not just 2...!).

You have come into a troubled world of spiritual warfare, sent by God to be a soldier for His Kingdom. I have dedicated you to this end that you might become mighty on earth (Ps 112), a strong follower of the King, a spiritually

DESTINY

5-31-89

Dearest Jonathan,

Welcome to the world, welcome to my life, son. You are greatly loved and appreciated—a precious gift from God, a long-expected privilege.

You arrived at 4:10 P.M. on Sun., May 21, 1989, after putting your Mom through 17 hours of labor! A strapping 9 lb. 13 oz. and 21" long, you were absolutely beautiful: so big, so healthy, so you. When I saw you emerge, big hands and stout body and all, I just began to laugh out loud! I was going to preach on Mark 3:20-35, "Getting Ready for Rejection"—but your arrival kept me out of church. All Irving Bible Church rejoices at your birth (brace yourself as a P.K., you have about 300 parents—not just 2...!).

You have come into a troubled world of spiritual warfare, sent by God to be a soldier for His Kingdom. I have dedicated you to this end that you might become mighty on this earth according to Psalm 112:1-2:

> Blessed are those who fear the Lord, who find great delight in his commands. Their children will be mighty in the land; the generation of the upright will be blessed.

As a strong follower of the King, you will become a spiritually powerful man of God whose life will make a difference in eternity. The life ahead of you will be an incredibly exciting adventure as you learn to know the God who made you, and to use the resources He's given you through faith. Heartache? Yes, there will be some. Suffering? Surely. But never despair. The battle is won; victory is already yours in Jesus. Hope will carry you through.

Jonathan, you are my son, but you are not mine. You are a sacred trust, placed in my care for a short time of training and equipping for a higher service. Never forget your destiny! I won't.

All My Love,
Dad

P.S. (2021): Through faith in God's promises, parents see the potential in their children to become spiritually mighty in the land.

જી   જી   જી

TRUST

2-22-90

Hi Jonathan!

The morals of our world seem to disintegrate a little bit more every day. I don't know what kind of world will greet you as you step into adulthood, but I believe it will be quite pagan. Son, you may deal with blatant persecution and rejection which is only latent today. If that's the case, I want you to remember that this life is temporary at best. We are pilgrims travelling to a better land. Sometimes, the longing for that better land is all we really have to keep us going. But it's enough.

When all is swirling around you and you feel discouraged and intimidated by sin's viciousness, remember Ps. 84:11-12:

> For the Lord God is a sun and shield; the Lord bestows favor and honor; no good thing does He withhold from those whose walk is blameless. O Lord Almighty blessed is the man who trusts in you!

Love,
Dad

P.S. (2021): No matter how hazardous the path, trust in God protects His children on the way.

೮೧   ೮೧   ೮೧

THE WORD OF GOD

8-28-91

Dear Jonathan,

You're a strapping 2 ½ year-old so full of curiosity and energy that at times you fairly burst. You're obviously a natural athlete. And you're mischievous. All marks of a person who will one day be a leader and make a mark. I can't wait to see what significant purpose God has for you to play in this world!

I want you always to have an anchor in your life, Jonathan—a reference point to define your values and give you direction. That's the Word of God. Learn to delight in God's ways as revealed in The Book, and you'll never be lost as are so many poor misguided wasters of life in this world!

Remember 2 Peter 1:20-21 when your faith needs bolstering:

No prophecy of scripture came about by the prophet's own interpretation. For prophecy never had its origin in the will of man, but men spoke from God as they were carried along by the Holy Spirit.

God is smarter than we are, and we're never smarter than when we listen to Him and do it His way!

Martin Luther said it this way:

Oh! How great and glorious [a] thing it is to have before one: the Word of God! ... He who loses sight of [it] falls into despair; he follows only the disorderly tendency of his heart and of the world's vanity, which lead him on to destruction.

The history of the world is a case in point of Luther's last line. But you and I don't have to learn the hard way. Thank God.

Love Always,
Dad

P.S. (2021): Direct me in the path of your commands, for there I find delight.
—Psalm 119:35 (NIV).

છ   છ   છ

SUCCESS

1/8/92

Hi Jonathan,

Last night at the dinner table I was reading about the prophet Elijah. I said to you, "Jon–can you say 'Elijah'?" You scrunched your nose up and pronounced with hilarious conviction, "Me no rike 'Lijah!'" You are a joy to be with–so positive, so fun-loving, so strong. God has made you special.

Special destiny however requires a special vision, a special perspective. One like that in Peter's consciousness following the incident in Luke 5:1-11. All night Peter had fished w/ no success. That was a blow. Financially, it meant Peter's family would struggle even more to make ends meet. But emotionally, it meant Peter would have to deal w/ the demons of failure, self-doubt, worthlessness, and embarrassment. "Others hit the jackpot w/ the nets last night; why didn't (couldn't?) I?"

Jonathan, you and I are subject to the very human craving to have success. We long for the respect of others, for self-respect, for a sense of significance and by the way, making good money wouldn't hurt! I relate to Peter's discouragement. I've known a lot of "failures" like Peter's. That's what amazes me in this account. Jesus, in sensing Peter's blue mood, decides to dispel it once and for all. How will Jesus cure Peter of the mad pursuit of worldly "success"–the accolades of people and money to spare? How will He relieve Peter of the craving to do and have all? By letting him!

At the very moment when Peter had all he had longed for–nets bursting, excitement, a legendary catch, a huge financial windfall– he let it go. Having finally grasped the prize, he relinquished it. Why? Because it was worthless? No. Because in that instant

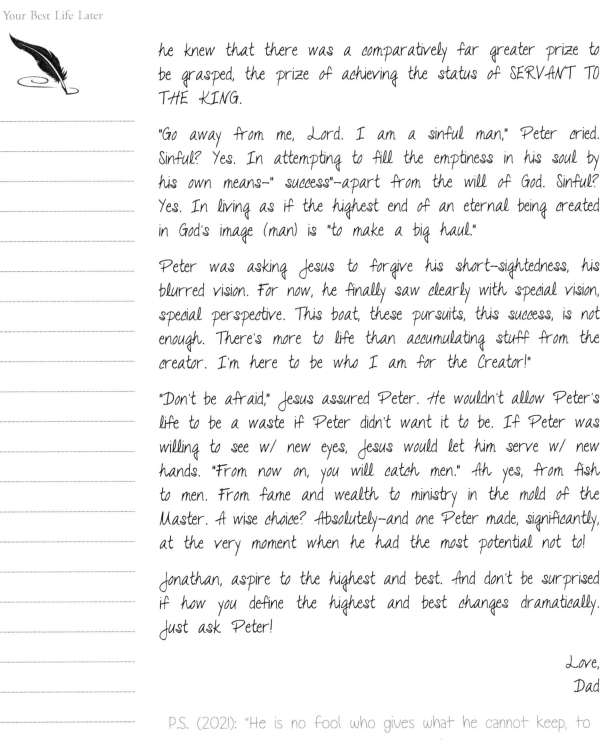

he knew that there was a comparatively far greater prize to be grasped, the prize of achieving the status of SERVANT TO THE KING.

"Go away from me, Lord. I am a sinful man," Peter cried. Sinful? Yes. In attempting to fill the emptiness in his soul by his own means—" success"—apart from the will of God. Sinful? Yes. In living as if the highest end of an eternal being created in God's image (man) is "to make a big haul."

Peter was asking Jesus to forgive his short-sightedness, his blurred vision. For now, he finally saw clearly with special vision, special perspective. This boat, these pursuits, this success, is not enough. There's more to life than accumulating stuff from the creator. I'm here to be who I am for the Creator!"

"Don't be afraid," Jesus assured Peter. He wouldn't allow Peter's life to be a waste if Peter didn't want it to be. If Peter was willing to see w/ new eyes, Jesus would let him serve w/ new hands. "From now on, you will catch men." Ah yes, from fish to men. From fame and wealth to ministry in the mold of the Master. A wise choice? Absolutely—and one Peter made, significantly, at the very moment when he had the most potential not to!

Jonathan, aspire to the highest and best. And don't be surprised if how you define the highest and best changes dramatically. Just ask Peter!

Love,
Dad

P.S. (2021): "He is no fool who gives what he cannot keep, to gain what he cannot lose.
—Jim Eliot, Shadow of the Almighty

80 80 80

WAITING ON GOD

4-9-92

Dear Jonathan,

As in any journey, life has its seasons when the going is tough. Sometimes, those difficult stretches seem interminable. Kind of like how it was for the Hebrew people when they were shackled in slavery by the Egyptians, crying out to God for relief. Same thing for Moses their contemporary—seemingly "shelved" in the desert babysitting sheep and wondering if his once-promising future held anything more than sand in his soup and numbing boredom.

You'll come into seasons of life like that. When you do, don't panic. It's not an aberration but an education. Two things to remember in the hard times:

1. What you learn while you wait is why you wait. That's why it's foolish to resent hard times. Resentment closes our hearts to God's voice, retards our progress, and delays God's freedom to deliver. Resenting hard times locks us into them. Only actually embracing them makes them our benefactor!

2. While you're waiting, God is working. Here are the Hebrews suffering and Moses vegetating and both parties crying out to God. Yet Exodus 3:7-8 says, "I have seen the misery of my people ... I have heard them crying out ... and I am concerned about their suffering. So, I have come down to rescue them."

While Moses and the people were suffering, God was acting. In bringing Moses to the Hebrews, the Lord answered both their needs. So, when the going gets tough Jonathan, don't give

up! God sees, God hears, and God cares. In due time, you will experience His deliverance.

All My Love,
Dad

P.S. (2021): Trials crowd our lives like friends bearing gifts that only by faith we can receive.

"When all kinds of trials and temptations crowd into your lives my brothers, don't resent them as intruders, but welcome them as friends! Realize that they come to test your faith and to produce in you the quality of endurance. But let the process go on until that endurance is fully developed, and you will find you have become men of mature character with the right sort of independence."

–James 1:2-4, JB Phillips

ಬ   ಬ   ಬ

GRIEF

7-15-92

My Dear Jonathan,

I came into my office early this morning and found a couple of letters waiting for me. The first was from the Dallas Chinese Bible Church. We'd sent them flowers as a memorial to five from their youth group who were killed in a blazing van accident. Nine others were injured. They were grateful for our sympathy.

The other letter was from a former pastor (E.W.) who now attends our church. He filled 3 typed pages with his despair at many personal failures and a sense that his life and future are worthless. As I sensed his grief and pondered the heartache of the Chinese Bible Church people, I remembered other griefs I'm dealing with:

1. D & J C lost their baby and face an uncertain future due to D's cancer.
2. S is a good friend of mine married to T ... a sweet girl tragically afflicted by anorexia. They've not had intimate relations due to her struggle and there is no end in sight. Recently, my friend broke down and visited a prostitute—a mistake for which he instantly confessed to his wife and God and others. But he had to leave home, and I'm trying to deal with both their heartaches and find a way to get them back together.

Other griefs on my heart this morning:

1. M R is an aged, godly woman who is in the hospital dying.
2. A major political Convention is in session and spotlighting candidates who boast of their commitment to abortion.

3. Bloody civil war is in session in Sarajevo, Yugoslavia. Thousands of civilians are starving and being killed.

Jonathan, this world is a stage upon which profound good and evil forces, seen and unseen, are playing out their drama. You and I are not only spectators of this spectacle. Often, we are compelled to be participants in the play, sometimes unwilling and always without recourse.

What do we do with grief? When it really hurts, where do we turn? To God. He alone can make sense of this mess. In their letter, the Chinese Bible Church people quoted Psalm 66:10-12,

> For you, O God, tested us; you refined us like silver ... we went through fire and water, but you brought is to a place of abundance.

Notice the sequence: agony, then abundance. Notice the purpose: testing. Notice the assurance: "You, O God." Life is not a capricious stage full of sound and fury, signifying nothing. It is God's proving ground for a forever people.

Never despair, then, Jonathan. No matter how bad it gets, rest in the Lord. Weeping in the night must become, in His good and powerful hands, joy in the morning.

Love,
Dad

P.S. (2021): Weeping may tarry for the night, but joy comes with the morning.
—Psalm 30:5, ESV

ଉ   ଉ   ଉ

THE PROBLEM OF EVIL

3-11-93

Dearest Jonathan,

Life holds a great many disappointments, injustice, and even tragedies. Bad things regularly happen to good people. And that raises a lot of questions about God.

"If God is all-powerful, He must not be good, or He would stop evil. If God is all-good, He must not be all-powerful, or He could stop evil."

The fallacy w/ these statements is in their assumption that the way things are is the way things always will be. They are not. The Bible is the story of how things are going to be different when God someday evens the score. Righteousness rewarded and evil punished are the great bulwark hopes of our hearts.

And as to God's goodness vs. His Power, "... you, O Lord, are strong and you, O Lord, are loving." (Psalm 62:11) Believe it, Jonathan. It's true—and the future will show it.

Love,
Dad

P.S. (2021): It's foolish to criticize the Author of history before reading the final chapter of His Book.

෫ ෫ ෫

OWNING YOUR VALUES

4-29-94

Dear Jonathan,

It's been a joy for me to watch you grow this last year. Though you're not even quite 5, I can already see that God has gifted you intellectually and athletically. You've also got a great sense of humor and spiritual tenderness. I'm torn between excitement to see what God will do with your life and the reluctance to see you grow up so fast! But I must remember you're not mine, but God's, and my job is not to cling to you but to launch you. You're already crawling up on the launch pad!

I played basketball yesterday w/ a group of high school guys. I was impressed w/ one of them in particular. He was confident without being cocky. He was friendly while competing fiercely. He was, though young, a real man in his own right.

That young guy, Jonathan, made me think of you. My greatest joy in you will come as I see you become your own man holding your own convictions and your own sense of servanthood to others. I will rejoice to see you undertake personal disciplines that you have decided are worthwhile and ministry concerns that you have received from the Lord. In short, I will rejoice to see you come into your own as a dynamic leader—knowing who you are, why you're alive, and determined to get there.

In that process and beyond, know that you'll always have a loyal fan over in the shadows, cheering you on. That's me!

All My Love,
Dad

P.S. (2021): "I press toward the mark for the prize of the high calling of God in Christ Jesus."
—Phil. 3:14, KJV

ဆ ဆ ဆ

Civil War brings out brotherly care

Leg wounds keep devoted sibling busy

A.C. GREENE

TEXAS SKETCHES

Tom Ellis and his younger brother Henry, of Lancaster, were in the 6th Texas Cavalry during the Civil War.

In July 1863, Tom — who had already spent eight months in a hospital in Mississippi — was wounded in Georgia and survived three hours lying in the hot sun shot in both legs.

Henry Ellis was told of his brother's injury and with the aid of Tom Dixon, another Texan, went back and loaded Tom and another wounded soldier onto a train. Then Henry and Tom Dixon ran to a spring to supply the wounded with water, and while they were gone, the train pulled out with the wounded men aboard.

A freight train followed the first train and Henry and companion jumped it, only to be ordered off by the conductor. After they were ordered "for the last time" to get off the freight train, Henry said, "I have a wounded brother in the train ahead with no one to attend to him, I am going to stay on this train and overtake him or die in the attempt." He stayed on.

They came to a large camp where the main hospital had been moved near a medical college, and a civilian came alongside the train calling for "a man name of Ellis."

He told Henry where to find his brother and while the surgeons were waiting for Tom to die, Henry cooled his wounded legs by carrying water from a spring and keeping a stream running on them day and night for 10 days.

Seeing that Tom would not die and his brother would not allow his limbs to be amputated, the doctors began treating him. Henry was allowed to stay with him for 30 days but he had to help care for the other wounded men.

Several months later Tom was sent to Jackson, Miss., on crutches. From Canton, Miss., he wrote for Henry to come and take him into the country where he could "get something to eat."

Henry made friends with an Uncle Jake Harmon who took the wounded Tom in, and there he stayed until the war closed. The brothers returned to Lancaster, and each lived well into his 80s.

In 1924 a friend reported Tom's legs kept him "from being as agile as a young man of his years might otherwise be, but Henry is as sprightly as a man who is all skin and bones is likely to be."

A.C. Greene is an author and Texas historian who lives in Salado. His newest book is 900 Miles on the Butterfield Trail.

10/16/94

THE GREAT CAUSES

10-17-94

Dear Jonathan,

I was touched in reading of Henry Ellis' sacrificial care of his older brother in the Civil War. Heroism need not be well-known or even grand in scale to be profound. One man looking out for his brother at all costs is as admirable as riding a space capsule or catching a winning touchdown pass-or is it? No, it's far more admirable!

God, family, and freedom-these are the great causes worthy of your heart and your sacrifice. Though in pursuing them you may remain unsung by the glitter-eyed world, you will be a hero to God, and of course, to

Your Loving Dad,
EAM

P.S. (2021): Stand for something worthy, or you'll fall for anything appealing!

"Finally, brethren, whatsoever things are true, whatsoever things are honest, whatsoever things are just, whatsoever things are pure, whatsoever things are lovely, whatsoever things are of good report; if there be any virtue, and if there be any praise, think on these things."

–Phil. 4:8, KJV

SABBATH

11-7-96

Dear Jonathan,

The "busy-ness" of life can be a great thief. We're taught to value the Puritan work-ethic and to push ourselves to excellence. Fine. But we're not taught to value the Scriptural balance to hard work known as "sabbath." Sabbath is ceasing, stopping, desisting. It is part of a universal life-rhythm established by God who created the world in 6 days and then "rested."

If we will follow His pattern, life will stay meaningful. We will remember that everything of value begins and ends by God's grace, not my effort, and we will therefore be able to relax and "smell the roses." There's more to life than work, effort, and achievement. There's mystery, wonder, and appreciation. Don't forfeit the latter in pursuit of the former! Keep sabbath. Love life.

Because I Love You,
Dad

P.S. (2021): The sabbath was made for man, and not
man for the sabbath.
—Mark 2:27 (KJV)

෨ ෨ ෨

STRONG IN THE LORD

Mon. June 2, 1997

Dear Jonathan,

Life can be a bewildering blur of appointments, duties, longings, disappointments, and joy— and if you don't have some "landmarks" by which to orient yourself, you can become lost, confused, and disillusioned. Skillful living is certainly a complex ability which takes many years to master. But it's also a fairly simple proposition. God says to prioritize certain values, and life for you will be good. A list of such values is given in Ephesians 6:10-18 (see my P.S. (2021) at end of this entry) in the context of spiritual warfare.

Satan does not want your life to be fruitful, but frustrating and empty, a futile tale of spun wheels and wasted opportunities. He is your enemy. Fight him! But fight smart by keeping these simple values your top priority:

1. Truth: Face the truth, tell the truth. Seek the truth. Love the truth. Don't tell lies or soon you'll be living a lie (which is the same as believing a lie).
2. Righteousness: Do right, period. Don't cheat, fudge, compromise, or rationalize. If you do right, the power of a clear conscience will pervade your soul.
3. Gospel: let the drama of a loving, dying, and rising God capture your imagination so completely that your own story becomes a subset of this grand story—God's story—that is playing out for eternity. Christ's love for you is really all you need to understand to become a hero yourself.
4. Faith: put yourself in God's hands, step out for His glory, calculate the risks—but then take them! Never let your soul

shrivel by hunkering down into the security of the seen. See with the eyes of faith and what you perceive will become reality.

5. Salvation: live out your deliverance from evil's power by redeeming each day for what is worthy. Eternal life is a present possession, the having of which should color every word you speak, every decision you make, and every attitude you demonstrate.

6. Word: God speaks! How foolish to ignore His voice! How wise to listen, learn, and obey.

7. Pray: talk much w/ God, for that is how you know Him. And knowing Him—well, isn't that the point?

I love you so much, Jonathan! Put on this armor, and you'll not only be my champion, but God's.

Dad

P.S. (2021): A good life flows from godly priorities.

"Finally, be strong in the Lord and in His mighty power. Put on the full armor of God, so that you can take your stand against the devil's schemes. For our struggle is not against flesh and blood, but against the rulers, against the authorities, against the powers of this dark world and against the spiritual forces of evil in the heavenly realms. Therefore, put on the full armor of God, so that when the day of evil comes, you may be able to stand your ground, and after you have done everything, to stand. Stand firm then, with the belt of truth buckled around your waist, with the breastplate of righteousness in place, and with your feet fitted with the readiness that comes from the gospel of peace. In addition to all this, take up the shield of faith, with which you can extinguish all the flaming arrows of the evil one.

Take the helmet of salvation and the sword of the Spirit, which is the word of God. And pray in the Spirit on all occasions with all kinds of prayers and requests."

–Ephesians 6:10–18

ဆ   ဆ   ဆ

JUDGING

Aug 24, 1999

Dearest Jonathan,

I see that I have been grossly negligent in my journaling for you. I will endeavor to improve. Sorry! It has been a busy couple of years, much of it coming from you! You have become a star athlete, playing on Coppell's Mustang-League All-Star team two years running. You're now playing in a Fall-ball select team (quite an honor just to be invited!). You are a fierce competitor. When Coach Bruce handed out different kinds of candy to symbolize each of you players at the end of the season, he gave you "Hot Tamales"-commemorating your now-famous temper. You're a great pitcher/ catcher/infielder. It's obvious to me not only from your natural talent, but also your internal drive, that you will excel at whatever you choose to do.

That's why I urge you always to choose the highest and best. Because you are gifted with high intelligence, physical ability, and personality, you will do easily what comes at great price to others. That is not justification for slacking off. God has given you much; He therefore expects much from you. Let your own best be always your standard. You will be tempted to rest on besting those around you. That is not good enough if it is not the best of Jonathan McQuitty.

Someone has wisely remarked that the unexamined life is not worth living. Examine constantly! Am I being faithful? Is my focus on true priorities? Am I honoring the Lord in what I seek? Will I be glad at the values I have chosen when the day of my death arrives? Do I have a pure heart? Am I giving life my best shot?

We had a good time at Pine Cone Family Camp last month—especially playing table tennis. So, we made it a priority to get ourselves a table at home. We found one on sale at Sears and have been happily banging away for a week now. Your Papa Eric came over this weekend (an avid player) and you beat him 21-19 in the first game you played him. I know because I kept score!

I took your older sister Julie to Texas A&M last weekend. My first to leave home. I have shed a few tears! I know that when my first boy leaves home someday (you!), it will be very hard on me. I do love you so. Yet, I want you to go far and high, and I must let go sometime. But not yet!

My dad came over from Shreveport to preach for me this weekend. I have this huge struggle when I'm around Eric. I love him, but he annoys me in a myriad of ways. I hate to admit this (to my own son, no less), but when he leaves, I always breathe a sigh of relief. I won't go into the details of what irritates me. It is far more an indictment of my own selfishness and impatience than anything he does. I just mention it because I'm wondering if, in this father-son relationship, some of this pressure is inevitable. I hope not, like it's some sort of separation/turf-making ritual that cannot be avoided. But on the slim chance that this is the case, I want to apologize to you in advance, Jon. If I'm insensitive, boorish, selfish, or otherwise embarrassing or annoying to you or your family, please forgive me. Know that years ago, I anticipated that I might do this to you and have suffered already for it! Try as I might to avoid, I realize I may cause you to shake your head or secretly roll your eyes. If it's any comfort, know that I once was wont to do the same. Perhaps you will find it in you to be merciful by the thought that you too will likely have a son someday.

As this eventuality has stricken me with my own need to show patience, perhaps the prospect of facing the same circumstance will help you cut me some slack.

I am now and will always be your biggest fan.

And Loving Father,
Dad

P.S. (2021): Do not judge, or you too will be judged. For in the same way you judge others, you will be judged, and with the measure you use, it will be measured to you.
—Matthew 7:1 (NIV).

℘   ℘   ℘

For Jonathan (an assignment I gave you
on the occasion of an altercation
you had with Jeffrey).   12/11/99

① How did Eliab treat David?
         He treated david very bad
because he accused david of coming
just to watch the war. He treated
him disrespectfully and did not
care about him.

② How should Eliab have treated David?
    Eliab should have said thank
you for the food row you did if
run and watch your sheep. He should
have been encouraging and
build david up and not to tear
him down.

③ What can big brothers learn from this story?
         to treat their little brothers
or sisters nicely and with as much
respect as you get from your parents
because you are older and could
hurt them easier.

LEADERSHIP

12–11–99

For Jonathan: an assignment I gave you on the occasion of an altercation you had with your kid brother Jeffrey!).

1. How did Eliab treat David? "He treated david [sic] very bad [sic] because he accused David of coming just to wach [sic] the war. He treated him disrespectfully and did not care about him."

2. How should Eliab have treated David? "Eliab should have said thank you for the food now you better run and watch your sheep. He should have been encouraging and build [sic] David up and not to tore [sic] him down."

3. What can big brothers learn from this story? "To treat their little brothers or sisters nicely and with as much respect as you get from your parents because you are older and could hurt them easier."

Love,
Dad

P.S. (2021): Anyone who wants to be first must be the very last, and the servant of all.
—Mark 9:35 (NIV)

    ഒ   ഒ   ഒ

LEGACY

2-15-00

Hi Jonathan,

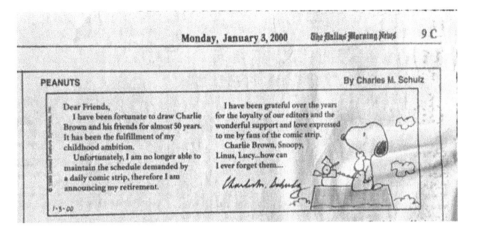

Here is the last strip drawn by Charles Schulz. He died a little over one month later. He'd drawn "Peanuts" for 50 years! I'm sure that sounds like an eternity to you. But when Schulz was a young man, I'm sure 50 years would have sounded like an eternity, too.

But for him, it came and went—quickly. So, will it do for you too Jonathan (I know it has for me!).

Schulz was a man of faith and integrity. Through a lifetime of hard and consistently excellent work, he created a legacy of wisdom and good will, which will long outlive him. He lived well, then he died. Now he enjoys an everlasting reward. I record this only to challenge you to live well too. Invest in faithfulness. Remember that all "this" will come to an end someday. Make each day count by daily praying, "Teach us to number our days right, that we may gain a heart of wisdom." (Psalm 90:12)

Love,
Dad

P.S. (2021): He is wise who seeks to use time well, rather than slow it down or regret its passing.

ର   ର   ର

GIVING BACK

2-18-01

Dear Jonathan,

You're really coming into your own in these days, and man, am I proud of you! I'm thinking of you in your 2nd year at Barbara Bush Jr High, now 7th grade. You went out for football, made the team, and started at QB and CB for the B-team. You threw touchdown passes, ran for touchdowns, made great tackles—all in the first season you ever played the game! Then, you made the basketball team and you're starting guard on the B-team there as well shooting 3's and making beautiful lay-ups. But sports aren't all. You're doing well in your classes, getting along with so many friends, and keeping us laughing with your impressions and "dialects." Not only that, but you're involved in youth group. Last night, I took you home after you spent 3 hours practicing your electric guitar w/ Joey W. You'll be playing with the band Wednesday!

Jon, you have great gifts. But best of all, you have a huge heart to drive those gifts. Use it all for Jesus, my son, and you will fly higher than you can ever imagine. I can't wait to see you up there in the stratosphere!

All My Love,
Dad

P.S. (2021): From everyone who has been given much, much will be demanded; and from the one who has been entrusted with much, much more will be asked.
—Luke 12:48

ဆ ဆ ဆ

IBC Youth Group variety show at the Irving Arts Center featured the whole McQuitty family performing a song from "The Sound of Music..."

So Long, Farewell

Key: C 9

Children.
There's a sad sort of clanging
From the clock in the hall
And the bells in the steeple, too.

And up in the nurs'ry, an absurd little bird
Is popping out to say, "Coo-coo."

Regretfully they tell us
But firmly they compel us
To say good-bye to you.

So long, farewell. Auf wiedersehn, good-night.

Elizabeth. I hate to go and leave this pretty sight.

Children. So long, farewell. Auf wiedersehn, adieu

Jonathon. Adieu, adieu to yieu and yieu and yieu.

Children. So long, farewell. Au' voir, auf wiedersehn

Julie. I'd like to stay and taste my first champagne

Julie. (Spoken) Yes?

Andy. No!

Children. So long, farewell. Auf wiedersehn, good-bye

Bonny. I leave and heave a sigh and say good-bye

Brigitta. Good-bye. I'm glad to go, I cannot tell a lie

Julie

PRAISING GOD

9-20-02

Dearest Jonathan,

I've been driving you to school every day at Ranchview where you are an 8th grader. Since your B-team football squad practices at 7:15 AM, you have to be out earlier than the bus runs, so I get to deliver you and all your stuff each morning. You carry all your books in your pack since the lockers are "too far," that plus your lunch & practice gear makes each morning like "moving day." You're quite a cool kid, too, with your bleached locks, necklaces, and "Chucks" with bright red shoelaces.

And how much you are achieving!

You start at QB for offence, at safety on defense. You're smart and scrappy and tough and a real competitor! I love to watch you play! Your grades are good (though we're trying to see you pull up that math a bit!). And you're really digging in at church. You play in the Middle school worship band, take guitar lessons from Joey W, and have started your own band called "SAR"—Some Assembly Required. I picked you up at IBC last night after you all rehearsed a new song that you wrote and sang for the group, "Calvary."

> You are a phenomenal young man, greatly gifted with world class potential.

> I am so proud of you!

> I thought of you as I read from Psalm 67:5-7 this morning.

Let all the peoples praise you, O God ... God, our own God, shall bless us ... and all the ends of the earth shall fear Him.

Why does God gift and bless you, Jon? Why does He prosper and help you? For your own joy and fulfillment, yes. But there's more. Our lives ultimately are not about us, but Him. In the final analysis, what matters in not that you were a talented, successful person, but that your success and blessing brought praise and glory to God. It's not about us. It's about Him. Ironically, the quicker and more completely we accept and live that truth, the happier and more fruitful we will be.

So, Jonathan, love the Lord first with all your heart and do all that you do for His glory and have a great time always!

All My Love,
Dad

P.S. (2021): Lord, make my way prosperous not that I achieve high station, but that my life be an exhibit to the value of knowing God.
—Jim Eliot, Through Gates of Splendor

ဆ   ဆ   ဆ

FATHERS

May 4, 2004

Dear Jon,

As you can tell by my long hiatus from writing, it's been a busy couple of years. But I'm not going to blow smoke. We do what we choose to do, and my priorities have not been what they should be. I've allowed work and the "urgent" demands of life to supersede the important and lasting things. I've noticed that pattern a lot in my life. So, I'm constantly adjusting direction to stay on course having learned that the last adjustment is never the last adjustment!

Well, I'm back and trying to be disciplined about matters that matter. And I want you to know—you matter a great deal to me—always have and always will.

You've turned into a man almost overnight in these 2 years. Transferred from Turner to Ranchview after a not-good experience playing basketball. Continued your band "Some Assembly Required" and played several cool venues (you're going to The Door in Deep Ellum in Dallas next month!). You've developed great friendships w/ your band guys, and of course with your old-time buds Chris and Tim. And now that we've just joined Hackberry C.C, you've lit up to playing golf.

You should know that one of the main reasons I took the plunge on that membership was to get a way to spend more time with you and Jeff while you're in HS. You're becoming your own man, and I understand that means a certain amount of pulling away from parents, especially dad.

But I want you always to know I'm all in for you becoming all you can be. I'm not here to hold you back but boost you up. There may be some rocky times ahead (fathers and sons, you know), but in advance I'm keen on you knowing that I'm taking steps to strengthen our relationship. God has given you great gifts, Jon, and I know He has great plans for you!

All My Love,
Dad

P.S. (2021): Lord, give me firmness without hardness, steadfastness without dogmatism, love without weakness.
—Jim Eliot, Through Gates of Splendor

ဢ ဢ ဢ

WEALTH

1-18-05

Dear Jon,

This morning at our little breakfast devotional, we read these words from Proverbs 22:4, "Humility and the fear of the Lord bring wealth and honor and life." (You were pretty bleary-eyed, so I wasn't sure you took it all in!). A similar sentiment is expressed earlier in Proverbs 21:21, "He who pursues righteousness and love finds life, prosperity and honor." This is so fundamental, so vital! Combining these two verses gives us this equation:

HUMILITY+THE FEAR OF THE LORD+RIGHTEOUSNESS+LOVE

=

WEALTH (PROSPERITY)+HONOR+LIFE

For one as gifted as you, Jon, it will often seem that life and wealth can be obtained in other ways. Are there not a multitude of wealthy and "honored" people in our world who walk with arrogance and mock God? Sure, there are. But their wealth is earth-bound, and their "honor" is the shallow adulation of mainly envious people. On the other hand, everlasting respect and blessing and honor comes from the Sovereign of the Universe, grants profound peace, and lasts forever.

God has given you many talents, and the temptation to "settle" for less than God's best (because it's better than most people's best) will be strong. Fight it, son.

Stay humble.
Fear God.
Walk in righteousness.

Love well.
The best is yet to be!

Love You,
Dad

P.S. (2021): God gives the most precious things in life, not to
those who seek them, but to those who seek Him.
—unattributed

ଚ୍ଚ   ଚ୍ଚ   ଚ୍ଚ

OUR DREAMS

March 9, 2005 4:30 A.M.

Dear Jon,

Last night I was driving you home from band practice at J.R.'s house and I asked you some questions about the future—your hopes and dreams concerning the band and your ultimate career. You told me you hope that all the guys will go to college in this area so that the band can stay together. "I'm not doing all this work for nothing" is how you put it! You said you'd like to make a career of music-recording with the band, forming your own record-company (and doing the graphic art for the album covers yourself!), and perhaps even finding time to be a worship leader as well. I am so excited to hear what God is putting in your heart to pursue in life. I know he has gifted you extensively. It's just fun to see His plan unfold in your life!

Rarely do our dreams and plans come true in exactly the way we imagined. So, I suspect that the Lord will introduce some twists and turns into your plan as you go along. But go with it, Jon. He is able to do exceedingly, abundantly above what you can even ask or think, and will do so as you honor Him. Someday I predict you'll look back with amazement to see that God's idea for your life was even more wonderful than you ever dared dream!

Know this, I am all for you in whatever you choose, in however things work out. Rich and famous or not, what matters ultimately is that you were faithful to God and did your best to love Him and others well. Whatever I can do to support and encourage you in that quest will be my honor and privilege!

Much Love,
Dad

P.S. (2021): Shoot for the moon. Even if you miss, you'll land
among the stars.
—Norman Vincent Peale

Dr. Andrew McQuitty
2230 Clearspring Dr. N
Irving, TX 75063

Dear Dad,

Service was awsome today. You told us all
to write these thank you cards to people who
have obscure jobs. I couldn't help it but to
write it to you. You took a step down tonight,
you told everyone that just bc your the guy
who's on stage, it doesn't make you more important than all the "little people." I've always
admired your humbleness. The main reason I try
to be humble in anything I do is because of
your example. Its an amazing thing to have

thank you

a father in "high place" but still gives credit to people, I'm so blessed. So thank you dad for being the boss who's on the same level as everyone else. I love you so much, your son,

Jonath

a 29 card

MOTIVES

Jan 4, 2006, Happy New Year!

Dear Jon,

You've been in the studio over Christmas break recording two new songs with Dave Y. Every day your band gets better and better. You've shown real dedication, leadership, and discipline in getting things to this point. I'm thrilled for you and proud of you.

I came across a question in scripture this morning that I'd like to raise for you. It's from John 1:35-39. John the Baptizer has pointed out Jesus as the Lamb of God, and Andrew wants to follow him. When he does, Jesus turns and asks: "What do you want?" It wasn't a rebuking question; "what do YOU want," or a frustrated question, "what do you WANT," but a probing question: "Before you commit to this, you need to have your values straight-what do you want out of this?" Had Andrew answered fame or success or wealth, I doubt Jesus would have encouraged him. But Andrew answered with a question of his own: "Where are you staying?"

Andrew didn't just want Jesus' gifts. Andrew wanted Jesus- to be with him and to know Him. "So, they went and spent that day with him." (John 1:39)

Jon, follow Jesus because He is the Lord, not because He is One who can bless you. He can and will, but always remember we're not here to use Him, but to be used by Him. What do you want?

Love,
Dad

P.S. (2021): A true disciple's primary motive in following Jesus is not to get a reward from Him, but simply to be with Him.

⬥ ⬥ ⬥

IN THE WORLD

1-21-06

Dear Jon,

It's 10 o'clock on Saturday and you're in Deep Ellum (Dallas) with your friends taking in a concert. Your mom really didn't like you going down there with no "adults" (you and Tim & Chris & Blake), but I told her you'd be fine, that you have a good head on your shoulders (can't say that about everyone in your group!) and that you can take care of yourself. And truly, Jon, you can. I've always believed you are extremely capable and a leader, and I trust you. So, get home safe and sound and prove me right!

One reason I'm willing to let you do some potentially dangerous things early in your young life is that I think the Lord is going to use you in the "Deep Ellum" type settings of this world. You have a flair for hip and cool, you're a poet and a musician, and you're a leader. You'll be able to go places and move in circles that I'll never even know about, and that's beautiful. Might as well get a head start! Just remember that wherever you go, whatever you do, whomever you're with, you are God's child and Christ's servant. Never forget Him, and He will never leave you. Follow Him and not only will you be blessed, you'll be a blessing to everyone around you. You already are to me!

Love,
Dad

(He made it home safely and under curfew! EAM)

P.S. (2021): Christ calls his disciples to be in the world, but not of the world.
—John 17:14-15

ജ   ജ   ജ

Hey Mom and Dad! thank you so much for spending thousands of dollars just to make me a hottie! haha. I'm so excited ~~that~~ now that they are off. It feels really strange, but I really enjoy it. Y'all are the best and I love you both very much! Thank you so much again!

your son,

Jonathan

TRANSPARENCY

March 11, 2006, Saturday 11:05PM

Dear Jon,

Again, as I write, you're with some friends at a concert in Deep Ellum. But this week you had another small adventure. Twice we let you drive to Austin for Ranchview's basketball playoff games. That's pretty heady stuff for a 16-year-old driving over 8 hours far away from your parents' watchful eyes, but even more significantly, far from their help and protection. I had to argue your mom into letting you go, but we do trust you implicitly. And sure enough, you proved out.

There is one small thing we'll need to discuss, however! You were in a little fender-bender that dented your bumper ... and you haven't told us about it yet! Always remember that no matter how far and wide you range, you're never alone. Jesus is with you. Never hesitate to call on His name.

BTW, love your teeth! (Jon had just had his braces removed. EAM)

Love,
Dad

P.S. (2021): The goal of this command is love, which comes from a pure heart and a good conscience and a sincere faith.
—1 Timothy 1:5

೮3   ೮3   ೮3

03/15/2006

I'M SO SORRY

July 28, 2006

Dear Jon,

I write with a heart still heavy from a bad day for us both yesterday. Buck R had invited you and me and Chris C for golf at the 4 seasons TPC (a big deal). You were late getting there so we waited and wound up not finishing the round because of darkness. I was embarrassed, disappointed, and finally furious, and when you did make it to the course, I didn't even speak to you.

Today I apologized to you for my atrocious behavior, and you graciously forgave me. What I didn't know yesterday was all the trouble you had getting to the course that was out of your control. I didn't know you'd tried to call and let me know what was going on. I didn't know you were upset and disappointed yourself. All I knew was I had wanted to go to the course with you, and you told me you had other plans, and then you didn't show without a word. I interpreted this as just not caring, and already feeling like I rarely get time with you, it also felt like a personal snub. I was so wrong.

If it's any consolation, those hours golfing yesterday were among the most miserable I've ever spent ... angry at you while at the same time desperately sad that this time of hanging with you that I'd so looked forward was ruined. It makes me cry even now. I'm so sorry for assuming the worst and jumping to conclusions and then acting like a baby. I never want that to happen again, not ever.

Upon reflection, I'm seeing that I'm too quick to impose my personality and thought process on you. That's not fair, because you are not me. And that's a wonderful thing, Jon, because there is so much about you that I admire and know is missing in me. Here are a few examples:

1. You are a caring, loyal person with an amazing capacity to make good friends and build strong relationships. I have a very few really good friends and find it hard to maintain relationship with people that are away or who have pulled some type of flakey shenanigans. It's not that I don't forgive. It's just that I am impatient and don't extend as much grace as I should. But Jon, you do! You are so much better at community and grace-giving and patience than I am. I don't suffer fools gladly, but since I often am one, I'm inspired by grace-giving people like you and want to be more like you (thanks for "suffering" me!)

2. You are far more patient and even keeled than I. I see you having a hard day playing golf for instance, and instead of throwing clubs or screaming (as I sometimes did at your age!), you just push on through. I know you're upset, but you just handle it so much better and more maturely than I do. I love that about you.

3. I also think you are quicker to forgive than I am, and more generous in spirit. When I get ticked at someone, it takes me a while to get over it (witness, yesterday!). But you are far more gracious than that, more easy-going, less demanding of perfection. You should be the pastor, not me! If I were your age now, I would treasure you as a friend.

4. You are an artist and a musician and have the ability to see goodness in the moment. I have always been driven, never quite satisfied with things the way they are, always living in the future while the present escapes me. I admire your perspective, your calm and agreeable nature, and your humor.

All of this is to say that I love and respect you so much, Jon. It kills me to think that I would ever discourage you from the wonderful good that God has made you to be in a selfish, foolish, misguided tantrum thrown to try and make you more like me.

Jonathan, you be you, your best self—always and the result will be glorious. I am your biggest fan, now and always.

All My Love,
Dad

P.S. (2021): Bear with each other and forgive one another
if any of you has a grievance against someone.
Forgive as the Lord forgave you.
—Colossians 3:13

ॐ   ॐ   ॐ

PAYDAY SOMEDAY

12-22-06

Dear Jonathan,

It's almost Christmas, and I'm sitting alone in my office at church thinking about the Christmas Story and Mary in particular. Having heard that she will be the Virgin mother of the Son of God, and having seen her miraculously pregnant cousin Elizabeth, she bursts out in a song of praise known through the centuries as "The Magnificent." The subject of her song is the character of God. Here are a few choice lines:

> ... the Mighty One has done great things for me—holy is His name...

> —Luke 1:49

> ... he has scattered those who are proud in their inmost thoughts.

> He has brought down rulers from their thrones but has lifted up the humble.

> He has filled the hungry with good things but has sent the rich away empty.

> —Luke 1:51-53

Mary knew what it meant to be humble and hungry, and what it meant to be oppressed by proud rulers and the wealthy. In spite of the poverty and hardships she endured, Mary still trusted in God—in His character, His goodness, and His promise ultimately to bring justice. Though Christmas means many things, one major meaning it held for Mary was that God keeps His promises. His choosing her for the honor of bearing the Messiah was an honor that Mary saw as God proving His faithfulness to her. And indeed, that's what it was. That being the case, we should listen to Mary's words carefully. Essentially, this is what I hear her saying for us all:

1. Ruthless, proud people will wreak injustice in this world. In Mary's day, it was Herod the Great & Romans. In our day, it's political rulers, terrorists, and crime lords. The wicked we have always with us.

2. But God is always mindful of the suffering of people. The existence of pain in the world doesn't negate the existence or goodness of a God who cares about suffering and will end it someday.

3. One day, God will humble the proud. What goes around, comes around. This life is but for a season, then either death and the judgment or Christ returns to judge. Either way, in time or eternity, the wicked are put down.

4. Also, one day, God will lift up the humble. The righteous will be rewarded. The humble will be honored. What was despised by the proud of this world will be esteemed in the next. Bottom line: Make sure you're on the side that ultimately wins—the side of the humble & righteous—God's side! Jesus was never to be found conspiring in the counsels of powerful, greedy, self-serving men. Rather, He welcomed those who were largely the outcasts of their day. He never let his head be turned by the overtures of cynics or the offers of powerbrokers.

Neither did Mary. Neither must we.

Love,
Dad

P.S. (2021): This is what the LORD says: "Let not the wise boast of their wisdom or the strong boast of their strength or the rich boast of their riches, but let the one who boasts about this: that they have the understanding to know me, that I am the LORD, who exercises kindness, justice and righteousness on earth, for in these I delight," declares the LORD.
—Jeremiah 9:23-24 (NIV)

๛   ๛   ๛

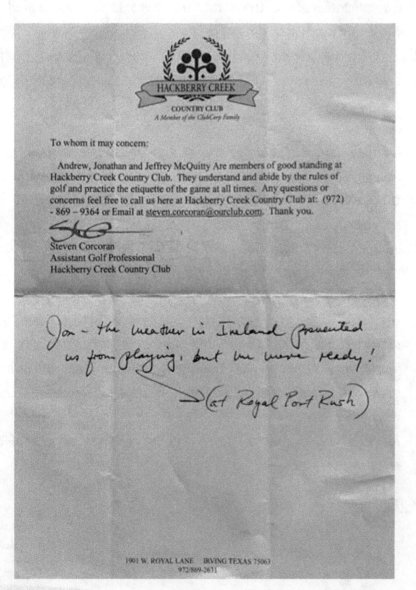

HACKBERRY CREEK
COUNTRY CLUB
A Member of the ClubCorp Family

To whom it may concern:

Andrew, Jonathan and Jeffrey McQuitty Are members of good standing at Hackberry Creek Country Club. They understand and abide by the rules of golf and practice the etiquette of the game at all times. Any questions or concerns feel free to call us here at Hackberry Creek Country Club at: (972) - 869 – 9364 or Email at steven.corcoran@ourclub.com. Thank you.

Steven Corcoran
Assistant Golf Professional
Hackberry Creek Country Club

Jon – the weather in Ireland prevented us from playing, but we were ready!
(at Royal Port Rush)

1901 W. ROYAL LANE   IRVING TEXAS 75063
972/869-2631

PRAY

12-29-06

Dear Jonathan,

Here's an interesting admission from your "professional Christian" father: I've been forgetting to pray. It's year-end and, as usual, IBC needs a lot of money to finish strong. I awoke last night and immediately it began to work on my mind: "How can we possibly get $350K in this week alone? What's going to happen if we don't get it?"

While I was in this anxiety mode, my mind also went in some other directions. "Is my heart getting more clogged? How should I lead IBC in the new year? Will our family have all we need financially as we enter the new year?" I was just going around and around in my head, getting more worried by the second when it struck me. "Why am I worrying about this stuff instead of praying about it?"

> Do not be anxious about anything, but in every situation, by prayer and petition, with thanksgiving, present your request to God. And the peace of God, which transcends all understanding, will guard your hearts and your minds in Christ Jesus.
>
> –Philippians 4:6–7

Oh yeah! Forgot about that one! When faced with problems and worries, we need not worry and stew, just pray. Think of it. We've been invited to an audience with the God of the Universe—the One who is all-powerful and good—there to lay down our burdens and cares. As we place our lives in His hands, the responsibility for what happens shifts from our shoulders to

His. No more worries—just be faithful to what you know He wants and go forward, knowing that He will see you through.

The thing is however, you can't forget to pray! When I finally remembered, it made all the difference.

Cast all your anxiety on Him because He cares for you.

-1Peter 5:7

Love,
Dad

P.S. (2021): Choosing prayer over worry is the path to peace.

ꙮ   ꙮ   ꙮ

PRAY, WORK, TRUST

May 3, 2007

Dear Jon,

My heart is full of excitement and joy because you are bound for college at the school of your dreams—Savannah College of Art and Design! We've been through a season of wondering and waiting. Having visited Savannah and auditioned musically, they awarded you $5K per year. That's great, but short of what you needed, and we were all disappointed.

But Jonny, you didn't let that stop you. You kept pursuing the dream. You wrote an essay, put together your art portfolio, got on the phone, and worked to get more funding. End result? They've now offered you $12K per year and you're on your way. Way to go, buddy—I'm proud of you! You have blessed and inspired me by your perseverance, and reminded me of some fundamental principles such as...

1. When God puts something in your heart, pursue it—even if it's hard, far-fetched, or put down by nay-sayers. You got a dream for attending SCAD and you went for it. God will give you other dreams in your life—pursue them just like you pursued this!

2. Combine faith with effort. You didn't just pray and trust. You worked hard. You produced. You remind me of the plaque that's hung for years in our kitchen at home! "Pray hard. Work hard. Trust God." The trust part doesn't stand alone. Like the farmer, you pray for rain and say "AMEN" with a hoe!

3. But the trust part is essential. Jon, you worked hard to get to SCAD. You never gave up. That's fabulous! But ultimately, you know that God opened the doors for you. You remembered

that all the hard work in the world means nothing apart from the blessing of God.

Jon, I believe your getting to SCAD is just the first step in God's grand plan for your life. You are on your way! This is your journey as an adult man making your own decisions and following your own path. Always remember to honor Jesus first, because He honors those who honor Him!

Always in your corner,
Dad

P.S. (2021): I ask—ask the God of our Master, Jesus Christ, the God of glory—to make you … grasp the immensity of this glorious way of life He has for His followers, oh, the utter extravagance of His work in us who trust Him—endless energy, boundless strength!
—Ephesians 1:19 (Message)

ᔕᔕ ᔕᔕ ᔕᔕ

Andy McQuitty

From: Travis Putman [travisputman@hotmail.com]
Sent: Tuesday, May 22, 2007 12:43 AM
To: Andy McQuitty
Subject: Just needing someone to listen

Andy,

Well, it's me again. You probably don't remember me, but I've emailed you a few times the past two years in regards to my job as a police officer. It's almost midnight and I've just arrived home from work. My wife and daughter are asleep and I'm needing to talk to someone. As I've done on several occasions, I've decided to email you for both therapeutic reasons and for your thoughts.

I've spent the last five and a half hours working a double homicide and suicide. At approximately 6pm, a man drove to his estranged wife's house, shot their seven year old son in the head, shot his ex-wife, and then killed himself. The nine year old daughter ran out the back of the house after seeing her mother and brother being murdered.

As an Investigator I have worked several similar scenes. I worked a similar homicide last October where a man shot his two sons, his wife, and then himself. In that case, I felt some comfort in knowing that both children were with Jesus. Tonight, I feel the same way regarding the seven year old boy and his mother. One of the mother's friends stated that she was the deceased's "Sister in Christ". I know that both she and her son are with Jesus.

Andy, it's the nine year old daughter that I can't stop crying for. I know that this world is full of sin and that Jesus hurts when we hurt, but how can he let a nine year old child go through such a tragedy. I'm 28 years old, have been a patrol officer, undercover narcotics investigator, and criminal investigator over the past several years. I've seen more dead bodies than I can count, and I still can't make sense of how and why things happen. How is a nine year old supposed to understand? People hear brief stories of tragedies on the news every night. However, very few people actually know what a traffic fatality or shooting victim looks like. The seven year old boy was missing half his face. I have nightmares regarding cases that I worked three years ago. How will this nine year old child ever forget the images she saw tonight? Why did God not let her die with her mother and brother? What good can God see in letting a nine year old be orphaned by such a tragic event?

This job has made me realize how fast life can change. That realization has made me a better husband, father, son, and brother. I never let a day pass without letting my family know that I love them. However, I feel that fear is taking over my soul. Not fear for my personal safety. I know where I'm headed when I die, and I do not hesitate to put my self in some pretty dangerous and often foolish situations on an almost daily basis. My fear is for my family, and more specifically my daughter. Since having her two years ago, police work has become ten times harder. Every dead child reminds me of her. I pray and pray, but I just can't let go of the fear of loosing her. Some nights I sleep on her bedroom floor out of fear that something will happen to her during her sleep (another fear resulting from a call years ago when a child died in her sleep). I know that Satan often works through our fears, but the nightmares and sleepless nights just seem to be getting worse.

I appreciate you taking the time to read this email. I just needed someone to "listen to me cry" for a minute. The truth is that it's hard to talk to people, even family, about nights such as tonight. You can't

5/23/2007

HOPE, NOT ANSWERS

5.23.07

Hey Jon,

I received this email the other day [written to express the grief of a police detective after just having spent over five hours working a double homicide/suicide]. Police in big cities have very tough jobs! Especially for a follower of Jesus, it's heartbreaking to see the kinds of tragedies on a daily basis that T describes. Even though most of us won't deal regularly with these kinds of issues, the questions he raises are questions we all raise. How can God let this evil happen? How can people, particularly children, get through this kind of trauma?

To the first question, there are many answers from the disciplines of philosophy and theology, all of which make rational sense but do not emotionally satisfy. God has simply not chosen to explain the "why" of evil. But what He has done is talk about the "how." How do we make our way through the troubles that life throws at us all? I love how Jesus answers this question in John 14. In trouble? Remember ... !

1. Your home is Heaven: "Don't let this throw you. You trust God, don't you? Trust me. There is plenty of room for you in my father's home. I'm on my way to get a room ready for you. I'll come back and get you ...." (John 14:1–3)

2. Your friend (Jesus) is the Father (God): "To see me is to see the Father ... don't you believe that I am in the Father and the Father is in me?" (John 14:10)

3. Your privilege is prayer: "From now on, whatever you request along the lines of who I am and what I am doing, I'll do it. That's how the Father will be seen for who He is in

the Son. I mean it. Whatever you request in this way, I'll do." (John 14:14)

4. Your comforter is the Counselor: "I will talk to the Father and He'll provide you another friend so that you will always have someone with you. This friend is the Spirit of Truth...." (John 14:15–16)

In other words, God doesn't give us an itinerary, but He packs us a lunch! How will we all handle our troubles? What is the way out? God doesn't say. His is not a way out, but a way through. It's a way "in spite of." We can find Him to be our Road, our Truth, our Life in the midst of tough times. Christians in the first century were hounded and persecuted for their faith. They weren't spared trouble. Yet they called themselves "people of The Way." That's what we are, too, if we trust Jesus.

Love You,
Dad

P.S. (2021): God leads his dear children along ... some through the waters, some through the flood, some through the fire, but all through the blood. Some through great sorrow, but God gives a song, in the night season and all the day long.
—God Leads Us Along, Gaither Vocal Band, 2013

ഔ   ഔ   ഔ

THE FRUIT OF SELF-DENIAL

August 28, 2007

Dear Jon,

You're leaving for college in a little over a week and I'm realizing that my time jotting in these pages is nearly at an end. I almost feel like these are my "last words" to you! Of course, I know that they are not; yet, in this particular venue, they are. That realization is bittersweet for me. It means that you've grown into manhood and are now ready to launch out into the wide world to live your life. That's wonderful! But it also means that a precious chapter in my life—having you as my son growing up under my roof—has drawn to an end.

You'll forgive me for feeling a bit of sadness here, if only momentarily! You've brought nothing but joy and pride and thankfulness to my life these 18 years, Jon. I know you will continue to do so as well in the years to come. I am so very grateful for you, and I anticipate that the best is yet to be.

I've been reading again Dallas Willard's book, The Renovation of the Soul (mine seems to need frequent tune-ups!). In one passage, he explains what it takes to love freely and spiritually.

> "Unless a grain of wheat falls into the earth and dies," Jesus said, "it remains by itself alone; but if it dies, it bears much fruit. He who loves his life [soul] loses it; and he who hates his life in this world shall keep it to life eternal."
>
> —John 12:24-25

This is a law of human life, partly visible at the level of purely human understanding and fully demonstrated by ...

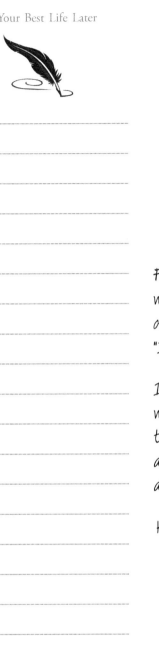

Jesus for all to see ... to accept, with confidence in God, that I do not immediately have to have my way releases me from the great pressure that anger, unforgiveness, and the 'need' to retaliate, imposes upon my life ... to step with Jesus into the path of self-denial immediately breaks the iron-clad grip of sin over human personality and opens the way for fuller restoration of radical good-ness to the soul.

–The Renovation of the Soul, pp 74-75

For so many, often (sadly) including yours truly, "getting what I want" is the driving force of the soul. That leads to all sorts of anger and frustration, because, as Mick Jagger famously sang, "I can't get no satisfaction!"

If, on the other hand, we can die to what we want and seek what Jesus wants, marvelous freedom results—freedom to forgive, to serve, to experience joy in the progress and success of others, and to hope. Paradoxically, in dying to what I want, I ultimately attain it. It's amazing but true:

He who hates his life in this world shall keep it to life eternal.
—John 12:24-25

Much Love,
Dad

P.S. (2021): The one principle of Hell is— "I am my own!"
—George MacDonald

꘠   ꘠   ꘠

LIFE'S GREATEST ASSET

September 1, 2007

Hey Jono,

Ask the famous people of our day what life's most important asset is, and you'll get varied responses. Hugh Hefner would say, "Lots of sex." Donald Trump would say, "Lots of money." Paris Hilton would say, "Lots of attention." Hillary Clinton would say, "Lots of power." But look in God's Word and you'll discover these all would be dead wrong. What is life's most important asset? The answer is in Psalm 112: "Blessed is the man who fears the Lord, who finds great delight in His commands." (Psalm 112:1) The blessing of God on your life is your life's greatest asset, bar none.

The greatest question then, is this: how does a person receive God's blessing? Answer: fear God. That just means taking Him seriously enough to listen to what He says and do it. What comes to the wise one who does so?

1. First, a legacy that endures. "His children will be mighty in the land; the generation of the upright will be blessed. Wealth and riches are in his house, and his righteousness endures forever." (Psalm 112:2) The wealth here is not necessarily of the monetary kind. It's joy, pride in one another, the satisfaction of making a difference, doing good, changing the world. You leave a legacy of influence and inspiration in the lives of all those you influence, beginning with your children but going out from there in ripples of respect.

2. Second, one receives hope that overcomes. "Even in darkness light dawns for the upright, for the gracious and compassionate and righteous man. Good will come to him who is generous

and lends freely, who conducts his affairs with justice. Surely he will never be shaken; a righteous man will be remembered forever." (Psalm 112:4-6) Does fearing God and obeying His commands insulate us from pain? No. Darkness comes even to the faithful in this broken world. But "even in darkness" the upright finds light. Those he has helped, help. Those he has loved, love. Those to whom he's shown justice, defend. What goes around, comes around. Be a good person and no darkness, no matter how deep, can overcome you.

3. Third, one receives a confidence that assures: "He will have no fear of bad news; his heart is steadfast, trusting in the LORD. His heart is secure, he will have no fear; in the end he will look in triumph on his foes. He has scattered abroad his gifts to the poor, his righteousness endures forever; his horn will be lifted high in honor." (Psalm 112:7-9) Fear is a dead give-away for going it alone. Show me someone who has walked away from the Lord, and I'll show you someone who fears what may lurk around every corner. On the other hand, show me a person who is trusting God and walking in His ways, and I'll show you someone who is as bold as a lion! Why would he not be? If your guardian is the Creator of the Universe, who or what could possibly push you around?

Not so, however, the wicked: "The wicked man will see and be vexed, he will gnash his teeth and waste away; the longings of the wicked will come to nothing." (Psalm 112:10)

Jon be blessed! Choose blessing. Reach out and receive what the Lord wants you to have! Fear Him; delight always in His commands. You'll never regret it!

All My Love & Blessings,
Dad

P.S. (2021): The greatest possible asset that anyone can have in their life is the blessing of God.

 howeve howeve howeve

Ranchview Baccalaureate
Class of 2007

LAUNCHING

9-5-07

Dear Jonathan,

I received an email from a 51-year-old gentleman today. He's been attending IBC for a year, checking out Christianity to see if he might believe. To date, he has not become a Christian because he just can't get around the "faith" thing. If God is real, why doesn't he just appear in our living room and reveal Himself? Why make it "so hard" for us who want to find Him to be able to do so? He also finds the concept of eternal separation from God in Hell distasteful and is troubled by "the problem of pain"—bad things happening to good people and indiscriminate suffering in the universe.

I suspect you have wrestled with these or similar questions, or if not, that one day you will. As you search for answers, I recommend the works of C.S. Lewis, Lee Strobel, and Brian McClaren (A New Kind of Christian). There are no easy answers to these perennial questions, but there are answers, though not of the type that most people seek. With regard to God and the Bible, we want empirical evidence of the sort we demand when making a purchase. "I won't buy that car until I can give it a test-drive." Reasonable. We want to believe, but only after seeing! Unfortunately, God has not left us that option when it comes to Himself. He says, "obey and understand ... believe and see," just the reverse order of what we desire. That means we are all faced with a simple but tough decision: even though I don't like the choice God gives me to believe by faith or not at all, will I? Or, because I'm ticked off that God hasn't structured Christianity the way I want, will I pick up my marbles and go home?

Confronted with this dilemma in John 6, Peter spoke for the disciples and for so many of us down through the centuries when he said: "Lord, to whom shall we go? You have the words of eternal life. We have come to believe and to know that you are the Holy One of God." (John 6:68-69)

I've gone through "mad" stages when, like the man who emailed me, I railed at God for making things so "unnecessarily" difficult. Here's what I found: being mad and rejecting God and His Word solves nothing. Rebellion produces no light. It may feel good for a little while but yields no answers and leads ultimately to despair. "Lord, to whom shall we go?" He is the only One to whom we can go. And mercifully, it's not as hard to do so, frankly, as we (I!) have often made it out to be. God has not left Himself without a witness, i.e., Romans 1. The miracles of Creation and Life and Beauty and Goodness all point to The Benevolent One. The Bible reveals His character, His Son Jesus, and our eternal hope. In other words, there's plenty enough to believe if only we can overcome our human pride that demands truth on our own terms. We can come to God on His terms only. That's the hard news. The good news is, we can come to God. He's there always!

So, Jon, believe Him and trust Him and follow and obey Him always even when the way seems dim, and you don't get what's happening. I've never regretted doing so in all this time. It hasn't been easy, and not always fun. But the Lord's goodness and blessing have followed me for simply choosing to trust what I know and simply believing for the rest. Jono, you are one of God's greatest blessings in my life. After your sister Bonnie was born so prematurely, the docs strongly advised us to let her be our last child. Alice could have died with Bonnie, and they were rightfully concerned her bearing any more children.

Had we heeded their warnings, you and Jeff would not be here! We just believed that God wanted us to raise more kids than just 3, and I also really wanted a son! We trusted the Lord, and here you come— healthy, full-term, the joy of our hearts then, now, and always! You have always been a miracle to us, Jon—truly a blessing from Heaven. More than anything, I desire that your life be filled with the same kind of blessing that you are to us. Follow Jesus always, and it will be so, even as it has been.

As you begin your college career at SCAD in just a few days, you have everything you need to become a stunning success in every way that word can be defined. You are smart and personable and talented and a true leader. I am so proud of what you've already become and anticipate joyfully all that yet lies ahead.

I love you, my son, and will always be here for you.

Your Biggest Fan,
Dad

P.S. (2021): "If you remain in me and my words remain in you, ask whatever you wish, and it will be done for you. This is to my Father's glory, that you bear much fruit, showing yourselves to be my disciple."
—John 15:7-8 (NIV)

℘   ℘   ℘

myspace.com/midweek
purevolume.com/midweek
midweekmail@yahoo.com

Part 5

A Journal For Jeffrey Lee

22 entries, beginning Jan 24, 1994–Aug 19, 2011

Hi Jeffrey!

Last Wednesday morning we all got up early to celebrate your very first birthday breakfast. I can hardly believe a year has flown since God brought you into our home. Already you've gone from a puckered (but cute!) little baby bundle to a strapping, laughing, almost-walking toddler! You have brought much joy – not only to your brother and me – but to Jonathan and your sisters as well. Suffice it to say from the very beginning: you are well-loved!

In this little book I'm going to attempt on occasion to write to you about things which are important in life. I know there will be times when God opens my eyes to some truth that I will want to tell you. This will be my means for doing so. I'll just store up a little idea-book – for you on these pages and share it with you when you're

GOD LOVES YOU

January 24, 1994

Hi Jeffrey!

Last Wednesday morning we all got up early to celebrate your very first birthday breakfast. I can hardly believe a year has flown since God brought you into our home. Already you've gone from a puckered (but cute!) little baby bundle to a strapping, laughing, almost-walking toddler. You have brought much joy—not only to your mother and me—but to Jonathan and your sisters as well. Suffice it to say that from the very beginning you are well-loved!

In this little book, I'm going to attempt on occasion to write to you about things which are important in life. I know there will be times when God opens my eyes to some truth that I will want to tell you. This will be my means for doing so. I'll just store up a little "idea-book" for you on these pages and share it with you when you're ready.

Let me close this first entry with the first idea—and the greatest of all—that you need to face life. I began by telling you that you are well-loved in the McQuitty family. But as deep and abiding as our love for you is, there is One Who loves you even more:

> God loved the world so much that He gave His one and only son so that whoever believes in Him may not be lost but have eternal life.

> —John 3:16 (NET)

The love of a father for his son can be surpassed only by the love of The Father for the Son. Yet God offered Him for us.

As a result, we can face whatever life may throw at us in the assurance that, no matter what men may do or circumstances may bring, God's love envelops us always.

In the Fathers Love,
Dad

P.S. (2021): The Father's love is His children's greatest gift.

       છ   છ   છ

A LIVED FAITH

Dear Jeffrey,

In his book The Return of the Prodigal Son, Prof. Henri Nouwen writes:

As I reflect on my own journey, I become more and more aware of how I have played the role of observer. For years I had instructed students on the different aspects of the spiritual life, trying to help them see the importance of living it. But had I, myself, really ever dared to step into the center, kneel down, and let myself be held by a forgiving God?

—The Return of the Prodigal Son, p. 12

I can identify w/ what Nouwen is saying, and I don't believe it's because we're both "religious teachers." I believe that all Christians find it easier to study faith than apply it, observe Christianity than live it, and analyze God than love him.

But life is to be lived, not documented; Christianity is to be experienced, not explicated. My great tendency is to get these confused. What a travesty to mistake facts about God for personal knowledge of Him.

Jeffrey, always test yourself with this question: "Am I living an authentic faith to impact this world, or am I living a theoretical faith to avoid this world?" If you do the latter, you'll be safe but sorry. If the former, you'll walk in joyful jeopardy—like Jesus, Peter, Paul, et al.

All My Love,
Dad

P.S. (2021): Learning charts our course, but action achieves our destination.

∞   ∞   ∞

DELAYED GRATIFICATION

7-5-96

Dear Jeff,

A great component of wisdom is the ability to take long-term effects into account when making short-term decisions. On the positive side, that's what a farmer does when he plants his seed in the spring. He's patiently tending to work now with the long-range view toward a Fall harvest. NOTE: he does not harvest immediately. There is delayed gratification. Thus, the wisdom is in the wait.

On the negative side, wisdom is required to avoid decisions now that will produce destruction down the road. This is what Paul had in mind in Romans: "What benefit did you reap at that time from the things you are now ashamed of? Those things result in death." (Romans 6:21) "For when we we're controlled by the sinful nature, we bore fruit for death." (Romans 7:5)

Here's the challenge: most often sowing good seed means delayed gratification while sowing destructive seed means instant gratification. Smoking is fun now but kills you later. Sexual lust is fun now but destroys your relationship and ultimately your soul later. Overeating is fun now but gives you heart disease later. Compared to the instant gratification of our flesh, godliness seems at first glance a poor alternative. But only to the foolish who aren't wise enough to take long-term effects into account!

Be wise, my Jeffrey! Do now those things you will be glad you did 15 years hence. Avoid now those things which God's Word says will visit only grief on you 15 years hence. "... the benefit you reap leads to holiness, and the result is eternal life." (Romans (6:22)

Love,
Dad

P.S. (2021): Wise people take long-term effects into account when making short- term decisions.

    ∫∫∫

PREPARATION

2/12/97

Dearest Jeffy,

The great Danish philosopher Soren Kierkegaard defined a saint as "one who wills one thing." Jesus put it this way: "... set your hearts on His kingdom first." (Matthew 6:33) Singlemindedness really does focus and simplify life. If you make God your central and defining concern, then all of your working and relating and praying is unified. You no longer have to "prepare" to be with people, to speak or minister, for you are living in a state of "preparedness." It is the disjointed, fragmented life that exhausts.

As the great spiritual writer Henri Nouwen expresses it:

> When God is my only concern, when God is the center of my interest, when all my prayers, my reading, my studying, my speaking, and writing serve only to know God better and to make Him known better, then there is no basis for anxiety or stage fright. Then I can live in such a state of preparedness and trust that speaking from the heart is also speaking to the heart.
>
> —The Genesee Diary, p 16

Saints and not just Boy Scouts need to be prepared!

All My Love,
Dad

P.S. (2021): Friends, don't get me wrong: By no means do I count myself an expert in all of this, but I've got my eye on the goal, where God is beckoning us onward—to Jesus. I'm off and running, and I'm not turning back.
—Philippians 3:13-14 (Message)

   ဢ   ဢ   ဢ

SUCCESS

1-14-98

Hi Jeffrey!

You're going to be a grown-up 5-year-old this month! What a joy you are to my heart! I look forward to seeing how God develops and uses you in coming years. You're smart, funny, and have personality galore. You'll probably be able to write your own ticket. That's why I wanted to share Kent and Barbara Hughes' 7 elements of success (Liberating Ministry from the Success Syndrome) with you. I want you to know what God says success is so that you'll seek it above all. "Success" according to Scripture:

1. First, success is faithfulness that shows itself in obedience to God's Word. (1Cor 4:1-2 NIV)
2. Faithfulness is not a cop-out for lethargy, apathy, or faintness of heart (Jesus' Parable of The Talents in Matthew 25).
3. There is no success apart from a foot-washing heart. "Now that I, your Lord and Teacher, have washed your feet, you also should wash one another's feet." (John 13:14, NIV)
4. There is no success apart from loving God with all that we have and are. "Hear, O Israel: The LORD our God, the LORD is one. Love the LORD your God with all your heart and with all your soul and with all your strength." (Deuteronomy 6:4-5, NIV)
5. Success must contain faith. "And without faith it is impossible to please God, because anyone who comes to him must believe that he exists and that he rewards those who earnestly seek him." (Hebrews 11:6, NIV)
6. Success comes to people of prayer. "True instruction was in his mouth and nothing false was found on his lips. He

walked with me in peace and uprightness and turned many from sin." (Malachi 2:6, NIV)

7. To be successful, we must be holy. "Be holy because I, the LORD your God, am holy." (Leviticus 19:2, NIV)

Jeff, you won't see these biblical descriptions of success written up in the Wall Street Journal! That's because they speak of a success far more profound than merely temporal worldly wealth & influence. They speak of the only success truly worth having—being pleasing to and blessed by God in time and for eternity.

Go for it, Jeff! Love,
Dad

P.S. (2021): God's definition of success is the only one that really matters.

ဆ   ဆ   ဆ

YOUR OWN PATH

Sept 1, 1999

Hi Jeffy,

Sorry it's been such a long time since I visited you in these pages! You've done quite a lot since I last wrote. You played admirably well on the Orioles, your first organized team sport (T-ball in Coppell). In that league, the Coach pitched you 2 balls. If you didn't hit them, you then got hit off the tee. I don't believe you ever used the tee. You hit the coaches' pitches every time! You've since even developed more confidence in your throwing and catching. Last night I was firing you tennis balls and you caught everything. Now if I can just get you to believe you can do the same with a real baseball, you will.

I'm watching with keen interest as you grow up in Jonathan's wake. You two love each other. Yet, I sometimes wonder if the day will come when you resent being "in his shadow." You're not, of course. God has gifted and blessed you in special and unique ways. Yet, it must seem so from time to time.

I see in you, Jeff, the capacity for seeing insightfully, thinking clearly, and feeling deeply. Your little face is the most expressive of any six-year-old I know! God is making you into a man of ability and passion. I don't know the specific assignment He has for you. But this I know—you will excel at whatever you do.

To this end, I am going to encourage you as you grow to follow in Jonathan's footsteps when you want to and when it is right and feasible. But I'm also going to challenge you to find your own way, too, even if it means taking a path not yet blazed by any of your older siblings.

I sure do love you,
Dad

P.S. (2021): When Peter saw him [John], he asked, 'Lord, what about him?' Jesus answered, "If I want him to remain alive until I return, what is that to you? You must follow me."
—John 21:21-22 (NIV).

   ❧   ❧   ❧

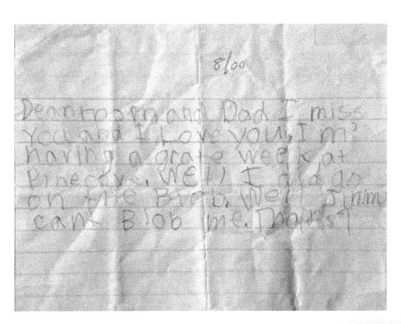

PRIDE

Aug 9, 2000

Hi Jeff,

Much has happened in nearly the year that has passed since I last visited you here. You learned to ride your 2-wheeler in the IBC parking lot, and we celebrated with ice-cream at McDonalds. You played coach-pitch baseball and starred as one of the team's best hitters and fielders. You have mastered "ollies" and several other skateboard tricks with Jonathan. You went to Pine Cove Towers for the first camp experience of your life—and had a ball. You start school at home Monday—the last of our children to be home-schooled. You make your mom and me proud. Always have, always will!

I had a scary experience yesterday. Sat with a married couple whose relationship has been destroyed by the man's immorality (he got involved in internet pornography and then later committed adultery) and financial irresponsibility. For 1.5 hours, I sat and listened to this proud man blame others for his sins. He blamed his wife, he blamed God, he blamed circumstances. He was defiant and stubborn. This was scary because I realized the destructive power of pride. When we become unwilling to face and admit and accept our own sins and failures and shortcomings, then we become unable to change. We doom ourselves to the unmitigated consequences of our sin. But is the price of pride and "saving face" worth destroying ours and other's lives? No way. This man has a young daughter. He will lose her, his wife, his happiness—all due to pride. And there's not a thing I can do about it. We all make choices and decisions for ourselves.

All of which is to say, dear Jeff: be humble and willing to learn. Stay teachable. Don't cover your mistakes or rationalize your sins. Confess and forsake them. Learn from them and go on to be a wiser, happier, and more blessed man!

All My Love,
Dad

P.S. (2021): "When pride comes, then comes disgrace, but with humility comes wisdom."
—Proverbs 11:2

꙰   ꙰   ꙰

DISCIPLINE

12-18-01

Dear Jeff,

During my (too long) absence from these pages, you have gone from a child to a strapping, lithe, 8-year-old boy. You're smart, personality-bursting, funny, and kind. I'm so proud of you!

It's both a blessing and a hardship for you to be the youngest of 5 kids in our home. On the one hand, you get to grow up faster. Hanging out with your older brothers and sisters, you do everything sooner, stay up later, see "real" movies earlier, and learn grown-up stuff faster. You're 8 going on 13 along with Jonathan!

But it's tough for you because it's confusing. You're treated almost like an adult, but you're not one—yet! The privileges and responsibilities of being grown aren't yours yet, but it's hard (at only 8) to understand why.

Two nights ago, I picked you and Jon up from church. I was running late. When you got in the car, you gave me quite a disrespectful tongue-lashing. Do you remember? I took you home, we went into my office, and I gave you 3 pretty crisp licks with a salad spoon! Ow! You were crying and my heart was breaking. (It really does hurt parents more than their kids—you'll find out someday!)

That was the first (and hopefully only) serious spanking I've ever given you and I want you to know, I had a deep struggle driving home that night. Spank Jeff, or not? I didn't want to at all. But Jeff, you're so precocious and smart, you'd been developing a bit of a snotty attitude. I realized you were getting

so big that spanking would soon be inappropriate and that allowing that attitude of disrespect to go unaddressed would not be to love you well. So, I decided that a spanking now would save us both a multitude of sorrows later.

So, I asked you to put your hands on my desk and whacked your wee bottom. It sizzled! You were first surprised, then mad, then dreading the knowing that you still had 2 to go. But you were so brave. You cried, but you stood there and took the other 2. How I admired you! I sent you to your room to think things over and went to the kitchen to rustle up something for you. I brought you up some cherry cheesecake and a coke (your mom didn't like that—junk food at bedtime?). We talked and hugged and laughed. I told you I love you so much. Then I went to bed feeling awful yet trusting that I had done the right thing by you. Time, as they say, will tell.

Here's what you must know. Great talent and ability channeled positively can accomplish extraordinarily good. But neglected and undisciplined, it can at best be wasted and at worst abused. Jeff, God has given you a wonderful mind, great presence, a big heart—so much giftedness! As your dad my longing is to see you fully reach all the potential God has built into you.

I Love You, Buddy-Boy,
Dad

P.S. (2021): "Whoever spares the rod hates their children, but the one who loves their children is careful to discipline them."
—Proverbs 13:24

છ્ર   છ્ર   છ્ર

BENCHMARKS

9-5-02

Hey Jeff!

It's been a momentous couple of weeks for you. On Aug 24, we dedicated our new buildings at IBC to the Lord. Part of those festivities was the first baptism ceremony in the new baptistry in the Town Square. Nearly 100 people were baptized, and you were the very first one! For almost 2 years you've been asking about being baptized. The look on your face that day told me it was worth the wait!

The other big event for you was the Monday before (Aug 19). You "attended school" for the first time! You are a proud 4th-grader at Las Colinas Elementary after being home-schooled to this point. How proud you were when we went to Walmart the night before to get your supplies and a bike-lock because you're going and coming all by yourself!

I want you to remember these 2 big events. Your baptism marks a point in time when your faith in Christ was publicly expressed from a sincere heart. Never forget, Jeff, that trusting Jesus doesn't just mean holding on to Him. When you trust Him for salvation, He begins holding on to you, too! There will be seasons in your life, perhaps even now as you read these words years later, when your grasp on God seems weak or even gone. Your baptism is a reminder, though, that the grasping that began when you put your faith in Christ goes both ways. You may have let go of God, but He has not and never will let go of you! You may feel far from Him, but He will never leave or desert you, never. "... if we are faithless, he remains faithful, for he cannot disown himself" (2 Timothy 2:13, NIV).

Second, remember your "coming out" into the world. Your first day, you got placed at a table next to Mike, an autistic child with behavior problems. But you were kind to him, and now he considers you one of (if not his only) friend. God places us in this world to love Him and serve others, Jeff, and you've made a stupendous beginning!

All My Love,
Dad

P.S. (2021): Trust in the LORD with all your heart and lean not on your own understanding; in all your ways submit to him, and he will make your paths straight"
—Proverbs 3:5-6 (NIV)

ॐ   ॐ   ॐ

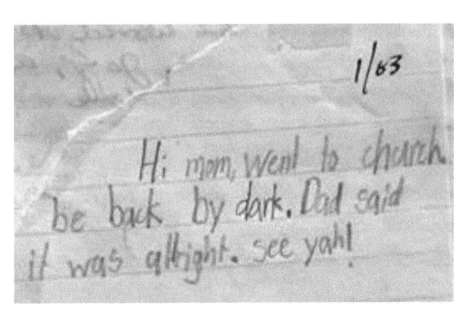

1/83

Hi mom, went to church. be back by dark. Dad said it was alright. see yah!

THE FEAR OF GOD

1-28-03

Hi Jeff,

You are an amazing little boy. So thoughtful and sensitive, so smart. Your mom and I are watching you walk through a formative time in your life in these days. It's not easy, but it's powerful. It all seems to go back to last Christmas. Mark Matlock preached a sermon at IBC on the subject of Hell, and how Christ's coming was to keep people from going there. You took that message so to heart. In fact, you began to let the dread of separation from God cause you to doubt your own salvation. You began to be sad much of the time, and sometimes you'd just begin weeping. Why? Because you weren't sure you are a Christian, that you "really believe." You'd say to me, "Dad, it's really hard to believe."

Well, in one sense you're right. It can be difficult to accept as true the existence of someone we've never seen! But on the other hand, it's not really all that hard at all if we exercise our intellect and a bit of faith. I've never seen George Washington, but I have faith in his reality based on the evidence of history and common sense.

It's the same with God. I don't need to understand all I know to use it and trust it. I'm no physics genius, but I trust electricity enough to know it's there and to flip on the light switch. There's an infinite amount I'll never know or understand about the Lord. But it's intellectually compelling that He exists, and so I am content to believe in Him with child-like faith. If a child can do it, it can't be that hard!

I just believe you have adopted a standard of absolute certainty for defining "belief" that has rendered "saving faith" in your mind an impossible attainment. I've been trying to help you alter your definitions, but so far you're not buying it! You bring a Bible in every night, desperate to have us read with you. And you actually find great comfort there (an unusual phenomenon if you're not a believer!). These are precious times. We'll read a whole chapter (we're in Matthew) and you'll come back later and raise questions about the text. You really want to understand!

Oh, by the way, your fear of Hell has now bled over into 2 other fears: 1. Your mom and me dying (thanks for not wanting that to happen!), and 2. of your brothers and sisters leaving home ahead of you thus rendering you bored & lonely. We've explained many times that yes, we'll probably die ahead of you, but hopefully not for another 30-50 years! And you will have a season as the only kid left at home, but that will be the time of your life—something to anticipate, not dread!

In the meantime, the tears and sadness and reading continue, and that's all fine and good. Why? Because it evidences within you a uniquely pure and sensitive spirit, an openness and desire for God, and a deep compassion for others. Time and maturity will allay your fears, Jeff. But I pray your heart and passion and care will never subside! God has made you special for a reason. Someday, we'll all know what it is, and it will be a glorious thing in our eyes!

All My Love,
Dad

P.S. (2021): "I give them eternal life, and they shall never perish; no one will snatch them out of my hand."
—John 10:28

ஐ   ஐ   ஐ

[Note stuck to cabin door at Pine Cove Christian camp]

Dad, went to play poker. Be back at 8:00pm. Were [sic] not betting! were [sic] going straight from summit to the pool party. See ya later after party. Jeff

HUMILITY

10-22-04

Dear Jeff,

Your mom and I have always said of you, "He's an unusual child!" The older you get, the more you prove us right! You're quite extraordinary in your sensitivity, talent, and personality. This has come through loud and clear recently as we've watched you perform the lead role of "Mr. Rabbit" in the Irving Children's Theater presentation of Alice in Wonderland.

You stole every scene you were in not intentionally, but by sheer talent. Miss Jill (the ICT Director) says you're the most talented child actor she's seen come along in many years. I am proud of you, and I can only wonder with anticipation what great things the Lord has in store for you to accomplish. God does not waste His gifts, and since He has so obviously lavished them upon you, I'm quite certain that He has significant work for you to accomplish for His Kingdom.

Here's the key to maximizing your formidable potential, Jeff— humility. Hold your talents graciously, thankfully, and with a humble heart and God will further His work through you in ways I suspect are unimaginable to you right now. Pride will diminish you, but a humble heart God will honor. Someday when you're operating in full power and all your glory—remember your old man that he was your first and greatest fan.

All My Love,
Dad

P.S. (2021): "Do nothing out of selfish ambition or vain conceit. Rather, in humility value others above yourselves …"
—Philippians 2:3

⫯ ⫯ ⫯

[Post-it note to Jeff from the director of his play]

Jeff, please learn your lines before first rehearsal. Thanks, Jill]

Jeff,

Please learn your lines before first rehearsal.

Thanks Jill

FAITHFULNESS IN OBSCURITY

January 3, 2006

Jeff,

I do apologize for the long hiatus since last I wrote you. I don't know, call it middle-aged distraction or something. I just fell away from recording these thoughts for you a time, but hopefully I'm back now!

You will become a teenager this month, officially surpassing the rank of little boy and becoming a young man. It's been fun watching you come into your own. I noticed your burgeoning big personality really coming out on our New York trip last Christmas (04) with your grandparents. You're funny and witty and aware and can carry on conversations with anyone. You're also a fun traveling companion-interested and fun and unselfish. What a great time we had!

You've been pursuing your acting as well, most recently in The Greatest Christmas Pageant Ever. No one has the expressions you do, Jeff! Plus, you're very bright, and this comes out more and more as you discuss films and world events. God has blessed you with a sharp mind and it's going to be an adventure discovering His plan and purpose for your life.

One thing I know, and that's that your life is significant for this world. I just finished 1 Chronicles 1-9, the genealogies. It amazed me to see how God recorded the names and lives and service of so many obscure people, from kings and generals to gatekeepers and musicians. Why? To show that every person matters, every person counts, every person can change the world through faithful service to God.

I also saw in Chronicles how every person can blow their chance! Saul was gifted by God and called to greatness. But he was proud and failed: "Saul died because he was un-faithful to the Lord; he did not keep the word of the Lord ... and did not inquire of the Lord. So, the Lord put him to death and turned the kingdom over to David ...." (1 Chron 10:13-14)

All of which is to say, Jeff, that if you will but keep the Lord first in your heart and ways, He will take those extraordinary gifts He's given you and do extraordinary things with your life! Stay humble, always "inquire of the Lord" by seeking His will in every matter, and He will guide you and bless you richly. Can't wait to see it!

Love You,
Dad

P.S. (2021): Only one life, 'twill soon be past; only what's done for Christ will last.
—C.T. Studd

಄ ಄ ಄

ENTHUSIASM

July 2, 2006

Dear Jeff,

I do believe the "golf bug" bit you, and he did it yesterday. For posterity, I thought this grand day should be duly noted! You and I went to the new Texas Indoor Golf facility in the morning. We rented one of their practice bays for an hour and proceeded to whack balls on camera. Each shot was reported back to us with all the stats, and we each recorded five swings to the internet.

You really did well! What's even more important, you looked good while you did well! I noticed that your right foot kept slipping because you were wearing tennis shoes. So, when we were done, I took you to the mall and bought you some cool Nike golf shoes. That afternoon, I dropped you off at Hackberry Creek to hit balls on the range at your request. I told mom you'd call when you were ready to come home. Two hours later, she called my cell phone, worried that you had not called. All told, you hit balls for 3 hours, and seemed to love it all. Welcome to the golf-bug-bitten ranks—I salute you!

Love,
Dad

P.S. (2021): "Whatever you do, work at it with all your heart, as working for the Lord, not for human masters, since you know that you will receive an inheritance from the Lord as a reward. It is the Lord Christ you are serving"
—Colossians 3:23-24 (NIV)

ဢ   ဢ   ဢ

ACCOUNTABILITY

12-20-07

Dear Jeff,

It's almost Christmas once again. I'm amazed that another year is nearly in the history books. But when I look at you, I can believe the time has passed. You have grown up so much this year. I think Jonathan leaving home for SCAD gave you some space to just "come into your own." I know that Jon notices your maturity too. Since he's been back for the holidays, he's been taking you around with him like one of his running buddies. Plus, you can now whip both him and me at ping pong—new respect!

You'll turn 15 next month, and the growth into manhood in your life is only going to accelerate. I am proud of the person that you are, and most especially of the man you're becoming! God has given you special gifts. You're very smart, have great social skills, and people listen to you and follow you. In other words—you're a leader. That's rare and wonderful. I am praying that Jesus will lead you into just the perfect sphere of influence that He has for you. It's one thing to have important gifts from God (and you do). It's quite another to employ those gifts effectively. We will all give an accounting one day for our stewardship. I want you to stand tall on that day—and I believe you will! BTW, stop beating me at Ping Pong, you're only 14!

Love,
Dad

P.S. (2021): "From everyone who has been given much, much will be demanded; and from the one who has been entrusted with much, much more will be asked."
—Luke 12:48

෨   ෨   ෨

HAPPINESS

January 3, 2008

A new year Jeff, and you are 14 going on 20! We're still in the holiday break, and you've been hanging out with friends away from home almost all the time! That's fine—I'm glad you're a social creature with great friends. But it does remind me that we're coming into a difficult transition in which your journey to manhood will be completed. Especially when you start driving, you will want more and more independence. I want you to have it. But the trick is maintaining a reasonable accountability while you're becoming your own man. That's where potential conflict lies. I want you to be your own man! And you'll get there, sooner than most! But while you're still in route, just know that I love you and want only the best for you, even if it seems I get in the way sometimes.

You and Jon and I got iPhones for Christmas. What fun! One lesson I always learn upon acquiring a new toy, however, is that "stuff" has an extremely limited capacity to provide happiness. Enjoy you phone but always remember that joy and satisfaction in life can never be bought. Happiness comes from a settled purpose, an integrous lifestyle, and a vibrant walk with Christ. May you always live in joy!

Love,
Dad

P.S. (2021): The grass withers and the flowers fall, but the word of our God endures forever.
—Isaiah 40:8 (NIV).

ജ   ജ   ജ

ENEMIES

5-6-08

Dear Jeff,

In just a few months it seems you have matured into a man—physically, intellectually, socially. Jonny came home from his first year at SCAD and I saw you beaming as you stood beside him. Why? You're now taller than he is! You'll be taller than me before long, too. You've finished your freshman year at Ranchview and will breeze through drivers' Ed this summer. My son—you're growing up so fast! And I'm proud of you for who you are and what God has made you to be—funny, smart, tender-hearted, integrous. The Lord has big plans for you Jeff, and I'm your biggest backer in fulfilling them all!

I'm 52 years old and, you might think, impervious by now to the passions and pratfalls of a younger man, NOT! I want to put down some lines here for you that will hopefully stand you in good stead as you move ahead to fight the good fight as Jesus' disciple. It's all about our neighbor, you know, the guy who hates our dogs, us, and the world (you'll recall he also chucked a golf ball at you one day but was such a sissy he missed and hit our house instead!).

I've wrestled mightily with my feelings about this guy. In the flesh, I just want to punch his lights out (like when he yelled at Mom that one day because the dogs barked at him). But Jesus calls me to love my enemies and do good to those who persecute me. What this has come down to for me is not a neighbor-dispute, but a test of faith. Do I trust God enough to obey Him in this situation or will I take matter into my own hands? So much of life comes down to this simple question.

This much I know: God will not work if I insist on doing what I want and not what He says. As he says to us, "Trust me and let go, or hold on and you're on your own." Jeff, I don't even want to be on my own, rebelling against God's best and living in the flesh, not the spirit. So, I'm fighting every day to turn this over to God. Faith, I think, is always like that—not a one-time decision, but an ongoing conversation (one that doesn't end by the age of 52! I'll let you know if it ever does, but I don't think so!). When you read these words, the situation w/ our neighbor will be long over— with ... hope I did well?

Love Always,
Dad

P.S. (2021): "You have heard that it was said, 'Love your neighbor and hate your enemy.' But I tell you, love your enemies and pray for those who persecute you, that you may be children of your Father in heaven."
—Matthew 5:43-45 (NIV).

ဆ ဆ ဆ

GRATEFULNESS

July 20, 2008, Sunday AM 7:35

Hey Jeff,

You just returned from the High School mission trip to Mexico yesterday. As you told us about all the hard work and especially about feeding the families living in the garbage dump, it struck me how much you learned on this trip that perhaps you're not even aware of yourself. Like this: "I don't know why I am so blessed and so many of these poor people aren't—all I know is I owe it to God and must be grateful."

I remember my first missions' trip in college. I spent a whole summer out in the Colombian rain forest. When I got back home, all I could do is stare at people living their comparatively luxurious lives and wonder if they had any clue how blessed they were? Of course, most don't. But you and I have been there; we do know how privileged our lives are. Don't be mad at the unaware. Just be grateful to God.

I'm so proud that you went and worked and served. I know we sometimes wonder if such trips really accomplish all that much good. Some probably are better than others. This much I'm sure of—those trips, even if they don't change the situation in the field that much, always change us. Perhaps that's the most important thing after all!

Love You So Much,
Dad

P.S. (2021): Our great blessings as God's children should not make us ashamed, just grateful.

☙ ☙ ☙

TRIALS

9-5-08

Dear Jeff,

You have your learner's permit and drove me for the first time the other night from Schlotsky's to Ranchview High for your golf team meeting. You did great! I was reminded of letting you steer golf carts over the years as a little boy on my lap. My how you have grown up! Driving a car is just one of many indicators of the great change you've accomplished in growing from a child into a man. And what a fabulous young man you've become, I'm so proud of you. Soon you'll be driving without me in the car with you, and then shortly after that you'll be making your way in this world as you trust God and live for His glory. I am excited for each step because I know you'll be ready, and you'll do wonderfully well.

As you gain complete independence (from parents) in life, you'll discover a corresponding need to become more dependent on God. No matter how grown-up or accomplished we may become, we still are weak and live in a sometimes harsh and unpredictable world. Hard things happen, disappointments pop up, seasons of difficulty and adversity grip us. These are not occasions of despair, however. They are opportunities to trust. Hard times test our character, deepen our trust, and strengthen our perseverance if only we walk through them at Christ's side.

We have a couple of huge controversies at IBC in those days. We had our first woman preacher 2 weekends ago, and our youth & children ministries are in a shambles. Lots of people are walking away from IBC, and I'm spending lots of time on the hotseat! This is one of "those" times! Yet hear some words that

I read this morning from Psalm 5:5: "Listen to my prayer, O God, do not ignore my plea. My thoughts trouble me and I am distraught. As for me, I call to God, and the Lord saves me ... I cry out in distress, and He hears my voice ... Cast your cares on the Lord and He will sustain you; He will never let the righteous be shaken."

Stay close to God, Jeff, and you'll never have to face anything alone!

Love You Buddy,
Dad

P.S. (2021): "When all kinds of trials and temptations crowd into your lives my brothers, don't resent them as intruders, but welcome them as friends! Realize that they come to test your faith and to produce in you the quality of endurance."
—James 1:2-4 (JB Phillips).

INDEPENDENCE

2-5-09

Hi Jeff,

It took several frustrating days after your birthday last month, but you and I finally got over to DPS for you to get your driver's license. We had a couple of little scares trying to get this done. We had to go by the driving school first to get your papers and permit. But the door was locked! We finally noticed their posted office hours, and they were to open in 5 minutes. They did, and we were on our way! I drove us up to the DPS (on Old Denton Rd) and found it wasn't where it had always been—and I couldn't find it! But we finally did. You passed your eye exam, I threw down $15, and you got it! We went for a Starbucks near home to celebrate (where you promptly got a call that you'd left your SS Card back at DPS! So back we went, and it's all good).

This marks a huge a benchmark in your life, Jeff. Though it's a little scary for parents to see their boy driving off the first few times, I have great confidence in you and know you'll be a great driver. Beyond the driving, however, is the independence driving affords. You can now go where you want, and when, and choose who knows what about it. In other words, you now have great freedom—and that's wonderful. But with freedom comes great responsibility. But no worries, you have that in spades!

Thrilled for you,
Dad

P.S. (2021): "I have the right to do anything," you say—but not everything is beneficial. "I have the right to do anything"—but not everything is constructive.
—1 Corinthians 10:23 (NIV)

BEAUTY

6-1-10

My Dear Jeff,

Much has transpired since my last entry. Tomorrow you will have completed your Junior year at Ranchview H.S. You have become an accomplished violinist in the orchestra and in your new band Seastroke. You took a lovely Iranian girl on a date in a limo with B & Z to your prom. This was a big moment for your mom and me as we took pictures of you all before and marveled at how adult and sophisticated you both are. Then yesterday you and Jon and I played 9 at HCCC and you're now hitting your irons the same distance as I do. You've caught me! (... and I love it).

I was diagnosed almost a year ago with Stage IV colon cancer, and it's been a ride since then not only for me, but also, I know, for you. But I must say your love and courage and support in walking through these days with me has been remarkable. God uses trials and even our suffering to grow us up and teach us things we'd never otherwise learn. I believe you are wise way beyond your 17 years because of what we've all been through, and that God has a purpose in this for your life.

You have recently become interested in attending U of Texas in their Arts Dept. Should that work out, I would not be surprised to see you hone your artistic skills there in preparation for communicating to people in this world truths that perhaps they can receive only through the medium of art. I have increasingly been touched by the power of art in touching hearts, conveying truth, and yes, changing minds. I fear that for most of my life I've been too enamored with the place of logic and scientific reasoning in our human quest. In this universe of mystery and transcendence however, it does "stand to reason" that some things will come clear to us (if they ever do) only through art not science. Music, poetry, films, literature, visual arts, and sculpture—all have the capacity to "speak" way beyond the reach of mere words.

I think I began to recognize this reality years ago when I read first read The Return of the Prodigal, a meditation by Fr. Henri Nouwen on Rembrandt's famous painting by the same name. So much in that piece of art ... so many books could be written about it! Yet, no number of books could replace it, ever. All of which to say, Jeff, you will change the world with your art, and I hope God lets me stay around long enough to see it happen.

Love Always,
Dad

P.S. (2021): Words and beauty both bear eloquent witness to the love, grace, and truth of our God.

෨ ෨ ෨

THE DESIRES OF YOUR HEART

2-18-11

Dear Jeff,

Finally, you received word yesterday of your acceptance into the Radio/TV/ Film Dept. of the University of Texas. Congratulations my son! I am rejoicing with you. This has implications for your future and for fulfilling your dreams. It's also a great affirmation of you as a person and to your skill. Your reputation now already at 18 years of age has gained you entrance into a prestigious program. I am so proud of you!

I'm also so grateful to God, as I know you are as well. I believe this is one chapter in your life that you'll always be able to point out as an example of God's reality in your life. Of course, He's always there and always faithful. It's just that, at certain times, He shows up in indisputable ways as if to say, "Don't forget ... I'm here, I love you, and I'm working out a stupendous plan for your life." He is, He does, and He's doing that. So, mark it down, you're on your way Jeff! Follow Him always.

Love
Dad

* * * July 8, 2011, Dear Jeff, As I write these words, you are in Austin for freshman orientation. U.T. for you has begun! Your future as a grown man of the world cutting your own unique swath on this planet is launched! And you're so ready. I'm proud of you.

Love,
Dad

P.S. (2021): "Trust in the LORD and do good; dwell in the land and enjoy safe pasture.
Take delight in the LORD, and he will give you the desires of your heart."
—Psalm 37:3-4 (NIV)

ත   ත   ත

FOLLOW HIM ALWAYS

August 19, 2011

Dear Jeff,

Today your mom and I have been married for 33 years. You've been a huge part (18 years' worth!) of those 33 for us. And tomorrow, we are taking you to Austin to move you into your dorm room at the University of Texas!

You knew I'd probably write this at some point in this journal! I can't believe how time has flown! Looking back over these pages has reminded me of so many beautiful times in our lives with you—our Jeff—our youngest, our buddy! Now, you're a man on the verge of stepping out as an adult into the wide world.

I couldn't be prouder of you, my son!

You are ready in every way.

I know you will seize the opportunity that these next 4 years present to you. I can't wait to see what you learn, how you grow, and where God leads you! I know it will all be wonderful.

Just follow Jesus, know and obey His Word, pray through everything, work hard, love well, and trust God. The sky is the limit!

And know that all along your way, I'll be praying for you and pulling for you.

Your greatest fan,
Dad.

P.S. (2021): "Come, follow me," Jesus said, "and I will send you
out to fish for people."
—Matthew 4:19

    ∞   ∞   ∞

Afterword

Julie Today and Her Tribute At Dad's Retirement Banquet

Dad,

As I look back at your career at IBC, I admit I'm limited by the perspective of a daughter. Alongside your tenure at IBC, I've been growing up—first as a six-year-old, then as a dorky middle schooler, then on to high school, college, marriage, career, and a family of my own. I've grown up alongside a church that was growing up with you. So, my perspective is totally, embarrassingly inadequate to fully capture all you've given to and created within IBC over these 31 years.

But I DO have my own perspective, limited as it is, and if there is one word that I think might describe you as a pastor and as a parent, it is the word: intentional. You are an intentional person. An intentional father. An intentional senior pastor. And that began way before you began at IBC.

When each of us McQuitty kids went off to college, you gave each of us handwritten journals that you had prepared for YEARS in advance, writing to us all through the years of our growing up, offering observations, musings about life and problems and God. It was an incredible gift to receive. I have mine here.

Your words, from August 15, 1986:

> As I write these words, I'm sitting in my little cubby hole office at Northeast Bible Church and glancing at a family picture in which you're about 4 years old. You're five now and growing and developing and learning so fast it boggles my mind. I guess this realization is what finally sparked my urgency level to the action point this morning. You see, I've been thinking about starting this journal to you for well over a year now—just never quite got

around to it. But "my little princess" is growing up (relentlessly!) and I must seize the moment and begin this prospect before it is too late.

Dad, you have always seized the moment. When I was an insecure middle schooler just beginning her time at a 'real school,' making the transition out of homeschooling and adjusting to the birth of another sibling, you saw a need for intentionality. You seized the moment, and you instigated our weekly Wednesday morning McDonald's breakfast dates which carried on throughout my junior high years. I treasured those dates more than you know.

You go on in your journal entry:

> And so, I have determined by God's grace to carry on a conversation with you which will be (obviously) totally one-sided for a good number of years! I look forward to the day when I can give you these ramblings of mine and, as a young woman, you can read them and understand them and (hopefully!) enjoy them and perhaps even humor your poor old daddy by giving him to understand that they were an encouragement to you.

Yes, Daddy, they have been an encouragement. Your one-sided conversation in this journal gave way to a burgeoning conversation at those early-morning McDonald's, which became an open camaraderie in high school, college, and beyond. Thank you for showing me what it means to love your daughter enough to take specific action.

I know you've seized opportunities and taken specific actions here at IBC as well which have transformed it into the amazing community it is today. That's a glorious thing. I celebrate that. But this little girl's life was changed not by the senior pastor of Irving Bible Church, but by my daddy.

I love you.

"Man After Your Own Heart"
Duet w Dad

Vs. 1

Oh God, Father in heaven and earth,
I call to you like deep calls
to deep over water.

Dad — Show me your endless measure of grace,
let tender mercies shine once again
from your Holy face

Both [Deep in my soul there's a craving
to please the one who has saved me.

Julie — O God, though I have fallen so far,
Dad — You know that I'm still a man after
your own heart.

Vs. 2 — (All Dad)
I am driven by rivers of pride,
You are my rescue, the maker and
keeper of my life.
Lead me by the still waters again;
use me in spite of the prodigal son
child that you know I am

Just as a deer runs to water,
so does my soul to you Father.

O God, though I have wandered so far,
You know that I'm still a man
after your own heart.

0000...
Just as a deer runs to water,
so does my soul to you Father →

JULIA KATHLEEN MCQUITTY RHODES - UPDATED C.V.

Julie was born in Tacoma, Washington on March 14, 1981. She grew up in Irving, Texas as the oldest of five siblings. In 2003 Julie graduated summa cum laude from Texas A&M University with a B.A. in English literature and a minor in business. She married Gordon Rhodes on December 4, 2004, and later gave birth to Andrew James on September 19, 2007, and to Madeline Mae on July 25, 2010.

Along with her parenting duties and volunteer work at her home church, Christ Chapel, Julie is an active freelance actor and writer in the DFW area. She writes regularly for MadeWorthy Magazine (40k readers) and the Tanglewood Moms blog (15K visitors per month). Julie has also performed in many DFW venues including Casa Manana Dallas Children's Theater, Circle Theater, Amphibian Stage Productions, Stolen Shakespeare Guild, and Lyric Stage. Julie is currently cast in a TV series being developed for streaming services and continues to pursue her stage career with regular auditions for lead roles in new professional productions.

~ ~ ~

ELIZABETH TODAY AND HER TRIBUTE AT DAD'S RETIREMENT BANQUET

Dad,

It has been almost impossible to be thorough in reflecting on your tenure as Senior Pastor at IBC, because the 31 years of your faithful ministry has filled up almost my entire life. So many of my childhood memories are connected to this church and you as its leader.

In the journal you wrote to me while I was growing up, on 12/14/01, you wrote these words:

Dear Elizabeth Grace,

It's wise to take the long view. Patience is not exactly a McQuitty trait. We generally like to go for something and get it quickly, or study something and understand it easily, or stand for something and be vindicated swiftly. But most of the really important things in our lives play out over decades. And I don't have to remind you that eternity lasts a long time! So then, it's just wise to take the long view.

Tonight, Dad, we celebrate that you have taken your own advice. You have taken the long view. Your ministry at IBC has played out over decades, and although it might have been marked by an impatient moment here or there, it amazes me to see all that God has done in and through you here.

There is such freedom in adopting your wise words, Dad. Taking the long view means that even if it's not all done today, it will be right there tomorrow when a new day begins. There must have been so many days that you were tempted to work late, maybe miss dinner at home, and burn the candle from both ends. As an ordained person now myself, I know from experience that the work never ends.

But in taking the long view, you didn't allow the weight and responsibility of your ministry at IBC to keep you from your family. I can remember when we lived in the Summit house, you would come home from church, and as many of us that were born and able to walk at the time would tackle you, screaming, "Daddy!" as you walked in. We were so excited that you were home, and just in time for dinner! You would often go outside with us after dinner and play street tennis, or we would play catch in the front yard with any kind of ball we could get our hands on; a baseball, a football, it didn't matter. And then later on when it was time for bed, we could always look forward to a thrilling bedtime story!

I so cherish those memories.

I had no idea at the time how weighty your days at IBC must have been. But because you were taking the long view, the mantle of your leadership and ministry was never so heavy that it kept you from being the fun and loving dad I got to have growing up, and still have today.

So tonight, I celebrate that you took the long view, both for what that allowed for God to do through you here at IBC, and also for what it did for me as your daughter. I love you, I'm so proud of you, congratulations!

ELIZABETH GRACE MCQUITTY - UPDATED C.V.

Elizabeth was born in Dallas, Texas on September 11, 1983. She grew up in Irving, Texas and later graduated from Texas A&M University in 2006 with a Kinesiology major and Psychology minor.

Elizabeth then studied at Fuller Theological Seminary from 2008-2013 and graduated with a Master of Divinity degree, emphasis in recovery ministry. She served a brief stint from 2011-2013 as a Chaplain in the US Army Reserves while simultaneously pursuing ordination as a priest in the Episcopal church.

Elizabeth was ordained as a Deacon in the Episcopal Church on June 3, 2017, and then to the Priesthood on January 13, 2018. Mother Elizabeth currently serves as the Vicar of St. John's Episcopal Church in La Verne, California.

~ ~ ~

BONNIE TODAY AND HER TRIBUTTE (SP) AT DAD'S RETIREMENT BANQUET

BACKGROUND

When IBC flew in all my grown children for my retirement dinner celebrating 31 years as Senior Pastor, one of them could not come.

Bonnie was then a full-time missionary finishing up her ninth year in China. Though she desperately wanted to come and give a tribute at the dinner along with her siblings, making a journey of that magnitude was simply impossible on short notice. So, Bonnie instead set out to create a video tribute which we played in her stead at the dinner. Following is the word for word transcription of that video which Bonnie began by reading one of my entries in her journal and finished with her words of appreciation ...

[On camera, Bonnie reads ...]

10-11-87

Sunday, 7:28A.M.

Dear Bonnie,

Since I wrote last, the Lord has answered our prayers for leading and brought us to Irving Bible Church. It's a great church with a rich tradition of Bible-teaching, and I'm honored and privileged to be here.

I'm also scared half to death! Last Sunday was my installation service and in just a few hours I'll be preaching my first message as pastor.

That's why I'm writing—to share a thought with you about facing scary experiences. I thought it would be more pertinent now since I'm facing one!

Here's the thought: time will propel us through scary experiences and inevitably deliver us to the other side. The way to get by hard experiences is to project through them and view them from a past perspective. Then, we can ask "How will I have wished that I handled this situation?" Such a perspective will make a difference. It will help you relax and even enjoy yourself. Don't worry: few scary things in our lives are potentially fatal!

We celebrated your first birthday Friday night! And, um, all these people were here. ["At the party were Steve/Julie/Blair Hart, Lee Thompson and Bob and June Armor." ... in the original entry.

Andy] We had chicken casserole and cake and sang to you and your sisters helped you to open presents. I think you had a good time ....

[Bonnie smiles and puts the journal aside. Looking into the camera ...]

Ah, Dad, just reading over such a special day in your life. This is just evidence of how you have continually opened up to not only me but how you have opened up to all of your children through the years—um, sharing how you were scared that you did not know what the outcome would be after the sermon or what you had gotten yourself into when you made the decision and were called to IBC 31 years ago. And, um, ...

I'm just so proud of you for the example you set for me and for all of your kids about facing your fears and trusting the Lord to bring you through them.

And, um, I'm excited about what the Lord has for you next. And as you said yourself, most scary things ... um, ... are not fatal, and the Lord to bring you through.

I love you and I miss you ... and I'm celebrating with you, today!

This was Bonnie's first address and phone number in China:

Bonnie McQuitty

亚东城 12-3-706, 仙林,南京,江苏,中国,25-210000
Yadong Cheng Apartment 12-3-706 XianLin, Nanjing, JiangSu Provence China, 25-210000
And my phone number to put on the bottom of the address is: 156-5193-5073

BONNIE CAROLEEN MCQUITTY – UPDATED C.V.

Bonnie was born in Dallas, Texas on October 7, 1986. She grew up in Irving, Texas and later graduated from Ouachita Baptist University in 2009 with a B.A. in Christian Studies (emphasis in ministry).

Bonnie serves as a full-time member with Cru (formerly Campus Crusade for Christ). Having moved to the far east and learned Mandarin, Bonnie completed ten years in country as a ministry leader before the 2020 pandemic prematurely forced her return to the States. Bonnie now resides in Austin, Texas where she serves with Cru's Bridges International Student Ministry at the University of Texas and also on the Chinese Network Team.

~ ~ ~

JONATHAN TODAY AND HIS TRIBUTE AT DAD'S RETIREMENT BANQUET

Dad,

To be honest, I'm not sure where to begin. A brief speech is hardly enough to adequately express how grateful I am for you and the impact you've had in my life. This will be a bit of a reduction as I home in on a couple of things I feel need to be acknowledged.

The way you treat mom.

Dad, I've never heard you speak a single poor word about mom. Partially because it's next to impossible to find something bad to say about her, but also because encouragement is what flows freely from your lips. "You know your mom, she's absolutely brilliant," or "There's nobody like your mother." "We are so lucky to have her," or my favorite: "Us guys are rather pathetic without a strong woman by our side. So, let's all just acknowledge the truth here ... this wouldn't be happening right now without mom."

Mom and Dad, your faithfulness to your first ministry—to each other and to your kids—I believe was the gateway to seeing God use you to do extraordinary things in your 31 years at IBC. On behalf of all of your kids and your congregation, thank you.

You were always there.

In an age where the 'absentee father' is a growing problem and wreaking havoc on the fabric of our society, you went against the grain (what else is new) and were always there. I can't remember a baseball game, a basketball game, a track meet, a musical, or a concert where you didn't show up.

I sometimes wonder what I was up to when you were writing to me in my journal. Perhaps playing in the other room with my action figures, or outside building skateboard ramps. Maybe I was fast asleep upstairs; or supposed to be asleep but was actually sneaking in one last round of video games. Maybe I was at band practice or at school, I don't know. Wherever I was, I know that we were physically part, but even still you were thinking of me, writing to me; even then you were there.

I decided to carry on the tradition and begin writing a journal for Eric Andrew McQuitty the second ... I have it here. In the first entry I write:

> You May be wondering what this journal is all about. It's actually something your Pops (after whom you were named) started with me when I was about your age. He wrote to me in a journal over the first 18 years of my life. He filled the pages with memories and with wisdom that he knew I was far too young to grasp. When I was 18 years old, I moved across the country to Savannah GA to begin college. On the last night before my parents left, Dad presented me the journal. I always knew my dad loved me ... I always knew he was proud of me ... he always affirmed that. But in that moment, my understanding of his love for me vastly deepened. I want the same for you.

Dad, even though it's the end of a season, it's not the end of your influence. You are a man with a legacy. The seed you've planted in the lives of your children and in this church will continue to grow and produce fruit for generations.

I closed the first journal entry with this:

> [Eric] I'd like to share with you the last words my dad wrote to me in my journal before giving it to me in 2007: 'Jon, be blessed. Choose blessing. Reach out and receive what the Lord wants you to have! Fear Him; delight always in his commands. You'll never regret it.' Eric, let Pops' parting words serve as my opening ones for you. "Delight in His commands and reach out for all that God has for you." With all my love—Dad

Mom and Dad, thank you. I love you and am so excited to see how God continues to work in and through you. Onward and upward!

JONATHAN ANDREW MCQUITTY – UPDATED C.V.

Jonathan was born in Dallas, Texas on May 21, 1989. He grew up in Irving, Texas and later graduated from the University of Oklahoma in May 2012 with a Bachelor's degree of Fine Arts (BFA) in Visual Communication. He then moved to West Palm Beach, Florida to join the staff at Journey Church as Worship Arts Pastor.

Jonathan married Andie on December 12th, 2014 and together they welcomed Eric Andrew (born October 15th, 2018) and Peyton Joy (born August 4th, 2020).

Jonathan continues to serve at Journey Church as an executive team member overseeing and leading worship, production, and creative ministries for this growing church of thousands on two campuses.

~ ~ ~

JEFFEREY TODAY AND HIS TRIBUTE AT DAD'S RETIREMENT BANQUET

Dad, tonight we celebrate you. These past 31 years, your faithfulness and dedication to the Lord has completely overflowed into IBC and its people, and by it, countless lives have been totally transformed by Christ. People all over have seen and felt your influence as "Pastor Andy," but only we have had the unbelievable privilege to know you as "Dad." When I look back at my childhood and teenage years and think of you, I don't think of the man on stage preaching or leading the church. I think of the man that picked me up from school every Tuesday to go to Grapevine Mills to share a blueberry muffin. I think of the man that  took me to countless biker rallies and taught me how to identify every type of Harley. I remember the man that coached my baseball teams, played hide-and-seek every night before bed, taught me to golf, and gave me my first Guinness. IBC may have been your baby too, but never once did you put it before us.

Dad, YOUR faithfulness to me has been one of the greatest earthly testaments to God's faithfulness I have ever known. To this day I don't understand how you managed to pour yourself into this church, yet still make each of us feel known and loved. You are the man I most aspire to be like, and I strive to make you proud every day. I can't wait to see what you do next—I know it will be great.

I love you!
Jeff

JEFFREY LEE MCQUITTY – UPDATED C.V.

Jeffrey was born in Dallas, Texas on January 19, 1993. He grew up in Irving, Texas and later graduated from The University of Texas at Austin in 2015 with a degree in Radio-Television-Film.

Jeff married Katy in October 2018 and works in Austin, Texas as a filmmaker and cinematographer with several feature films and award-winning documentaries in his portfolio.

CPSIA information can be obtained
at www.ICGtesting.com
Printed in the USA
JSHW021944200222
23148JS00003B/11